The
Carolingian Renaissance
and the
Idea of Kingship

The Birkbeck Lectures 1968–9

The
Carolingian Renaissance
and the
Idea of Kingship

The Birkbeck Lectures 1968–9

WALTER ULLMANN

METHUEN & CO LTD

First published 1969 by Methuen & Co Ltd
11 New Fetter Lane, London EC4
© 1969 Walter Ullmann
Printed in Great Britain by
Butler & Tanner Ltd, Frome and London

SBN 416 11770 8/33
1.1

Distributed in the USA by
Barnes & Noble Inc

Table of Contents

v

Lecture *VII*

THE CAROLINGIAN BEQUEST

Preface

The Birkbeck Lectureship in ecclesiastical history approaches its first centenary: to be elected Birkbeck Lecturer has always been regarded, within and without the University, a mark of special distinction. And indeed, the noble line of Birkbeck Lecturers is awe inspiring, because their lectures either by reason of their subject-matter or the discovery of new material or new interpretations, have proved themselves seminal far beyond the topics immediately treated. As may be imagined, I am deeply sensible of the honour which the Council have conferred upon me by electing me this year's Birkbeck Lecturer: I have thereby incurred a very great debt of gratitude to the Electors as well as a very high degree of scholarly responsibility. For who would not feel a sense of profound humility when confronted by the names of those in medieval ecclesiastical history alone who have been Birkbeck Lecturers?

I have only to single out three of them, all in the appropriate ecclesiastical language, *bonae ac piae memoriae*, whose lectures have proved so basic that they have given entirely new directions to historical research or historiography. In the very first year of this century John Neville Figgis, appropriately enough a pupil of Maitland himself, opened up in the master's presence hitherto unknown vistas in the constitutional and legal field by his studies in the conciliar and post-conciliar periods: the extent to which his lectures have fertilized research, is still not fully acknowledged – in fact, there runs an almost continuous line of research down to this day, for he was one of the first, if not the first, who correctly assessed the doctrinal value of Bartolus and the Bartolist school for the study of the history of political ideas; and it was Figgis himself and a few years later his own pupil, Cecil Woolf, a Fellow of Trinity, who introduced Bartolus to the English-speaking world and fundamentally influenced continental scholarship. In the second decade of this century the great Oxonian of *Illustrations of the History of Medieval Thought and Learning* fame, Reginald Lane Poole, gave in his lectures the fruits of years of studies on the papal chancery: he was the first English scholar to make the intricate machinery of the papal nerve-centre his special métier and to introduce the subject to English historians and a wider English public. By virtue of the soundness of his research and penetration, and despite the great and detailed work that has since been carried out in this field, his lectures have stood the test of time. And in the third decade of this century Zachary Brooke's Birkbeck Lectures introduced still another genre to English historical scholarship: he was the first to realize the role of Lanfranc as the *fons et origo* of post-Conquest English ecclesiastical law; it was Brooke who by virtue of his monumental and yet so modestly displayed scholarship was able to discover Lanfranc's copy in the Wren Library and above all else to demonstrate the stages by which the *ecclesia Anglicana* absorbed the common canon law and thus became an integral part of the universal Church. Who, then, in the face of such talent, scholarship, insight and historical penetration and perception, would not feel daunted and sense the *onus gravissimum* which rests on him who tries to fill the office of a Birkbeck Lecturer?

The choice of a subject is always fraught with danger. In the main there were two reasons which made me select the Carolingian period: (1) as far as I could find out, no previous Birkbeck Lecturer had ventured into this period of early medieval Europe which is, so to speak, a no-man's land: and yet I believe that this epoch – roughly the second half of the eighth and the ninth centuries – represents an age which holds the key to a better understanding not only of the subsequent medieval centuries, but also of modern Europe: it was the age which showed the amalgamation of the Greco-Roman heritage with the Germanic civilization and yielded the kind of Europe which we have inherited: *nostra res agitur*. (2) In perhaps no other period of European history can the contribution of the ecclesiastics to problems of public government be better demonstrated. We can here watch how a new society, a European society, that is, is welded together by the application of religious and ecclesiastical as well as royal norms, in a word by the co-operation of the Carolingian kings with the ecclesiastical hierarchy. The result of this team-work was the emergence of a European, cosmopolitan society, Roman in one sense, Christian in another, and Germanic in yet another: in brief, the Carolingian period was the age which gave birth to Western Europe in all its multifarious complexity, because it was that epoch which witnessed the fusion and adaptation of heterogeneous forces with the result that, from the ideological angle, a new community came into being.

The crucial and determinative part which the Carolingian ecclesiastics played in this historical process, may indeed cause a certain detachment, if not positive aversion, in twentieth-century man. However understandable this may be, it is a thoroughly unhistorical attitude. After all, it is one of the tasks of a historian to discern and to lay bare what is hidden beneath a surface the outward appearance of which may well be deceptive. Perhaps you will allow me to quote one of the great sons of Trinity, Lord Macaulay, who glimpsing something of the magnitude and the dimensions of the problem, said à propos this very point that the encroachment of the sacerdotal order on the functions of the civil authorities would be considered in his own time a great evil, but, he continued, what is an evil in some circumstances, may in others be a blessing. For, 'a society sunk in ignorance and ruled by mere physical force, has great reason to rejoice when a class of which the influence is intellectual and moral, rises to ascendancy. Such a class will doubtless abuse its power; but mental power, even when abused, is still a nobler and better power than that which consists merely in corporeal strength.'

What I hope to do within the confines of a limited number of lectures is to interpret one segment of the Carolingian Renaissance. It will be my privilege to propound before you the view that the Carolingian Renaissance had a meaning to which (to make no higher claims) insufficient attention has been paid by modern historiography, but which I believe was a Renaissance not quite in conformity with the usually accepted canon. In trying to demonstrate the Carolingian conception of the Renaissance and its relation to contemporary Rulership, I shall have to go into a number of what may at first sight seem somewhat abstruse religious and biblical points, because without them that age is simply incomprehensible. For we must not import our own conceptions, or rather pre-conceptions, into so distant a period as the Carolingian age – some 1100 years separate us from it – if we wish to understand the epoch as it understood itself: this requires the elucidation of the epoch's own premises and presuppositions, in order to see it from within and with the eyes of its own contemporaries.

The treatment my subject demands – and I think it is only fair to give a warning of this by way of a preface – is overwhelmingly analytical and exegetical, for I am convinced that historical progress, that is, a better comprehension of an age that rested on premises somewhat different from those to which we have grown accustomed, can be achieved only by analysis in depth rather than by a synthesis in width. We can no longer afford the luxury of wielding the painter's brush and of painting a picture of the past in vivid colours and lively images, suitably interspersed with moralizing value-judgments. Nor must we fall into the other extreme – antiquarianism, that is, the very earnest but quite profitless, because historically irrelevant, exposition of mere *trivia*: luckily, the antiquarians have never found the Carolingian period a rewarding pitch. The analysis of so important an ideological and conceptual development as the Carolingian one, is too serious a business to be presented in an essayist's manner, for the analysis must perforce embrace a variety of disciplines, including law, liturgy, symbolism, as well as patristic lore and the remnants of hellenistic and platonic doctrines: in short the analysis to be striven for must of necessity be integrative, because the development it attempts to subject to exegesis, itself constituted an integrated whole. After all, history is not a self-contained, compartmentalized, anaemic, intellectual pursuit, but a living thing and is shaped, like life itself, by a variety of formative forces and agencies. In no other age was this more discernible than in the Carolingian era.

In order to keep the slightly expanded lectures to a manageable size and also to save costs, I have in the final version pruned the footnotes severely and restricted them to their barest essentials. In the Addenda I have appended a few references which may be of interest to some readers and to which (except on p. 7 n. 1) I have drawn attention in the relevant notes by adding (A).

My thanks are once more due to the many colleagues, friends and former research pupils who have sent me their offprints and books, from which I have derived the greatest profit. That some of my recent research students have stimulated me greatly, should be put on record, and in singling out Dr Janet Nelson no reflexion is intended on my other research students. It is in the same spirit that I must record my gratitude to an old friend of mine, Professor Percy Ernst Schramm, for his numerous suggestive observations and for keeping me abreast with his own researches by a constant flow of offprints: my disagreement with him on the one or the other point only goes to show how intellectually challenging and penetrating his views are. To all those colleagues and undergraduates who offered me constructive criticisms I must express my thanks. It is particularly gratifying to find that relevant and fundamental topics in medieval history unfailingly evoke a strong and sympathetic resonance amongst intelligent and historically discriminating undergraduates. Finally, to my wife – once more – I am deeply grateful for the loving care with which, in rather adverse circumstances, she has handled the text and helped me in numerous other ways.

Cambridge   W. U.
Spring 1969

Abbreviations

AD	*Archiv für Diplomatik*
AKG	*Archiv für Kulturgeschichte*
Ann.	*Annales*
BM	Böhmer-Mühlbacher, *Die Regesten des Kaiserreichs unter den Karolingern*, vol. I, 2nd ed. by J. Lechner (Innsbruck, 1908)
Cap. followed by number	*Capitulare* in *MGH. Capitularia* I–II
Chron.	*Chronicon*
CSEL	*Corpus scriptorum ecclesiasticorum latinorum*
DA	*Deutsches Archiv für die Erforschung des Mittelalters*
D(D).	*Diploma(ta)*
Hist	History; historical; histoire; historique; historisch
HJb	*Historisches Jahrbuch der Görresgesellschaft*
HZ	*Historische Zeitschrift*
JE	Ph. Jaffé, *Regesta pontificum Romanorum*, 2nd ed. by (F. Kaltenbrunner), P. Ewald (and S. Loewenfeld) (repr. Graz, 1956)
Kern–Buchner	F. Kern, *Gottesgnadentum & Widerstandsrecht*, 3rd ed. by R. Buchner (Darmstadt, 1962)
Liebermann	F. Liebermann, *Die Gesetze der Angelsachsen*, 3 vols. (Halle 1905–13)
LThK	*Lexikon für Theologie und Kirche*
M.A.	Middle Ages; Moyen Age; Mittelalter
Mansi	J. D. Mansi, *Sacrorum conciliorum nova et amplissima collectio* (Florence, 1759–98)
Manitius	M. Manitius, *Geschichte der lateinischen Literatur des Mittelalters* (Munich, 1911–31)
MGH. AA.	*Monumenta Germaniae Historica: Auctores antiquissimi*
— *Capit.*	*MGH. Capitularia*
— *Conc.*	— *Concilia*
— *Const.*	— *Constitutiones*
— *DD.*	— *Diplomata*
— *Epp.*	— *Epistolae*
— *Form.*	— *Formulae*
— *SS.*	— *Scriptores*
— *SS. RR. GG.*	— *Scriptores Rerum Germanicarum*
NA	*Neues Archiv der Gesellschaft für ältere deutsche Geschichtskunde*

xiii

NT	New Testament
OT	Old Testament
PG	W. Ullmann, *The Growth of Papal Government in the Middle Ages*, 3rd ed., London, 1965
PGP	W. Ullmann, *Principles of Government and Politics in the Middle Ages*, 2nd ed., London, 1966
PGr	J. P. Migne, *Patrologia Graeca*
PL	J. P. Migne, *Patrologia Latina*
RAC	*Realenzyklopädie für Antike und Christentum*
Reg.	Register
RHE	*Revue d'histoire ecclésiastique*
RHEF	*Revue d'histoire de l'église de France*
Sav. Z., GA; KA	*Zeitschrift der Savigny Stiftung für Rechtsgeschichte: Germanistische Abteilung; Kanonistische Abteilung*
T.U.	*Texte und Untersuchungen zur Geschichte der altchristlichen Literatur*
W.L.	Wattenbach–Levison, *Deutschlands Geschichtsquellen im Mittelalter*, ed. H. Löwe, 4 fasc. (Weimar, 1953–63)
ZKG	*Zeitschrift für Kirchengeschichte*

All other abbreviations are self-explanatory.
Biblical references are to the Vulgate.

The Renaissance of Society

There is ample justification for considering the Carolingian age as an entity: its sources are readily at hand; the period lends itself to an easy delineation as it spans a time of no more than a hundred and fifty years; the ruling dynasty was the same throughout and exhibited the same basic, but characteristic features; and, above all, Frankish society and its government underwent what may in modern parlance be called a radical ideological transformation within these chronological limits. Lastly, from a wider historical point of view the Carolingian age deserves particular attention, because it constituted the period of Europe's gestation and apprenticeship, the period in which the concept of Europe as a cultural, social, religious and especially political entity, sustained by its own forces, became for the first time an operational concept. For Europe was not a geographical expression, but denoted a perfectly well understood conceptual structure characterized on the one hand by the multiform if not heterogeneous complexion of the inhabitants under Carolingian rule, and on the other hand by the unifying and cementing bond of the Roman-Latin, Western as opposed to Byzantine, Christianity. It is these main features which, I believe, furnish sufficient justification for subjecting the period to a fresh analysis and interpretation within the confines of a limited amount of lectures.

The beginning of the Carolingian period coincides with the rapprochement between the Franks and the papacy in the early fifties of the eighth century. To be sure, the initiative rested entirely and exclusively with the papacy which pursued a policy towards the Franks that can be understood only against the background of Byzantine–papal relations reaching right back to the fifth century. In its dealings with the Franks the papacy followed what might be termed an ideological blue-print which despite the different guises, norms and changes of nomenclature, was in substance a christianized Roman cosmology. The change of the historical map in the fifties of the eighth century by the papacy signified the execution of the papal blue-print and had as an immediate effect the Europeanization of the Franks by which I mean that the Frankish kingdom became an integral part of the historical process, the springs of which were of Roman-Latin parentage. In fact, the Franks were the only available instrument by which papal policy could be put into practice. The Visigoths had been wiped off the face of the map; the Lombards had, rightly or wrongly, been looked upon as a threat to the existence of the papacy; for geographical reasons the Anglo-Saxons could not serve as instruments in the hands of the papacy.

That the Franks responded favourably to the full-scale integration into the Roman-European framework finds its ready explanation in the fertile soil that had been methodically and systematically cultivated by St Boniface and the other missionaries. The conditions were therefore particularly propitious for implanting Roman–Latin–Christian cosmology. The firm organizational ecclesiastical structure proved its great value by providing a most suitable framework for this process of adoption and consequential adaptation, for strong footholds had been created which served as secure bases for the deployment and dissemination of these Roman-Christian ideas now engulfing the Frankish kingdom with great rapidity. Indeed, the Franks were, in a quite peculiar way, susceptible to this Roman-Christian influence, because in comparison with, say, the Visigoths or the Anglo-Saxons their soil was fallow: the educational and literary attainments during the Merovingian rule or even during Pippin the Short's government cannot in any sense compare with those prevailing in the Iberian peninsula or in Northumbria or Mercia or Kent. It is no exaggeration to speak of the first half of the eighth century as a period of intellectual stagnation:[1] there was nothing even faintly approaching a plan for educating the clergy, and no sustained efforts were made to preserve even the low level of clerical literacy.[2] In other words, as far as intellectual and cultural and literary pursuits were concerned, the Frankish soil was virgin in every respect.

However badly informed we are about the formative educational influences on Charlemagne[3] the fact is incontrovertible that his government exhibited a quite definite and sharply profiled educational policy.

---

[1] Cf. M. L. W. Laistner, *Thought and Letters in Western Europe A.D. 500–900*, 2nd ed. (London, 1957), 191, speaking of an all-pervading decay in the gloomiest terms; no less gloomy was W. v. d. Steinen in *Karl d. Gr.*, ed. B. Bischoff (Düsseldorf, 1965), ii. 9, who refers to a process of barbarization between the sixth and eighth centuries. Cf. also following note.

[2] So excellent a connoisseur as P. Lehmann said: 'Der schulische und wissenschaftliche Tiefstand ist bis etwa 770 das Normale' in 'Das Problem d. karol. Renaissance' in *Erforschung d. M.A.* (Stuttgart, 1959), i. 102 ff.

[3] Cf. Lehmann, loc. cit. 125 f. (Charles' Latin education negligible: *unbedeutend*); see also J. Fleckenstein, 'Karl d. Gr. & sein Hof' in *Karl d. Gr.*, ed. H. Beumann (Düsseldorf, 1965), i. 24 f.

One may even go further and say that for him as king (in contrast to his father Pippin) the issue of religion and of a dynamically conceived Christianity[1] was a living issue, and one that basically and fundamentally affected his government and therefore also the kingdom itself. He realized that one of his main functions as a Christian Ruler was to provide the kingdom with a quantitatively as well as qualitatively improved clergy: his kingdom needed not only a larger body of ecclesiastics than it already possessed but above all a better educated and better trained clergy, if indeed, as his biographer tells us, his kingdom was to be modelled on the *civitas Dei*, an aim which we should not consider a hagiographic overstatement or a romantic ascription by a biographer. But for the realization of the programme he envisaged, the supply of suitable men to carry out his highly ambitious plan was wanting: these men just did not exist. At this stage we might well think of Charlemagne as a kind of missionary who intended to christianize the vast territories which he had conquered, but had not the men to accomplish the task. For to him Christianity was not merely a matter of intense personal belief, but perhaps more a matter of profound public and social concern. Nevertheless, there were respectable and flourishing schools with quite well developed schemes of study which could indeed boast of a reservoir of talent in men and of a supply of books, but they were not in the Frankish realms. The initiative of Charlemagne harnessed this talent of men and this reservoir of books to his court: these men came either from conquered territory, such as Lombardy, or were recruited from the refugees of enemy occupied territory, such as Visigothic Spain, or were invited to join him, as were the men from Anglo-Saxon England. He thereby secured what one might term a nucleus of literate and extremely gifted men who, by all accounts, were also productive and able teachers. To have detected this talent when he himself was barely capable of writing, and to have drawn it into his orbit and kept and multiplied it there, is certainly an achievement that has few, if any, parallels in European history.

It was in pursuit of this educational policy – exclusively a royal measure and carried through at royal expense – that the literary and cultural phenomenon of a Carolingian Renaissance emerged.[2] Whether

---

[1] For more recent expositions of Charles' Christianity, see A. Waas, 'Karls d. Gr. Frömmigkeit' in *HZ* 203 (1966), 265 ff.; above all the imaginatively painted pen portrait of Charles by P. E. Schramm, *Kaiser, Könige u. Päpste* (Stuttgart, 1968), i. 302 ff., esp. 305–8, 310. Cf. further E. Delaruelle, 'Charlemagne et l'église' in *RHEF* 39 (1953), at 197, quoting appropriately Ganshof's apposite statement.

[2] See the balanced and sensible presentation by Laistner, op. cit. 189 ff.

or not the name is justified[1] is of lesser concern than what this phenomenon represented. In general, it would be right to say, I think, that
there was a marked endeavour to resuscitate ancient and quite especially
patristic literature, and to some extent also to imitate and to develop its
thoughts. This resuscitation of what the protagonists viewed as classical
Christian models led, we are told, to the Renaissance of letters, to a
revival of all relevant branches of learning, to a re-birth of studies in general; it was a *Bildungsreform*.[2] This Renaissance was, the best authorities inform us, a *kulturelle Bewegung*[3] or a *grande movimente culturale*[4]
or *un mouvement intellectuel*. One of the pressing tasks which the king
faced – so we are furthermore told – was the purification of Latin,[5] no
doubt in order to promote a correct Latin prose, if not also poetry.
Indeed, Charlemagne is said not only to have been a purifier of Latin,
but also a passionate advocate of precision and succinctness in the use
of terms and words, hence his personal supervision of the corrected
texts and writings.[6] There is alleged to have been the self-less Carolingian devotion to philology, to studies in grammar, to orthography,
glossography, epistolography, and so forth, in other words a veritable
re-awakening of the human mind singularly directed towards (ancient)
literature and culture, in the midst of all the din of battle and military
campaigns and marches.

Now there is rare unanimity amongst all scholars that this literary and
cultural Renaissance was set on foot by the direction and initiative of
Charlemagne in his function as a king. And let us remind ourselves: it
was a movement, hence something that continued to develop, to grow,
that was in continual motion and was kept in motion by its own inner
force and for the sake of better Latinity, better Latin prose, better Latin
syntax and style, and so on. This literary movement was an official
royal movement, stimulated, propagated and enforced by the king
whose knowledge of written Latin was admittedly a little shaky. I can-

---

[1] Cf. on this A. Monteverdi in *Settimana Spoleto*, 1 (1954), at 366 ff.

[2] The expression is Schramm's, op. cit. 338.

[3] P. Lehmann, *Erforschung*, cit., ii. 125 and *passim*.

[4] A. Monteverdi, art. cit. 366.

[5] See P. Lehmann, op. cit. ii. 132; or 114: 'eine *Wiedergeburt der Studien überhaupt*'
(italics original). For the literacy of the Carolingians see the balanced exposition by
H. Grundmann, 'Litteratus-illitteratus' in *AKG* 40 (1958), 1 ff., at 39 ff.; see also the
realistic assessment of Latin knowledge in educated quarters by D. A. Bullough, *The Age
of Charlemagne* (London, 1965), 100 f.

[6] For this see Schramm, op. cit. esp. 327 ff.; cf. 329: 'Er begnügte sich nicht mit An-
regungen oder Anweisungen an die Geistlichen als die Sachkundigen, sondern über-
wachte die Durchführung persönlich.'

not help asking this question: is it at all likely that a man of Charlemagne's statesmanship, practical wisdom and calibre, with an unerring eye for assessing concrete reality, should have devoted so much energy to this purely literary and cultural movement? Does this sort of educational policy about which we read in literally speaking countless modern books, articles, dissertations and so on, not resemble education based on what one might call a liberal arts course?[1] Is it, to continue the questioning, not a little unrealistic, if not also anachronistic, to assert a literary Renaissance which was, on all accounts, an end in itself? If indeed this was all that is embraced by the term Carolingian Renaissance, it would at best have amounted to nothing more than an aesthetic movement which kept a number of scholars and their assistants busy in their studies and cells, a movement which, to be sure, preserved a number of ancient works for posterity – after all, the men had to keep themselves busy to justify their existence as 'educated' men – but which was an early example of scholarship for the sake of scholarship, learning for its own sake, evoked and engendered and exclusively supported by a man who was experienced with horses and swords rather than with the Latin language either in its purified or impure form. What I fail to understand, what I cannot see and what I am bound to question is how there could be a literary and cultural movement – call it Renaissance or what you will – floating in a vacuum, and having no links with the society surrounding it. Is it really compatible with any kind of historical, let alone ordinary human, experience that upon an educationally and intellectually barren and untilled Frankish soil – for that was what Frankish society was by the mid-eighth century – should be grafted a literary and cultural Renaissance of the dimensions as we know them? Are not in fact at all times cultural and literary phenomena intimately and indissolubly linked with society in which they occur? Can the one be divorced from the other?

The view of the Carolingian Renaissance with which one is constantly confronted, seems to me – and I say this not without a little hesitation – somewhat unreal and therefore unhistorical. No doubt, in the age of Charlemagne, as in every age, there were men who lived only for their scholarly work – men like Petrus of Pisa, or Paulus Diaconus, or Paulinus of Aquileja spring to mind – but I find it extremely difficult to believe that the promotion of their studies was the special and official concern of Charlemagne as king. For what purpose did the king advocate and decree this *mouvement intellectuel*, this Renaissance? This seems

---

[1] Indeed, this is what is implied by Schramm, op. cit. 331.

to me a crucial question to ask. I do not wish to be misunderstood: that there was a revival of learning during the reign of Charlemagne – and afterwards – is undeniable; what I seriously question is whether this literary and cultural Renaissance can be said to have been an end in itself. It would seem that this literary Renaissance was an epiphenomenon, was a by-product, of a much more profound and more fundamental Renaissance. The literary and cultural Renaissance was conditioned by a Renaissance which took its essential features, its physiognomy, its complexion, in short its inner substance and essence, its life-blood, from the religious field. The Renaissance with which Charlemagne was primarily concerned, aimed at a rebirth, a regeneration of the whole Frankish people. We must try to follow the thought processes of a man such as Charlemagne, whose educational attainments, it is agreed on all sides, were not conspicuously high: not even his most uncritical admirer could present him as a literate person. But he was, as I have already indicated, a very devout Christian, for whom the Christian religion was, in a very literal sense, a driving force, individually as well as socially or collectively.

According to one of the few undisputed Christian axioms, through the working and infusion of divine grace the baptism of the individual effects a new creature,[1] in other words, baptism has always been understood to bring about a rebirth, a regeneration, a Renaissance of the individual. This individual Renaissance became during the reign of Charlemagne the pattern for a collective Renaissance, that is, the attempt at a regeneration, at a *renovatio* or renewal, at a rebirth of the Frankish people. Differently expressed: the rebirth of the individual consisted in his shedding his naturalness, the very being which nature had given him and which had made him 'a man of flesh'.[2] As a 'new creature' the baptized Christian shaped his life – or was said to have shaped it – no longer in accordance with the natural laws, because he had become a participant of the divine attributes themselves; he thus stood on a level entirely different from that of 'the man of flesh'. This was held to have been a veritable transformation of the individual: through the working of divine grace the individual was said to have undergone a metamorphosis.

With regard to the collective Renaissance a great many similar in-

---

[1] The *nova creatura* of St Paul, II Cor. 5. 15 and 17; for some details of this individual renaissance cf my *Individual & Society in the M.A.* (London, 1967), 7 f., with further literature.

[2] See further St Paul in I Cor. 2. 14 and 3. 3; Gal. 5. 24; Col. 2. 12.

gredients may be discerned. A careful reading of the official documents emanating from the royal chancery as well as of the contemporary literary and epistolary products, shows the frequency with which certain terms are employed, such as *renovare, emendare, revocare, reformare, renasci*, and their respective nouns, such as *renovatio*, or *regeneratio*, and so on.[1] This is not and cannot be coincidence. There is, I think, ample justification for saying that the Renaissance aimed at by Charlemagne was the transformation of contemporary society in accordance with the doctrinal and dogmatic notions of Christianity, as it was seen in the light of patristic lore. It is not necessary, before this forum, to point to the historic significance of this social or collective idea of a Renaissance or, what has recently been termed, an 'institutional Renaissance'.[2] For the first time, at least as far as Western Europe is concerned, we are here confronted by the conscious effort to shape the character of a society in consonance with the axioms of a particular doctrine, here the Christian norms. Although the actual doctrines intended to refashion society may differ radically, this Frankish-Carolingian experiment begins the long and distinguished line of many similar efforts in both Western and Eastern Europe, one of which is being re-enacted almost before our own eyes on a global scale.

Let us be quite clear about the substance and the implications of this Carolingian Renaissance. In essence it was not different from the Renaissance which was said to apply to the individual Christian. This means in the present context that what had hitherto been the result of the working of natural factors, such as custom, experience, tradition, history, was now, by the direction of the king himself, to yield to the overriding authority of doctrine and dogma; the royal government postulated a programme that was in conformity with a definite doctrinal

[1] Schramm has correctly assessed the significance of these terms, see op. cit. 330 (the work by J. Fleckenstein referred to ibid., n. 61, was not accessible to me). And yet Schramm rejects the whole idea of a Carolingian Renaissance and wishes to substitute 'Carolingian correctio' (336 ff.), because (1) the Carolingian Renaissance would become a preliminary to the late medieval and early modern Renaissance and, more important, (2) Renaissance presupposes something akin to the biological process of birth. I would never maintain that there was a link between the Carolingian and the later Renaissance, but the second ground adduced must, I am afraid, be rejected, precisely because baptism effected a *nova creatura* and brought about a *renovatio* or *regeneratio* (cf. Tit. 3. 5). But above all, Schramm's objection based on biological considerations, had long been answered in St John's gospel, 3. 5 ff. Because of its central importance let us quote this biblical passage: 'How can a man be born when he is old? Can he enter the second time the womb of his mother, and be reborn (*renasci*)?' To which Christ answered: 'Unless a man be reborn (*renatus*) of water and spirit, he cannot enter into the kingdom of God.'

[2] G. Ladner, art. 'Erneuerung' in *RAC* vi (1966), 262 ff.

set of principles which – and let us be clear about this point too – were not of the king's making, but were adopted by him and possibly adapted to actual contingencies. In other words, the naturally evolved Germanic past, the natural experience gained in the course of the antecedent Frankish development, the naturalness of Frankish society were now, by law and decree and statute, to be overlaid by principles, axioms and norms derived from an a–natural, a–human source, a source that had nothing to do with history, custom, experience and with all the other features belonging to natural humanity, but all the more with features which originated in, and belonged to, divinity. The effect which this Carolingian Renaissance in the social sense was to produce in the public field was a 'baptism' on the largest conceivable scale.[1] This, indeed, was not only the standpoint of Charlemagne, but also of his contemporary papacy which in a manifesto to the whole Frankish nation specifically applied in a collective sense to the Franks the baptismal terms of 'the holy nation', 'the royal priesthood' and 'the people who had acquired their salvation'. 'Of all the kingdoms the Frankish shines forth in the sight of the Lord.'[2]

The conceptual handle by which this transformation or regeneration was to be carried out was what I might call applied ecclesiology. That is to say, ecclesiology had become an integral part of the governmental outlook, programme and plan: ecclesiology had been absorbed into the governmental system itself. For what had hitherto been conceived as a mere conglomeration of families, tribes, conquered peoples, became in the course of the ninth century ideologically and conceptually transformed into one body public, the Church, which *au fond* disregarded the natural, linguistic and tribal differences of peoples and regions. The application of the ecclesiological theme radically and fundamentally shifted the ground from the haphazard, chancy and fortuitous conditions of society to the charismatically understood body that was held together, not by ties of blood, but by a common and articulated faith. This is not, of course, to deny that in practical life differences continued to exist, but the essential and basic Christian themes imprinted themselves upon the physiognomy of this unit. As Gabriel Le Bras once remarked: 'La Chrétienté se compose de chrétientés.'[3]

---

[1] The fairly recent conversion of the Eastern regions should be noted, and also the continuous territorial expansion of the kingdom by means of conquest and the subsequent necessity of converting the pagans.

[2] *Cod. Car.* no. 39 in *MGH. Epp* iii. 552, lines 6 ff.; the biblical reference is I Pet. 2. 9.

[3] See G. Le Bras, *Hist. du droit et des institutions: Prolégomènes* (Paris, 1955), 125.

This public body, the Church, was a corporate and juristic entity, one that was not only conceived to be in direct communion with divinity, but also to originate from the same source: it was divinity which was alleged to have brought into being this unit, the Church, and its very existence depended on the same divinity. This unit was ideologically superimposed upon an accidental assemblage or a diversified collection of families, tribes and groups. The one body was the product of natural forces, the other the product of the mind, of the spirit. To the former corresponded 'the animalic man', to the latter 'the new creature' of the baptized Christian. In each case there is a Renaissance, the one individual, the other social. And just as the individual, through the juristic effects of baptism was incorporated in, or absorbed by, the Church, in the same way the component groups of Frankish society were absorbed within the corporative union of the Church.[1]

It is clear that this intended Renaissance of society was bound to have radical consequences with regard to the concept and structure of Rulership, for society and government were then – as now – complementary. Seen from the angle of this Renaissance the title which Charlemagne as the first Carolingian took and which was not to disappear again, has additional significance: the 'king by the grace of God' signified precisely the radical shift which the concept of Rulership had undergone.[2] In fact, this title in some respects epitomizes the break with the past better than any learned exposition by a Carolingian writer could have done.[3] An intellectually conditioned or ideologically conceived change of character in a society necessarily involves a change in the conception, structure and purpose of its government. One can go further and say that the Renaissance of a society involves a Renaissance

---

[1] Although he sets out from different premisses, E. Delaruelle's view has everything in its favour, when he says that the significance of this age lies 'dans son idéologie', *RHEF* 38 (1952), at 70.

[2] See in this context the important exposition by Th. Mayer, 'Staatsauffassung d. Karolingerzeit' in *HZ* 173 (1952), 467 ff., esp. 469, 475 where he speaks of the Germanic (corresponding to what I have called the ascending theme of government) and the Christian-theocratic conception (corresponding to my descending theme): 'Die zwei Staatsauffassungen standen sich klar und scharf gegenüber und ergänzten sich dennoch gleichzeitig.' Cf. also the remarks of H. Fichtenau, *Das karol. Imperium* (Zürich, 1949), 63 f. See also in this context the interesting jurisprudential dichotomy of *Herrschaft* and *Genossenschaft* (corresponding to the descending and ascending themes) by G. K. Schmelzeisen in *AKG* 44 (1962), 137 ff., at 141 f. Cf. also below 31 n. 11.

[3] In so far there is a close parallel with Clovis, also called *novus Constantinus*. I entirely agree with M. Wallace-Hadrill, *The Long-Haired Kings* (London, 1963), 172, who in discussing his conversion says: 'By the mere fact of conversion to Catholicism Clovis is a *new kind* of barbarian king . . . the *break with the past* is as complete as the bishops can make it' (italics mine).

of its government or Ruler and that the changes in the conception of a society are conspicuously and intensively focalized in the changed conception of the Ruler himself. As we shall presently see, the Renaissance of society substantially strengthened the monarchic role of the king, and none realized this better than Charlemagne himself. The descending theme of government and law was the conceptual complement of the Renaissance of Frankish society. Perhaps nothing shows the Renaissance of the Ruler more convincingly than the displacement of the *Geblütsrecht* by Rulership resting on divine grace conveyed through the unction: what had hitherto been the result of biological transmission, became now the result of a transmission of divine grace. To this topic I will return in its proper context, when we will have to examine the most conspicuous and practical effect which this applied ecclesiology was to have in the course of the ninth century, that is, the incorporation of the Ruler *qua* Ruler into the body of the Church.[1]

The doctrinal implementation of the transformed status of the Ruler presented far fewer difficulties than might have been expected. Here doctrine could look back to a distinguished ancestry beginning in the Roman Church during the pontificate of Leo I: it was during the second half of the fifth century that seminal and basic (papal) ideas relative to Rulership in a Christian society came to be enunciated. Here was one of the openings for the literary Renaissance, and here we find an explanation for the predilection of the Carolingian scholars for the patristic writers and, in short, for anything that might be considered classical Christian literature. To this subject of Christian Rulership we shall also return in due course.

But this topic is merely a segment of a much larger one. You may recall that the realization of the social Renaissance was to be in conformity with the accepted Christian doctrines, dogmas and principles. The isolated efforts of individual scholars and of specified schools had shown that there was in fact an untapped reservoir of a great variety of doctrines. It seemed a dictate of statesmanship as well as of commonsense that for the successful implementation of the Renaissance programme the hitherto evolved doctrine should be made available, studied and distilled, but these tasks necessitated the availability of a much larger body of qualified scholars than had hitherto been the case.

---

[1] With reference to Pippin's anointing H. X. Arquillière, *L'augustinisme politique*, 2nd ed. (Paris, 1955), had magisterially pronounced: 'C'est l'incorporation officielle de l'institution royale dans l'église . . . c'est la traduction liturgique du "ministerium regis" ' (43). For further details of this theme see below 60 ff.

Differently expressed: the programme of the Renaissance of society necessarily involved a literary Renaissance potently orientated towards the Renaissance of society itself. And since in substance this social Renaissance was the practical application of the ecclesiological theme, the bearers of the literary Renaissance suggested themselves to the king in the shape of the ecclesiastics. As the sole bearers of the literary and cultural Renaissance they were destined to play a crucial role in a two-fold capacity, that is, as clerics and as scholars. Their ecclesiastical status provided them with the platform from which they could effectively disseminate the resuscitated doctrines and ideas. It is indeed very seldom that scholars themselves have also been the organs by which their abstract ideas were translated into concrete governmental terms. For it was the ecclesiastics who staffed the royal chancery and thus became instrumental in the formulation of government measures[1] or acted in a corporate capacity as diocesans or as advisers to their bishops in the numerous Frankish councils of the ninth century, which were to become the chief media of ecclesiastical legislation upon which the Rulers relied. In whatever capacity they were engaged, they were vitally concerned with one of the major instruments by which the Renaissance of Frankish society and government was to be implemented – the law applicable to the whole of Frankish society.

It is only when Charlemagne's overriding aim of a Renaissance of society and the concomitant need for better equipped and organized ecclesiastics is considered that his republication of the canon law collection called the *Dionysio-Hadriana* at the Diet of 802 can be understood. This collection was originally made by Dionysius Exiguus in the early sixth century but was enlarged by Pope Adrian I and handed by him to Charlemagne on the occasion of his visit to Rome in 774.[2] Evidently, the purpose of this legislative measure was to provide the ecclesiastics with a unified body of law by which a homogeneous ecclesiastical body was to be created in his realms. The collection was given by Charlemagne the simple title 'Codex canonum' and was known in the court itself as *codex authenticus*.[3] A similar measure was envisaged by him for

---

[1] The anecdote reported by Notker is worth recalling. Charles on one occasion complained to Alcuin about the lack of trained clerks in his chancery: 'I wish I had a dozen Jeromes and Augustines in my chancery' whereupon Alcuin replied: 'Even the Almighty had only these two, and you want a whole dozen of each' (cit. from Fichtenau, op. cit. 40).

[2] See H. E. Feine, *Kirchl. Rechtsgeschichte*, 4th ed. (Weimar, 1964), 151, here also further literature.

[3] About the fate of the collection in the Frankish domains and the numerous copies made in the ninth century, see especially R. Kottje, 'Einheit u. Vielfalt d. kirchl. Lebens in d. Karolingerzeit' in *ZKG* 76 (1965), 323 ff., at 335 ff.

the reform of the monasteries. Charlemagne himself had a copy made from the supposed original of the Rule of St Benedict in Montecassino (*ca* 787), but this attempt at a monastic unification did not bear fruit until Benedict of Aniane joined the court under Louis I and became 'General abbot' for all Carolingian monastic establishments. What was done in 802 in regard to the 'codex canonum' was now in 816 done for the monasteries when an 'institutio' for all of them was issued.[1] Since the programme presupposed firm control of the ecclesiastical body, it is understandable that Charlemagne (and his successors) insisted on the individual churches supplying detailed inventories of all their goods for the inspection of the royal officers (the *missi*).[2]

A reflexion should precede the attempt to characterize this literary Renaissance in the service of the Renaissance of society. Nowadays it is an article of faith that intellectual pursuits in order to merit the designation of scholarship, must be uncommitted and stand aloof from a cause. The justification of this point of view is that scholarship otherwise loses its objectivity and its prime aim of discovering the truth. I do not and cannot express myself on the validity of this standpoint, but within the precincts of Carolingian scholarship – and not even its severest critic can deny that it was scholarship – we have a scholarship which is so much committed that it would be difficult to find an appropriate parallel in history. The scholar-ecclesiastics were *engagé*, for they were committed to exactly the programme which was the official royal plan, the programme of Charlemagne himself. This scholarship served the purpose of resuscitating, discovering and rediscovering the doctrines with the help of which the social Renaissance was to be effected. It is this purely practical complexion of Carolingian scholarship which marked it off from other similar scholarly pursuits in later ages. There was a single-mindedness, a purposefulness in this royally advocated and encouraged scholarship, harnessed as it was to the programme of the Renaissance. One can also advance the view that precisely because they committed the (modern) unforgivable sin of being committed to a programme, their scholarship exhibited vitality, relevance and realism which were presuppositions for its astonishingly rapid success within so short a span of time in excruciatingly difficult conditions.

It is nowadays fashionable to refer to the alienation of creative man,

[1] For this cf. *PG.* 124 and n. 1; Fichtenau, op. cit. 196 ff.; Kottje art. cit. 331 ff.; and esp. J. Semmler, 'Reichsidee u. kirchl. Gesetzgebung' in *ZKG* 71 (1960), 37 ff., at 43 ff.; id. ibid. 74 (1963), 15 ff., esp. 65 ff.

[2] For this see the exhaustive study by E. Lesne, *La propriété ecclésiastique*, iii (1936): *L'inventaire de la propriété*.

be he scholar or writer or artist, from the government and the society surrounding him. The repeated assertion that there exists an unbridgeable division between the politician wielding power and the scholars and thinkers concerned with matters to which no power is attached, seems to contain a kernel of truth. The reason why I mention this feature of withdrawal or indifference, is simply to demonstrate the contrast between this modern phenomenon and the world upon whose consideration we have embarked, for in the Carolingian epoch there was, as far as the littérateurs and scholars were concerned, no such divisive gulf, but on the contrary an intimacy and closeness of contact between government and scholar without which the evolving governmental doctrines, the vigour of intellectual pursuit and the radical change in the field of public government, would be well-nigh incomprehensible. For there was mutual dependence between the government and ecclesiastical thinkers: the latter supplied the intellectual equipment for the former to execute the Renaissance of society; and the government provided the right conditions under which the latter were enabled to pursue their vocation. The relationship between government and scholar in the Carolingian age was *mutatis mutandis* not intrinsically different from that which prevails today between government and atomic physicists and the technocrats of the various denominations. Present-day Harwell or Porton or Cape Kennedy were preceded by the Carolingian centres of Rheims, Le Mans, Metz and Fulda.

Yet, I would not convey a realistic picture if in this same context I were not to draw your attention to the alienation that emerged on a different plane: it was the incipient and rapidly evolving alienation of the broad masses of Carolingian society from the government itself. This alienation of the *populus* from the *gubernatores* is easily understandable in view of the very ideas which were to bring about the Renaissance of Carolingian society. There can be little doubt that the estrangement or dissociation of the people from the government was inherent in the ecclesiastical ideology of theocratic Rulership. For with the conferment of power on the Ruler the people had nothing to do and could not, therefore, interfere in its execution; power was held to stem from divinity. Within this descending theme of government there was no possibility that the people could emerge as a politically creative and active organ: the succeeding centuries right down to the threshold of our time bear witness to the barrier that existed between people and government.

Nevertheless, the monopoly of education and literacy which the

Carolingian ecclesiastics obtained for reasons which should not be difficult to understand, was unaccompanied by the benefits which a later age was to confer upon scholarship, that is, the benefits which the mechanics of higher education and the organized regularity of advanced academic training produced. For in the ninth century there were no universities and this precluded the training of a regular supply of younger scholars.[1] The absence of universities on the other hand had the advantage that the scholars had a degree of freedom in scholarly pursuits of which later generations might well be envious: they were thrown back upon their own resources, their self-reliance and ingenuity. This institutional lack of universities must be held responsible, in great part any rate, for the absence of a third and fourth generation of scholars, and partly explains the gradual intellectual decomposition which is noticeable in the beginning of the tenth century. But on the other hand this freedom from academic burdens permitted the scholars to concentrate on topical and practical issues and especially on legislating in their own ecclesiastical assemblies or through the instrumentality of the king. And this legislation concerned itself overwhelmingly with precisely those issues, subjects and topics which were held relevant for the Renaissance, the rebirth or renewal of the Frankish people. Next to the practical work of legislation – to which I will turn in my next lecture – the Carolingian age also saw for the first time in European history the emergence of a special genre of literature, that is, the monographic literature devoted to the exegetical treatment of certain problems falling within the orbit of the public government. The literary species of *specula regum*[2] also begins to make its tentative début. In short, the social Renaissance entailed a literary Renaissance which was scholarship devoted to the rebirth of Frankish society, a rebirth in the Christian sense as understood at the time. The literary Renaissance was a means to an end.

This character of the literary Renaissance evidently imprinted itself on its own manifestations. If we keep in mind that the Renaissance of society was, so to speak, to work from top downwards, we shall find it easier to understand the character of this literary Renaissance. To begin with, it was exclusively Latin: one or two exceptions apart, there was

---

[1] The disadvantages arising out of the absence of universities become all the more conspicuous when the social links of the universities in the high M.A. are considered, about which see P. Classen, 'Die hohen Schulen u.d. Gesellschaft im 12. Jh.' in *AKG* 48 (1966), 155 ff.

[2] For a useful conspectus of these see L. K. Born in *Rev. Belge de phil. et d'hist.*, 12 (1933), 583 ff.

hardly any worthwhile attempt to translate Greek material or to study Greek in depth.[1] This feature quite obviously had repercussions beyond the immediate literary confines, because the works resuscitated and analysed and applied, transmitted the Roman–Latin tenor and thus potently and crucially assisted in the task of reorientating Frankish society in conformity with the underlying Roman thought-processes, overwhelmingly manifesting themselves in the reawakened patristic lore. It was Tertullian, Cyprian, Jerome, Augustine, Boethius, Cassiodore, and a host of others who were now studied and who shaped the minds of those in the inner cabinets of the kings and their advisers. Herewith was transmitted and absorbed a good deal of ancient and notably hellenistic Ruler ideology and Ruler cult through the medium of early Christian writings in Latin translation and consequently of patristic authors.[2] But it was not mere resuscitation which one here sees at work, because in resuscitating patristic or classical writers of Christian antiquity the ecclesiastical scholars at the same time made these authorities applicable to their contemporary conditions and hence an integral part of the process of remodelling. Society began to be conceived in terms of its adaptation to the programme extracted from the ancient Latin–Christian writers rather than in those of its own history and experience and its own inner-native forces.

No doubt, the Latin[3] character of this literary Renaissance gave Carolingian (and for that matter subsequent medieval) scholarship an international or, if you like, an inter-regional character. There was, as yet, no more than the amorphously conceived, dimly felt and wholly inarticulate awareness of the differences between French and German;

[1] See Laistner, op. cit. 238 ff., on the superficiality of Greek knowledge in the ninth century. For John Scotus as the translator of Pseudo-Denis, see below 114 f.; see further, B. Bischoff, *Mittelalterliche Studien* (Stuttgart, 1967), ii. 246 ff.

[2] Here the influence of Eusebius in the Latin translation by Rufinus of Aquileja is noteworthy. Cf., e.g., L. Bréhier and P. Batiffol, *Les survivances du culte impérial romain* (Paris, 1920), esp. 6 ff.; F. J. Dölger in *Antike & Christentum*, iii (1932), 119; N. Baynes in *Ann. de l'institute de philologie et d'histoire orientales*, ii (1934); E. Peterson, *Theol. Traktate* (Munich, 1951), esp. 49 ff.; L. Prestige, *God in patristic thought*, 2nd ed. (London, 1952), 92 ff.; L. Cerfaux and J. Tondriau, *Un concurrent du christianisme: le culte des souverains* (Paris, 1957); J. A. Straub, *Vom Herrscherideal in der Spätantike* (repr. Darmstadt, 1964); F. Taeger, *Charisma* (Stuttgart, 1960), esp. ii. 246 f.

[3] Clearly as a result of the awakened interest in education, style and grammar and the consequential zest for collecting all sorts of works – notably in Charles' own court library as well as in Fulda, Lorsch, Lyons, St Thierry, etc. – even minor ancient pagan writers found a niche in the libraries, quite apart from Cicero, Virgil, Horace, Ovid. But this didactic aspect of the Renaissance falls outside the scope of my enquiry. For some magnificent reproductions of artistic, cultural and generally literary products, see D. A. Bullough, *The Age of Charlemagne*, cit.

and when on the political map of Europe the treaty of Verdun (843) made changes which were to endure beyond the Middle Ages, it was scholarship once more which in this very same decade provided an ideological supra-regional link in the shape of another Latin – though this time spurious – document, the Pseudo-Isidorian concoction which, too, was to display its effects far beyond the Middle Ages. Yet this supra-regional scholarship couched as it was in exclusively Latin terms, enveloped Western Europe in a veritable protective cocoon: Western Europe came to be quite effectively immunized against Greek–Byzantine influences. In any case, Latin was no 'native' language and therefore the impact which this Carolingian scholarship and education was able to make upon the layman was bound to be restricted.[1] Attempts at an education on a broad scale floundered on the medium of communication, the Latin language. What training there was available, was vocational, such as training in chancery work, training for the profession of a notary, training for the correct performance of the ecclesiastical chant, and so on. Teachers and pupils in these vocational 'training schools' were clerics. The very idea of vocational schooling would in-indicate its overwhelming utilitarian character: it was the kind of society which determined its primary needs, hence also the legislatively enforced establishment of cathedral and monastic schools for the education of the succeeding ecclesiastical generation.[2]

Once more we find here a feature which was to accompany the observer right through the greater part of the Middle Ages: the conscious cultivation of an intellectual élite consisting of the higher ecclesiastics on the one hand, and the neglect of the vast mass of the agrarian population in intellectual and educational respects on the other.[3] These two layers of the population found it very hard to bridge the gulf separating them. It is as well to invite your attention to these features: to the extent to which this literary Renaissance was supra-regional, to the same extent it was restricted to Latin literature and to the same extent it was confined to an élite, the ecclesiastical intelligentsia, who were to be the actual manipulators of the social Renaissance. This literary Renaissance stood to the social Renaissance in the same relation as theology stood to Christianity. Just as theology without Christianity would have been

[1] Charles seems to have realized this as his encouragement of the native language would demonstrate, see Einhard, *Vita Karoli*, c. 29.

[2] Cf. also E. Lesne, op. cit. v (1940): *Les écoles de la fin du VIII* à la fin du XII* siècle*, 27 ff.

[3] Cf. the excellent observations by J. F. Lemarignier in F. Lot-R. Fawtier, *Hist. des institutions françaises au M.A.*, iii (1962), 3–4.

unthinkable in that epoch, in the same way the literary Renaissance made sense only against the larger background of its social counterpart. And just as the theologians oftentimes spoke language barely comprehensible to the ordinary Christian, in the same way the doctrine set forth by the adepts of the literary Renaissance would not have always been understood by the mass of Frankish society in whose Christian interests the movement was entertained.

In pursuit of the ecclesiological theme Frankish society was to be clothed in the basic characteristics of christian religion as understood at the time. If for that period one feature was outstanding, it was the wholeness (or 'totalitarian') character of the Christian theme itself. Accordingly, it was one society which received its determinant marks from its alleged origin in divinity: this one society was the Church, and in the as yet barely noticed change from the *populus* (or the *gens*) *Francorum* to the *populus Dei* (or *christianus*) lies the proof for the operation of the ecclesiological theme, by the instrumentality of which the Renaissance of society was to be realized.[1] Hence in conformity to and in accordance with the basic premisses of the ecclesiological theme and the wholeness point of view, there was no conceptual separation between the religious, political, moral, etc., norms.[2] Moreover, there was no conceptual distinction between a Carolingian State and a Carolingian Church,[3] nor anything approaching a pluralistic society and on these premisses none could come about. This undifferentiated cosmology reflected the ancient Christian point of view that life on this

---

[1] Cf. E. Delaruelle in *RHEF* 39 (1953) at 191–2. Some notice of this was taken by E. Ewig in *Das Königtum: seine geistigen & rechtl. Grundlagen*, ed. Th. Mayer (Darmstadt, 1965), 45, but he did not pursue it: 'Das neue Königssakrament (sanktionierte) zugleich die Stellung der Franken als Gottesvolk des neuen Bundes.' Cf. also 69, note 288. In his *Laudes regiae* (Berkeley, repr. 1958), E. H. Kantorowicz, 57, came near the point by saying that 'the king began to represent a type of Ruler modelled on David. He was the *novus Moyses*, the *novus David*. He was the priestly king, the *rex et sacerdos*.' M. Wallace-Hadrill, art. cit. (below n. 3), 38, rightly points out (though with reference to Louis I's downfall) that 'the *universus populus* was conceived in biblical and not in Germanic terms'. Cf. in this context also H. Löwe, *Die karol. Reichsgründung u. der Südosten* (Stuttgart, 1937), 137 ff.; and G. Tellenbach in *HJb* 69 (1949), 103 ff., at 122 ff.

[2] See also E. Delaruelle, *RHEF* 38 (1952), 71: this age did not know 'notre distinction du profane et du sacré'.

[3] Cf. also L. Halphen, *A travers l'histoire du M.A.* (Paris, 1959), 92 ff., for whom the distinction between Church and State is rightly 'une méprise complete'. What there is, is 'ce fait capital que l'église et l'état ne font qu'un' (100). Cf. also the very apt remark of M. Wallace-Hadrill, 'The via regia of the Carolingian age' in *Trends in Medieval Politica. Thought*, ed. B. Smalley (Oxford, 1965), 39: 'I am not positive what this (distinction) means.' Cf. also now D. Köhler in *Adel u. Kirche: Festschrift G. Tellenbach* (Freiburg, 1968), at 156 ('peinlich anachronistisch').

earth was no more than a preparation for the next – hence a pluralistic atomizing standpoint would have been quite incomprehensible to a contemporary – so that this-worldly and other-worldly issues flowed into one. Indeed, here we move entirely within the precincts of a doctrinally preconceived programme which by reshaping Frankish society attempted nothing less than the conquest of a historically evolved society.

No other single factor was more instrumental and crucial in the process of transforming Frankish society than the Bible. The Bible was credited with the status of a textbook containing all the relevant maxims, axioms and norms relative to (private and) public life. To Charlemagne and his advisers the Bible was not only a book of religious edification or instruction or divine revelation but also and above all a book which between two stiff covers, so to speak, embodied the sum-total of all knowledge necessary for the ideological Renaissance of Frankish society. Charlemagne, himself apostrophized as (the Old Testament) David in his inner circle, is on record as having expressed himself on the value of the Bible in these words:

> For it is a treasure store which lacks in nothing whatsoever, is abundantly provided with all that is good; whoever approaches this treasure with a devout mind and searches for anything in good faith, will profit from this knowledge and enrich himself.[1]

Several other statements of Charlemagne to the same effect could be quoted: they all sufficiently explain his insistent advocacy of the study of the Bible by his contemporaries, notably the higher ecclesiastics. For, as he once more declared,

> In the Scriptures there will be found the norm, on the basis of which authority is instituted, and according to which the superiors should act towards their subjects and the subjects towards their superiors ... how secular counsels are to be taken with prudent deliberation, how the fatherland is to be defended, how the enemy is to be repelled.[2]

Hence his proclamation of the utility and beneficial effects of biblical

---

[1] *Libri Carolini*, ed. F. Bastgen (suppl. vol. to *MGH. Conc.* 1924), ii. 30, p. 96, lines 18 ff. For the *Libr. Carol.* on which Charles lavished great care and which were written for him by Theodulf of Orleans, see now A. Freeman in *Speculum*, 40 (1965), 203 ff.; here also, 287–9, some emendations to the *MGH.* text. This study would seem to have settled the problem of authorship.

[2] *Libr. Car.*, pp. 92 ff., esp. 96, lines 12 ff.

studies and scholarship, because it is in any case pure truth, is immutable and undefiled: the Bible was to him the instrument of celestial governance through which the pattern of the right kind of earthly government may be discerned; in brief, it was the beacon for mankind.[1]

It is only when due emphasis is given to the views which Charlemagne held in regard to the value of the Bible for purposes of government that one can understand his royal programme of promoting biblical studies. On the other hand – and I must strongly emphasize this – there was no royal programme which made the revision of the Bible its goal nor is there any evidence that the king himself had ordered a new text of the Bible.[2] Hence there was no such thing as a specific Alcuin Bible[3] nor was there a royal command to revise the Bible and establish a new 'purified' text. What Charlemagne did – and in this he merely followed up his own programme of a Renaissance of society – was to create conditions favourable for the study of the Bible, to stimulate and further these scholarly efforts and to promote the exchange of biblical-exegetical works.[4] We ought to be clear about this: it was not biblical exegesis *per se* which Charlemagne had at heart, but an exegesis and study of the text in order to find the divinely inspired pattern for contemporary Frankish society, the *populus Dei*. The presupposition for this purposeful task was, however, the availability of a Bible text, that is, a sufficiency of copies. It is not necessary to remind you that this royal furtherance of biblical studies was clearly formulated within the last ten to fifteen years of the eighth century, just the time when the frontiers of his kingdom had been vastly expanded: the newly conquered people were, so to speak, 'raw', and in order to provide the missionaries and intellectual and religious leaders with the model which contained the eternal truth, an adequate number of copies had to be made available.

Two material consequences followed. First, the quite rapid and accelerated production of Bibles within the last two decades of Charlemagne's reign. I do not exaggerate that, in relative terms, at no other time in European history was the Bible so frequently copied within so short a time. So far from his having ordered a revised text, the extant copies abundantly prove that there was no uniformity of the text, nor

---

[1] Ibid., pp. 98–9.

[2] The common opinion was effectively demolished by Bonifatius Fischer, 'Bibeltext u. Bibelreform unter Karl d. Gr.' in *Karl d. Gr.*, cit. ii. 156 ff.

[3] Id. ibid., 169–75.

[4] Id., 162–3, 216.

c

could this ever be achieved,[1] because the 'printing houses' were dispersed throughout the realm. This fact is linked with the second consequence: these *scriptoria* were not only wholly and exclusively staffed by ecclesiastics, but were also under the supervision of ecclesiastics. The result was that the circle of ecclesiastics came to be drawn larger and larger, since the copyists invariably and understandably belonged to the lower echelons of the hierarchy, largely also to monkish establishments, so that in this way literacy spread at least to the inferior clerical sections. The need for a greater number of copies of the Bible, for the reasons stated, stimulated the extension of literacy downwards, and not incomprehensibly reacted most favourably upon the execution of the Carolingian enterprise of renewing Frankish society. It is time we considered some of the ways and means with which this was done.

[1] Cf. also Laistner, op. cit. 205–6.

The Instruments of the Renaissance

If any particular date is to be assigned to the beginning of the process in the course of which the Franks came to be – in the ecclesiastical sense – reborn or regenerated, it would be conveniently and justifiably be that of the council convoked by Karlmann, the maior domus and son of Charles Martell; this was presided over by St Boniface in 742. The reason why he had convoked this council was, as he explained in the *Capitulare*, to have the benefit of episcopal advice in the task he had set himself of establishing the 'lex Dei et ecclesiastica religio' for his *populus Dei*.[1] This concept of the *populus Dei* signifying nothing less than the Frankish people, was to become the crucial and basic idea throughout the next century and a half. Charlemagne himself in his 'Admonitio generalis' found this concept of the *populus Dei* a convenient operational instrument, when he laid down certain duties of bishops and dukes towards the Frankish population.[2] It would only be tedious to give more instances of this ideological device in the subsequent period. Its meaning seems clear enough: the educational and instructional and disciplinary measures enjoyed by the Carolingian kings in their numerous decrees and laws (the *Capitularia*) were addressed to the Frankish people as the 'people of God', so as to broadcast their regeneration and rebirth as the *populus christianus*. This transformation or rebirth was to do away with the customs, traditions and practices as they had developed in the past: the *populus Dei* was to live and to arrange its public (and private) matters, was to organize itself by shedding its outdated laws and manners[3] and by following the norms, the laws, the

[1] *Cap.* 10, pref., and cc. 3, 5, p. 25 = *MGH. Conc.*, pp. 2–4. In this context the prologue to the *Lex Salica* is noteworthy, cf. *PG.* 61 f., with sources and literature. The comment on this prologue by D. A. Bullough, *The Age of Charlemagne*, cit. 39, is worth quoting: 'The God of the Old Testament and the New had acquired a new chosen people.' In comparison with the Merovingian charters the royal charters of the Arnulfings and early Carolingians show considerable differences which reveal ecclesiastical influence to a marked degree; cf. the highly meritorious study by I. Heidrich, 'Titulatur und Urkunden . . .' in *AD* 12 (1966), 71 ff.; cf. 137 f., 169 ff., 228.

[2] *Cap.* 22, p. 53 = Ansegisus, *Coll.*, pref., in *MGH. Capitularia*, i. 397.

[3] The notice of Einhard, *Vita Karoli*, c. 29, that Charles had ordered the redaction of the laws and customs of his subject peoples, deserves special attention in this context.

prohibitions and injunctions germane to the *populus Dei*. Society, in other words, was to be viewed entirely from the ecclesiological angle and was to be based, not on Frankish or Germanic or any other naturally grown habits and usages, but on the laws of God.

This was exactly the significance of one of Charlemagne's *Capitularia*, possibly the most important of his reign in this context. It was the *Capitulare* which he issued at Aachen in 802 and in which he gave precision to the oath to be taken to himself by everyone in the Frankish realms. This oath imposed upon everyone the duty of observing the divine precepts as well as the law of the Church in the interests of service to God.[1] The programme of a rebirth of the Franks in the ecclesiological sense could not, I am inclined to think, be expressed better than by this legislative measure. Moreover, in this whole lengthy *Capitulare* the Franks themselves were spoken of in only isolated instances, and then only in reference to the past. Indeed, seen from this angle, the expression on Charlemagne's seal of the *Renovatio Romani imperii* gains in this context added significance.[2] This idea of a rebirth of necessity led to a monopoly of power on the part of the ecclesiastics, because they alone were credited with the knowledge of God's laws and precepts. Hence it is – I mention this as a mere instance – that from the moment the process of the Frankish Renaissance became operative, episcopal visitation became an invariable and inevitable governmental public measure aimed at controlling not only the clerics, but also, as Pippin in 744 had already clearly laid down and as it was repeated throughout the following decades, the laymen.[3] Charlemagne ordered annual episcopal visitation extending at the same time the competency of the bishops.[4] Evidently, the needs of an ecclesiologically conceived society were different from those of a purely natural entity, and consequently it is understandable why the chief criterion of all Carolingian legislation and its enforcement was the *salus et necessitas* of the Franks in their regenerated status as the *populus Dei*.[5] Differently expressed: the well-being and the requirements of a people depended no longer on the observance of custom and historically or genetically developed usages and corresponding laws, but on the element that alone imparted life to

---

[1] *Cap.* 33, cc. 3–5, pp. 92–3.

[2] For this see the interpretation in *PG* 110 ff., and also below 139 f.

[3] *Cap.* 12, c. 4, p. 29. Episcopal visitation for purely clerical supervision had of course been practised since the late fourth century.

[4] *Cap.* 19, c. 7, p. 45 (the visiting bishop should 'populum confirmare et plebes docere et investigare'); further *Cap.* 22, c. 70, p. 59; etc.

[5] Cf., e.g., *Cap.* 255 of June 844, cc. 5–7, p. 257.

the *populus Dei*, the faith as expounded by the ecclesiastics: this was the element that vivified and animated and maintained the fabric of this body. It seems comprehensible that in this process of Renaissance the Frankish people came to be compared with, and also to take the place of, the Old Testament Jewish people.[1]

This process of transformation presents the spectator with a singularly persuasive demonstration of the capacity of ideas to conquer the slowly matured and apparently firmly entrenched habits, traditions and customs. The 'new society' was to absorb these established features of the Frankish people, and thus to render them harmless. The rapidity with which this process advanced, was not only due to the dynamic royal policy, not only due to the ecclesiastical talent the kings could muster, but above all to the absence of any defence on the part of the conservative and traditional forces: for who was there to represent their interests in the face of the ideological avalanche that was to engulf men and society from the mid-eighth century onwards? Had the 'Establishment' anything that seemed worth defending? Had it anyone capable of putting forward its own case, if there was one? To ask these questions seems to me advisable, if only to make more easily accessible to understanding the historically highly significant process that unfolded itself in the Carolingian era.

I

It would therefore appear profitable to look at the instruments by which this Frankish rebirth came in actual fact to be effected, or perhaps we should say by which its realization was attempted.

One of the oldest means of supplying a Christian body public with appropriate norms of living was the ecclesiastical council. And here indeed the Merovingian period had quite effectively prepared the ground, although for reasons irrelevant to my main topic, Merovingian and Carolingian Frankish councils showed some differences.[2] There was in fact more kinship between Visigothic and Anglo-Saxon councils on the one hand and the Carolingian assemblies on the other than between the latter and their immediate predecessors. Visigothic councils showed

---

[1] Cf., e.g., *Cap.* 293, c. 29, p. 406.

[2] The main difference was that the Merovingian councils were exclusively clerical assemblies; their decrees related to the clergy predominantly; royal officers did not enforce the decrees; the councils themselves were as often as not merely consultative assemblies for the kings.

considerable Byzantine and late Roman imperial influence,[1] and since Reccared's government the kings leaned heavily on them. The councils approached the function of royal diets, since apart from the ecclesiastics a number of palatine officers and other (well-selected) laymen took part. The competency of Visigothic synods embraced purely ecclesiastical and royal matters, including even royal succession, protection of the royal family, definition of high treason, imposition of taxes, and so on.[2] That the Anglo-Saxon councils had much in common with the Visigothic conciliar practice, has long been noted,[3] with one qualification, however. For in Anglo-Saxon England the Witan to all intents and purposes had absorbed the ecclesiastical council,[4] though the intellectual leadership belonged to the ecclesiastics.[5] The subject-matter of the Anglo-Saxon conciliar decrees was both clerical and royal.

In regard to the Carolingian councils, there is no doubt that they were convoked by the king and could not become lawful assemblies unless and until the king had done so. The composition of these councils was mixed, hence they are rightly called *concilia mixta*, so that one can indeed speak of them as royal assemblies in which ecclesiastical as well as lay persons participated and in which the ecclesiastics functioned as experts whose opinions in the numerous religious and semi-religious questions submitted to them, was decisive – and was soon to become directive. And these questions related to the ideological substructure and doctrinal superstructure of the new 'society', in other words to the fundamental issues with which any society in the process of transformation is faced. The role of the higher ecclesiastics as experts in the royally convened councils was due to their forming an integral part of the kingdom itself, of the *populus Dei*, and consequently of its diet which was the council. That the ecclesiastics came to change their role from consultants to determinant organs, seems to me in the main due to two factors, and both already displayed their force in Charlemagne's reign.

The one is to be sought in Charlemagne's immediate institutional surroundings, that is, what has been called his own ministry of public education and spiritual instruction situated in his own court or what

---

[1] See K. F. Stroheker, *Germanentum & Spätantike* (Zürich, 1965), at 207 ff., esp. 234 ff.; here also further literature.

[2] For details see in *PL* 84: Toledo IV, c. 75, col. 384 ff.; Toledo VIII, c. 10, col. 425 f.; Toledo XIII, cc. 1, 3, 6, col. 489, 491, 493–4.

[3] W. Stubbs, *Constit. Hist.*, i. 252.

[4] P. Hinschius, *Das Kirchenrecht* (Berlin, 1883), iii. 546 n. 2.

[5] F. Liebermann, ii. 737 sub no. 7, and 676 sub no. 1.

some of his contemporaries, notably Alcuin, called the academy.[1] In this court academy its members debated in the presence of the king, who was ever hungry for more knowledge, the kind of questions relevant to the attempted transformation of the society under his control; and it was this scholarly and informed dialogue that prompted some literary productions on the questions debated as well as some instructions which were given to royal and episcopal officers: in one way or another this court academy constituted a reservoir of ecclesiastical personnel as well as a vehicle for the dissemination of ideas: in personal and impersonal respects it potently fertilized the ground upon which synodal decrees were eventually to fall.

The second factor is intimately linked with the first, for it was to a very large extent the same personages who had frequented the academy, who became bishops and abbots and as such participated in the ecclesiastical councils of the time; moreover it was sometimes the pupils of these scholars who continued the work of their teachers in the practical workaday world. What I would like to stress here is the added weight which these 'courtly' scholars were to assume: indeed, it does not need particular acumen or special insight into group psychology to realize how much more effective and influential the corporate personality of a synod was in comparison with that of an individual; although the individuals were the same they assumed when once assembled by the king's order in the synod a corporate and organic personality, the authority and influence of which was understandably greater than the statement of one or two individual scholars, however eminent in themselves. The synods presented a closely knit front which by virtue of their group personality manifested in the synodal decrees and decisions, had in contemporary conditions the weight of a modern parliamentary assembly. To this in itself highly significant feature one more must be added: the decrees had to be republished in the hierarchically placed lower churches, and it was at this juncture that an intimate contact between the people at the grass roots and the formative organs of the 'new society' was established. In the last resort, however, the synodal decrees and canons – we shall presently have to deal with some of them – distilled into the language of the law the doctrine or dogma long before discussed in the academy or set forth in some epistolary product or even, as we shall see, in what with every reason can be called a monograph that appeared before the respective synod.

[1] For this see F. Brunhölzl, 'Der Bildungsauftrag d. Hofschule' in *Karl d. Gr.*, cit., ii. 28 ff. and J. Fleckenstein, ibid., i. 41 ff.

Against this background the ascendancy of the ecclesiastics from the role of consultant experts to that of determinant organs becomes understandable. Evidently, the actuality of the situation had something to do with this ascendancy. Frankish society became more and more soaked with religious and ecclesiastical elements, especially from the second decade of the ninth century onwards. It would be a facile explanation if this acceleration and depth of penetration were to be sought in Louis I's government or in the difficulties which the unexpected addition to his family created. What must not be forgotten is that his father had in a most effective and enduring way set the ecclesiastics on their successful path and that as a result of this royal initiative in the last years of his reign they showed a considerable degree of self-awareness, self-realization as well as self-assertion, and also some not negligible independence from the king himself.[1] Clearly, the weakness of Louis I's government facilitated this progress greatly, but it did not create the conditions upon which the ecclesiastics were able to act in a determinative manner: was not Louis himself the very product of this royally initiated and ecclesiastically inspired education? By the time of Charlemagne's death the ecclesiastics had emerged as a most capable, dynamic and alert intellectual élite – who was there to counterbalance their weighty and determinative influence? They were the ideological and religious offsprings of Charlemagne – the implications were and are plain.

It is assuredly no coincidence that the brisk conciliar activity of the ninth century began in 816 at Aachen and continued for exactly one hundred years. And the subject-matters which engaged the synodists belonged overwhelmingly to the public sphere, belonged to those matters which in all societies formed their structural background and ideological sustenance. What is of at least equal significance is that the synod began to split off from the royal (or imperial) assembly.[2] Although the right of the king as the sole legitimate organ to convoke the synod remained untouched through the subsequent period,[3] it is nevertheless worthy of remark that when Louis I summoned no less than four large councils in one year (829) to be held at Mainz, Paris, Lyons and Toulouse, the framework of the discussion allowed considerable freedom; and of particular concern is the enlargement of ecclesiastical legislative competency. Louis ordered the archbishops, bishops and abbots

---

[1] Cf. *PG* 123 ff.

[2] For this see P. Hinschius, *Kirchenrecht*, cit. iii. 554.

[3] For an early instance of a purely ecclesiastical assembly summoned by Louis I, see the Council of Aachen in 817, *Conc.* ii. 312 ff.

of virtually the whole Frankish realm when treating of the matters pertaining to religion, to declare what was and what was not to be accepted by the princes and the people: the synodists should make known what divine authority teaches ('ut divina auctoritas docet').[1] It would be erroneous to hold that this highly significant royal (imperial) purpose of summoning these four councils amounted to an abdication, amounted to handing over to the ecclesiastics matters which directly and intimately affected the kingdom and all its people. Yet I do not think it is an exaggeration to say that in these councils we have the concrete and visible proof of the higher ecclesiastics reaching the height of legislators and relinquishing the status of mere consultant experts. And indeed, this development was unmistakably pre-portrayed in Charlemagne's own thought-pattern, his own aims, his own governmental framework. It would seem quite superfluous to draw any comparison between the status of the ecclesiastics in the second and third decades of the ninth century, let alone of later decades, with that of barely a generation earlier. The knowledge of what the *divina auctoritas* teaches, to use Louis' own words, constituted the special qualification of the ecclesiastics: and no other qualification was more vital and necessary for the Renaissance of Frankish society than this one. And joined to it was great talent, training in scholarship, and purposefulness – all presuppositions for successfully effecting a very real Renaissance. What body or movement should have impeded this evolution, this 'ecclesiastization' of Frankish society?

To these observations on the ascendancy of the ecclesiastics in their corporate capacity should be added at least a brief reference to the material which enabled them to produce the transformation of Frankish society. Their own native contribution was on the whole limited: originality of thought was certainly not their strength. But this was of lesser concern than the dexterity and the skill with which they applied ancient material to the exigencies as they saw them. There was adoption, there was adaptation, there was adjustment of a Cyprian, an Ambrose, an Augustine, an Isidore, let alone of papal and conciliar statements of an early period: what all these sources propounded in an abstract way, was now brought down to the grass roots of a very concrete social entity. Thereby these authorities not only became part and parcel of the Frankish intellectual equipment but also the doctrinal forces upon which Frankish society was to rest. It was the fallow yet fertile soil of the

---

[1] *Cap.* 184, pp. 2–3; the same in the convocation preamble for Aachen in 836: *Conc.* ii. 56, p. 705.

Frankish realm which at once explains and made necessary the utilization of this ancient material as well as the resulting syncretism. Here again the briefest comparison between this state of affairs and the one prevailing a generation earlier shows the advance made. Seen from this angle, the lack of originality dwindles into insignificance. By absorbing ancient material of patristic, papal, conciliar provenance, the Frankish ecclesiastics whether alone or much more frequently in their corporate capacity as synodists, supplied the legal instruments by which the transformation or the rebirth of Frankish society was to be carried into effect. For the conciliar decree was law properly conceived; it was a law which was focused as much on the external as on the internal side of man; it was a law which embodied the very essence of Christianity, its 'wholeness' character, and therefore embraced the whole man. As yet there is no distinction between (enforceable) law and (unenforceable) morals.

I cannot conclude this section without mentioning an epiphenomenon of this Carolingian Renaissance. The more the ecclesiastical scholars occupied themselves with the sources and with turning them into concrete synodal decrees and laws to realize the Renaissance of society, the more it must have appeared to them that in order to be complete, in order to suppress the numerous surviving Germanic customs, and so on, some more radical measures were called for. But these, with the means at their disposal, could hardly be put into practice without some additional measures. The point I wish to make is that the concoction of the forgeries in the mid-ninth century – to wit, Pseudo-Isidore, Benedictus Levita and Angilramn – were means partly to accelerate the progress and to help along the process of transformation, and partly to eradicate customs and practices which the ecclesiastics considered obnoxious to the whole idea of a Christian body public. These practices – to mention but one or two, the proprietary church system, or the hitherto undisputed right of the king to summon councils which legitimately could issue laws, or the subjection on the part of the clerics to royal jurisdiction – in their aggregate constituted weighty impediments to a fully-fledged transformation in the opinion of the ecclesiastics (engaged in these forgeries). Hence not only the 'supplementation' of the genuine material with the spurious, but above all the provision of proper legal material in the shape of papal decretals from the time of the very first 'popes' in Rome.

The result was that a bridge was thrown between the Frankish ecclesiastics – we might call them the radical wing – and the Roman

Church, for in order to achieve the full transformation, the total rebirth of Frankish society, it appeared to these radicals necessary to take the logically imperative step, that is to withdraw entirely from the royal side and to subordinate themselves in a wholly institutional and jurisdictional respect, to the Roman Church by recognizing its primatial authority. From the papal point of view the gift which the Frankish forger-ecclesiastics made to the Roman Church was as unexpected as it was to prove useful, but from the domestic Frankish standpoint the forgeries provided an anchor, the safest possible platform for the subsequent generations, for in these documents the earliest extant statements of the papacy were made on precisely those issues which these ecclesiastics considered to be in need of drastic curtailment, if not of total abolition.[1] The reason why these forgeries, notably Pseudo-Isidore (produced within the decade of 845 and 855) did not at once make their full impact in the Frankish domains, is understandable: for the great majority of the ecclesiastics this material appeared too radical, but as it always is in such situations, it is the small radical purposeful minority which gradually makes headway and becomes the dominant majority. This state of affairs was reached in the closing decades of the century. From the genesis of the European point of view it is necessary to draw these forgeries into the orbit of historical consideration.

II

The prime concern of Rulership in all civilized societies is the establishment and maintenance of those conditions which are conducive to the realization of society's basic aims. These conditions are commonly regarded as public peace and order and welfare which are, however, merely short-hand devices for expressing that kind of ideology of which they are the outward manifestation. The kind of public order and peace and welfare encountered in a communist society is assuredly different from that to be found in a capitalist society. By their legislation governments and Rulers attempt to establish the conditions which facilitate, if they do not guarantee the free deployment of those principles upon which their society rests, so that the fulfilment of its purpose becomes feasible. These considerations apply with particular force when a new society is

---

[1] So profound a connoisseur of Frankish diocesan and provincial councils as Ch. de Clercq also considers the appearance of Pseudo-Isidore a decisive moment in the evolution and eventual triumph of Frankish ecclesiastical thought, see his 'La législation religieuse franque' in *Rev. de droit canonique*, 8 (1958), 122 ff., at 145–6.

to supplant its predecessor: not only will legislation be especially plentiful, but it will also be replete with precisely those measures by which the old society is to be reshaped, renewed, in short to be reborn. We have some examples of this renaissance of society very much within our own generation: but exactly the same reflexions can be made about Frankish society in the Carolingian age. Here the *Capitularia* were the royal instruments by which this process of regeneration or rebirth was to be implemented. And indeed in one of his *Capitularia* Charlemagne himself made the establishment and preservation of public peace and order (understood in a Christian sense), the programmatic point of his government.[1] In this very same programmatic pronouncement the idea of the *populus christianus* or the *populus Dei*, just as much as the *filii Dei*, had replaced the *populus Francorum* and the Franks altogether.[2]

This overriding idea of the Carolingians as legislators found concrete expression in the most minute, if not sometimes trivial, details which formed the subject of the *Capitularia*. To be sure, this law-creative device was not the invention of the Carolingians, though there is nothing before which compares in size, scope, substance and extent with the Carolingian *Capitularia*.[3] Although some of them were called *capitularia ecclesiastica* it should not be assumed thereby that the *capitularia mundana* did not deal with ecclesiastical matters: in a society which is in the process of being reborn as the *populus christianus*, there is barely an item that does not exhibit some Christian ingredients, a standpoint at once comprehensible if it is remembered that Christianity seizes the whole of man. Again, the *Capitularia* made synodal decrees their own by excerpting from them or simply repeating them. Since they were, or were intended to be, mainly administrative instructions, the *Capitularia* do not, as a rule, contain much doctrinal argumentation, but as far as the Carolingian Renaissance comes into question, they were first-class transformative agents. It is the great variety of topics which makes the *Capitularia* the royal instruments of the Renaissance – from the detailed regulations concerning baptismal fonts to feast days, Sunday observance, procedural matters concerning clerics, fasting, perjury, matrimony, usury, and so on and so forth. Leaving

---

[1] *Cap.* 22, c. 62, p. 58 = Ansegisus, I. 59, p. 401.

[2] And in fact once more approximating the people of Israel to the Franks, see ibid., c. 61, p. 58.

[3] The most recent and exhaustive study is by F. L. Ganshof, 'Wat waren de capitularia' in *Verhandelingen van de kon. Vlaamse Academie: Kl. d. Letteren*, 22 (1955). See further R. Schneider, 'Zur rechtl. Bedeutung der Kapitularientexte' in *DA* 23 (1967), 273 ff. (in minor respects modifying Ganshof's firm conclusions).

aside Justinian's *Novellae*, it would be hard to find anything in medieval or modern legislation that approaches the amount of ecclesiastical or religious material with which the *Capitularia* are suffused. There was virtually no item that was left untouched: and it is the earthiness of the *Capitularia* which shows them to be also first-class social documents.

A few instances might perhaps be helpful. Charlemagne himself legislated that the women had the specific duty to prepare the linen for the altars;[1] or the clerics were enjoined not to offer drink or meat to a penitent:[2] every parish priest was instructed to have ready the eucharist for cases of imminent death;[3] no parishioner was allowed to attend the services in a neighbouring parish:[4] even the contents of the clerical sermons formed the subject of *Capitularia*;[5] what work may or may not be undertaken on Sundays;[6] the detailed fixing of feast days and holidays of obligation;[7] the duties of godfathers.[8] Of greatest moment, at least from the constitutional-historical point of view, was the standing and position of the ecclesiastics: this was a topic of a number of *Capitularia* and in one way or another protected ecclesiastics from accusations by the lay people;[9] thereby the spurious *Constitutum Silvestri* was turned into an honest legal enactment. To a Christian society it was evidently of some considerable moment that not only ecclesiastically decreed excommunication, that is, exclusion from the benefits of the society, formed the subject of conciliar as well as royal legislation, but it was also of great social significance that in order to give proper effect to excommunication, contact with persons excommunicated by a synod or a bishop was prohibited.[10] Law is not merely a mirror of society: it also is a rather faithful mirror of its underlying conceptions and aims; above all it is a very effective educator and guarantor of social stability. Although no such highfalutin term as teleology would ever have entered the mind of any Carolingian Ruler, there can be, I think, little doubt that their legislation as exhibited in their *Capitularia*, constitutes an almost classic instance of a teleologically conceived creation of the law. Law was at the service of an ideological programme; law was conceived in functional terms.[11]

[1] *Cap.* 81, c. 7, p. 178.   [2] Ibid. c. 12, p. 179.   [3] Ibid. c. 16.
[4] Ibid. c. 8.   [5] Ansegisus, I. 76, pp. 404–5.   [6] Ibid. I. 75, p. 404; II. 7, p. 416.
[7] Ibid. I. 158, p. 413; II. 33, p. 422; *Cap.* 81, c. 19, p. 179.
[8] Ansegisus, I. 35, p. 422.   [9] Ibid. I. 133, p. 411.   [10] Ibid. I. 7, p. 398.
[11] *Mut. mut.* the same may be said about the royal law as has been said about conciliar law, above 27 f. In this connexion special mention should be made of the penetrating study by H. Krause, 'Dauer und Vergänglichkeit im ma. Recht' in *Sav. Z.*, *GA* 75 (1958), 206 ff., esp. 211–31; see further R. Sprandel, 'Ueber das Problem neuen Rechts im früheren M.A.', ibid., *KA* 48 (1962), 117 ff., at 121 ff.

In view of the aim of Carolingian legislation and the purported transformation of Frankish society another topic demands some attention.
Enforcement of the law is perhaps the most serious problem that faces
any legislator. This was a topical problem in the Carolingian age: since
Frankish society was to be sustained by religious principles and since
their enunciation was understandably in the monopolistic hands of the
higher ecclesiastics who, however, had not as a rule the paraphernalia
of effective power at their control, the problem of law enforcement was
solved by the Carolingians, beginning with Charlemagne himself, by
imposing upon the counts the duty to assist the bishops in the exercise
of their judicial functions.[1] And in 813 shortly before his death Charlemagne made obedience of counts, judges and the whole population to
the bishops a general legal and constitutional principle.[2] Throughout
the subsequent decades of the ninth century there is legislation on the
part of the Carolingians to turn royal counts and other officers into
lieutenants and auxiliary organs of the bishops in the exercise of their
episcopal duties.[3] As a matter of fact, Charlemagne himself had once
more initiated this development by laying down that tithes were to be
exacted by royal officers and that if there were disobedience, the guilty
officer was to be convicted of sacrilege, his goods confiscated and handed
to the fisc.[4]

In view of the direction in which Frankish society was moving it
cannot cause much surprise that in the royal *Capitularia* the bishops
were charged with inquisitorial activity: incest, adultery, murder, robbery, rape of nuns, sacrilege, were some of the crimes which were allocated to the bishop's judicial purview:[5] if convicted, the culprit was
forced to do public penance.[6] Moreover, the bishops had acquired very
real powers of controlling the machinery of public government, as, for
instance, the *Capitulare* of Pîtres in 862 made clear when it declared that
negligent royal officers might be compelled to attend to their duties by

---

[1] See the decree of the Frankfurt synod in 794 in *Conc.* ii. 166, c. 6: 'Statutum est a
domino rege et s. synodo ut episcopi faciant iustitias in suis parochiis . . . comites quoque
nostri veniant ad iudicium episcoporum.'

[2] Ibid., *Conc.* ii. 296, c. 10: 'Ut comites et iudices seu reliquus populus obedientes sint
episcopo.'

[3] Cf., e.g., Louis I's *Cap.* 150, c. 7, p. 304; Ansegisus, II. 6, p. 416; II. 23, p. 419:
'Comites . . . adiutores fiant in omnibus' and if found negligent after a second admonition,
notification to the king 'ut auctoritate quod in nostro capitulari continetur, subire cogatur'.

[4] *Cap.* 93, c. 8, p. 197; further Ansegisus, II. 37, p. 422; Louis II in 850, *Cap.* 211, p. 84;
etc.

[5] See, for instance, Lothar in 850, *Cap.* 203, c. 6, p. 66.

[6] This, too, was begun by Charlemagne, see *Conc.* ii. 297, c. 25.

ecclesiastical sanctions, notably excommunication, to be decreed by the bishop.[1] The statement made in a *Capitulare* of Karlmann in 884 expressed the public role of the higher ecclesiastics in this regenerated Frankish society very well: it was the bishops, he said, who attended to the exigencies of the Church as well as of the kingdom.[2] To my mind the ecclesiological transformation of Frankish society, that is, its Renaissance, cannot be better illustrated than by the role which the ecclesiastics were to play in the management of this entity: towards the end of our century King Arnulf at the synod of Tribur in 895 made a programmatic declaration to the effect that it was his royal duty to see that the kingdom entrusted to him by divinity was governed and ruled in accordance with the ecclesiastical law – '*iure ecclesiastico* regere et gubernare'.[3] Or seen from yet another angle, the legislative acts of the Carolingians manifesting themselves in their *Capitularia* were to a not inconsiderable extent the concrete enactments of the theoretical point of view postulated by Isidore of Seville and the fourth Toledan Council; it was the same doctrine also which was now restated by Regino of Prüm at the very end of our Carolingian period: he maintained that if sacerdotal exhortation to implement justice was to prove insufficient, royal power should, then, employ the means of coercion at its disposal.[4]

Considering the ecclesiological complexion of Frankish society it will not be difficult to understand one of its most significant effects. Once more, there is a fairly clear division between the pre-Carolingian and the proper Carolingian periods. Ecclesiastical censures, notably excommunication, displayed no effects outside the immediate ecclesiastical sphere during the Merovingian and very early years of the Carolingian era. The more the changing and changed character of society is taken notice of, the greater the scope will be which excommunication will display in what *prima facie* may be considered non-ecclesiastical spheres. The consideration that the Frankish kingdom was nothing more or less than the realization of the idea of the Church, could not lead to any other view but the one which became prevalent in the ninth century and was expressed in numerous testimonies, namely that an excommunicate

[1] *Cap.* 272, c. 4, p. 308, lines 27 ff.

[2] *Cap.* 272, c. 7, p. 373: 'episcopi qui nostris et suis et communibus ecclesiae atque totius regni necessitatibus occupati sunt'.

[3] *Cap.* 252, c. 3, p. 214: 'Nos igitur quibus cura regni et sollicitudo ecclesiarum Christi commissa est aliter regnum et imperium iure ecclesiastico regere et gubernare non possumus . . .'

[4] Regino of Prüm, II. 296 in *PL* 132, 341: 'Ut quos sacerdotalis admonitio non flectit ad iustitiam, regalis potestas ab improbitate coerceat'; for Isidore, cf. *PG* 28 ff.; Toledo IV, c. 32 in *PL* 84. 375.

person was excluded from practically all relevant public activities in society. Those who were solemnly and publicly excommunicated were unable to live a civic life and were considered, from the social, public and legal point of view, dead persons.[1] On the other hand, the outlawry decreed by royal court or by the Ruler himself, was not by itself credited with these comprehensive effects nor did it on its own account affect the purely ecclesiastical sphere of the culprit. In other words, what primarily mattered, was not the law and the sanctions of the king, but those of the ecclesiastical authorities, and from the point of view of Frankish rebirth this is what one would have expected.

It was particularly the criminal sanctions employed which showed plainly enough how much royal legislation was suffused with purely ecclesiastical criteria, ingredients and modes of thought. A character-istic example was usury which was originally a purely ecclesiastical or if you like religious offence: by royal legislation it became a civil crime as well.[2] The refusal to pay tithes was threatened with exile and con-fiscation of goods.[3] Lords who would not acquiesce in any ecclesiastical punishment of their inferior personnel, incurred both excommunication and the *bannus regius* which carried the appropriate payment for such contempt of royal power as well as an additional defamatory penalty.[4] Similarly, the harbouring and giving comfort to those who had incurred ecclesiastical censure, entailed excommunication as well as the with-drawal of the king's grace.[5] In general, anyone who stood in contempt of ecclesiastical censure, was to be exiled by the king, as the *Capitulare* of Pîtres declared: he was to be persecuted as 'God's and the Church's enemy and as a ravager of the kingdom'.[6] These are mere instances which could easily be multiplied, but I think that they sufficiently demonstrate the strong suffusion of royal legislation with purely ecclesiastical ele-ments: and I think that one can appreciate this ecclesiological develop-ment if, say, one casts a glance back from the just-mentioned *Capitulare* of Pîtres to the time of Pippin the Short's last years of government.

In some respects the Carolingian *Capitularia* may be compared with the *Novellae* of Justinian, especially when the ecclesiastical enactments

---

[1] For details see E. Eichmann, *Acht & Bann im Reichsrecht des M.A.* (Paderborn, 1909), 14 ff.; *PG* 140 ff.

[2] Cf., e.g., *Cap.* 163, c. 5, p. 327.

[3] *Cap.* 191, cc. 6, 7, p. 13.

[4] See *Cap.* 259, c. 9, p. 269. For the Harmscara here mentioned, see H. Brunner, *Deutsche Rechtsgeschichte* (Leipzig, 1908), ii. 596.

[5] *Cap.* 258, c. 10, p. 266: 'excommunicationem ecclesiasticam et motum indignationis regiae'.

[6] *Cap.* 272, c. 4, p. 309.

are considered. Despite a superficial similarity I do not think that the two legislative devices have much in common; nor is there sufficient evidence to show that the *Novellae* exercised influence on the Carolingians. What in the first place distinguishes the *Novellae* from the *Capitularia* is that the latter have been transmitted only at second hand, that is, they were drafted after the kings had orally pronounced them,[1] whilst the *Novellae* were chancery products in the most formal sense and, above all, finely composed legal enactments. Secondly, the *Capitularia* focus attention on the concrete, on the actual situation and aimed at the implementation of certain ecclesiastical principles and canons by every stratum of Frankish society down to its grass roots: they never lost this earthy character; the *Novellae*, whilst they also pursued this aim, nevertheless showed the individual legal enactment as a specific application of some general jurisprudential or ideological or religious or ecclesiastical point of view – hence the extraordinary fascination and beauty of their Arengae; in the *Novellae* the monarchic will was always shown to be the source as well as the point of return of the individual enactment. With this is linked the third difference: the *Capitularia* do not exhibit this monarchic-autonomous will, for they overwhelmingly presupposed ecclesiastical rulings which they endowed with royally supplied enforceability: these ecclesiastical norms or statements or rulings were thereby made into royal law, whereas perhaps the most outstanding feature of the *Novellae* was their emphasis on the expression of the imperial-monarchic will.

III

In modern societies which undergo, or are subjected to, a transformation, press, wireless, television, hand bills, pamphlets, paper-backs, play an increasingly great role in shaping public opinion and in achieving that transformation of society which governments have set themselves as their aim. In our highly sophisticated age it is difficult to visualize a society in which none of these mass media existed. True enough in the ninth century there was a beginning of publicistic literature in the shape of monographs on certain topics: Smaragdus, Agobard of Lyons, Jonas of Orléans, or a little earlier Alcuin himself or Theodulf of Orléans – to mention just a few outstanding contributors – had written at length on the topic of government in a Christian society, whilst a great many others wrote monographically on questions of liturgy or of

[1] For this see F. L. Ganshof, op. cit. 16 ff., 97 f.; also R. Schneider, art. cit. at 278 ff.

D

pure theology and related subjects. It is also true that the synodal decisions and decrees were reproduced and copied in a great many manu-
scripts for the guidance of at least the principal churches. Although, as
I have mentioned earlier, there were no institutions of higher learning,
the quite rapid growth – rapid in comparison with only a generation
earlier – of learned monographs would incontrovertibly prove what a
great reservoir of talent had been released and by the same token adequate evidence is furnished that for the monographic literature there
was at least a restricted readership available.

But all these literary efforts could at the very best reach a very small
section of the population only: admittedly, the stratum addressed was
the *tonangebende Schicht*, that section which to all intents and purposes
set the tone in society. Yet, if the intended ecclesiological transformation of Frankish society was to assume concrete shape, it was assuredly
imperative to engulf the whole *populus* in the process itself. To some
extent, the *Capitularia* and synodal decrees shared the same fate as the
monographic and epistolary productions: however influential and determinative, it was still an infinitesimal part of Frankish society which
was the recipient. The vehicle which was to supplement these means
effecting the rebirth of Frankish society and which was intended to
reach all sections of the populace, was the sermon. The sermon was
considered by the Carolingians, especially by Charlemagne himself, as
the most appropriate instrument with which to get down to the grass
roots of society. However poor, however deficient, however unlearned
and unintellectual, the sermon was certainly the most easily accessible
vehicle to serve the purpose of the government as well as that of the
illiterate and yet largest section of the population. It was an instrument
of education as well as of instruction:[1] I do not think it is too much to
claim that the Carolingian sermon constitutes one of the earliest attempts at a *Volksaufklärung*: it was to an extent and a degree not hitherto envisaged to inculcate ethical precepts in the guise of religious principles upon the whole population. This purpose of the sermon was to
achieve on the lower and lowest levels of Frankish society what the
royal and synodal legislation tried to do in the higher echelons of

---

[1] The best general introduction is still A. Linsenmayer, *Geschichte d. Predigt in Deutsch-
land* (Munich, 1886), esp. 14–61. The whole problem is really one of interest to religious
sociology which has been greatly promoted by G. Le Bras, *Études de sociologie religieuse*
(Paris, 1955); cf. also id. in *Settimana Spoleto*, 7 (1960), 595 ff. For the lay people in the
eighth century see J. Chélini, 'La pratique dominicale des laïcs dans l'église franque' in
RHEF 42 (1956), 161 ff. For the high M.A. cf. now J. B. Schneyer, *Wegweiser zur lat.
Predigtliteratur des M.A.* (Munich, 1965).

society. Ethical standards were to be equated with religious standards and precepts.

In view of the end pursued by Charlemagne himself, his legislative enactment in the so-called 'Admonitio generalis' of 789 deserves special mention. In it he imposed on the bishops the duty to send out priests for preaching purposes – not, be it emphasized, as missionaries into heathen lands, but as preachers in order to explain and interpret the Scriptures; he did not omit to stress that this measure was to strengthen them and to deepen the understanding of the gospels.[1] Regularity in the instruction by qualified preachers was one more item he stressed – hence the frequently expressed insistence on an adequate clerical education – and he linked this with the visitational circuits of the bishops. All this was repeatedly re-enacted throughout the subsequent period.[2] And regularity meant preaching on all Sundays and holidays.[3] Even the subject-matter of the sermons was laid down: apart from the obvious religious or dogmatic expositions, such as instruction on the essence of divinity, on the mystery of trinity, on the incarnation, resurrection, and so on, the government as well as the councils were particularly anxious to drive home in suitable manner and language such virtues as chastity, humility, modesty, charity, liberality, moderation in eating and drinking, abstinence from all carnal works and from marital relations on Sundays, and so on.[4] The sermons of the parish priest remained virtually the only channel through which any kind of moral-religious instruction was purveyed.[5] The so-called carnal deviations formed a large part of this sort of instruction, because on the basis of St Paul, they were held to be impediments to obtaining salvation.[6] It is advisable to mention this in particular, because it is hardly ever realized that these moral inculcations were to be the presuppositions of an important sequel, that is the saturation of the criminal law with these self-same moral ingredients.

The sermons of this popular type familiarized the populace with the Bible,[7] and thereby in an unostentatious manner the people at large

---

[1] *Cap.* 22, c. 82, p. 61.

[2] Cf., for instance, Louis I, *Cap.* 150, c. 9, p. 304.

[3] *Cap.* 36, cc. 4 ff., p. 106.

[4] Cf., e.g., *Conc.* pp. 194–5, c. 13; and Council of Chalons, c. 10, p. 276.

[5] For a good example cf. the report of Hrabanus Maurus to Haistulf, the archbishop of Mainz, *ca.* 825, in *MGH. Epp.* v. 391, no. 6: no doubt the standard of Hrabanus' sermons was somewhat higher than that of ordinary priests. For examples of actual social conditions cf. H. Fichtenau, *Das karol. Imperium*, cit. 153 ff., esp. 170 ff.

[6] *Cap.* 22, c. 81, pp. 61–2, referring to Gal. 5. 19–21.

[7] Christianity was purveyed 'in a somewhat abridged form' (Fichtenau, op. cit. 164).

came to absorb a number of biblical themes: after all, the sermon according to St Paul was the means whereby the word of God became known.[1] Hence the sermons put Christ's teaching into contemporary framework, that is, in space and time. Moreover, according to the same St Paul, the preacher was held to be Christ's legate and the mediator between Christ and the people.[2] But in order to achieve the end of the sermon and to bring home some of the basic tenets of Christianity to a largely illiterate populace, recourse had to be made to allegory and typology, because thereby the abstract doctrine was clothed in a concrete and sensual garb, with the consequence that not only could the biblical theme be suitably driven home, but it was also remembered much more easily than the possibly intricate doctrinal point itself. That is, I think, at least one of the reasons for the exuberance of allegory and typology in medieval sermons. Naturally, these sermons did not excel in originality: in fact, even if this had been possible, to have propounded original ideas would in all likelihood have defeated the very purpose of the sermon. Moreover, the frequently enacted precept that sermons should be in the vernacular so that the 'vulgus' could understand[3] had evidently the same purpose, that is, to enable the illiterate men and women to follow the exposition of the biblical theme.

Closely linked with this feature of the sermon and its lack of originality was the perusal of models. For there was a very real need for them, since the kind of preaching required and prescribed by both royal and conciliar legislation was new and had to have some pattern which could be adopted. This explains not only the strong patristic influence in the Carolingian epoch, but above all shows how it was possible that an ideological and intellectual bridge between Frankish ecclesiastics and the great masters of the sermon, such as Ambrose, Augustine, Leo I, Gregory the Great, and so on, could be so firmly established. A by-product of this was a very great improvement of linguistic expression and precision by the Carolingian disciples of the great masters as well as a far greater penetration into, and a far wider scope of, biblical exegesis than could be observed less than a generation before.[4] In a word,

[1] I Thess. 2. 13; Rom. 10. 14, 17; etc.

[2] II Cor. 5. 20.

[3] *Cap.* 78, c. 14, p. 174: 'ut vulgus intelligere possit'; Council of Rheims (813), c. 15, *Conc.* p. 255: '. . . secundum proprietatem linguae praedicare'. For other examples see Linsenmayer, op. cit., 53 ff. and also D. A. Bullough, op. cit. 117–18.

[4] In this context the emergence of the Carolingian Homilies should at least be mentioned, for instance, those by Paulus Diaconus made upon order by Charlemagne (*Cap.* 30, p. 81, lines 1 ff.) or by Alcuin; the Homilies by Hrabanus Maurus and Haimo of Halberstadt were particularly useful, because they were clearly the result of practical

the sermon became a means whereby the gulf between the somewhat rarefied ecclesiastical thought and the practice of popular religion could be eradicated: the abstract theme was distilled into the language of ordinary folk. After all, the sermon formed an essential part of 'the art of arts' which was the government of the souls.[1] In the transformation of Frankish society the sermon played a most important role: by the employment of imagery, allegory and other suitable means not only was the christocentric theme driven home effectively, but Frankish society itself became christocentric, with consequences which have barely been appreciated.

Partly for ecclesiological reasons and partly for reasons which will become presently apparent, royal as well as synodal legislation from the late eighth century onwards insisted on what may be called the incorporation of every subject of the king into a parish. This measure of parochial organization contributed to a very great and hardly appreciated extent not only to the effectiveness of routine preaching, but also, and perhaps more so, to making the parish the very real centre of religious and ecclesiastical life: the parish became, for practical purposes, the nerve centre of every parishioner as well as the day-to-day focal point of social, if not also, legal life. That everyone had to belong to one particular parish was laid down as a matter of law at the very end of the eighth century and was observed throughout the ninth.[2] Hence every inhabitant of any locality was tied to one and only one parish and could not even – apart from narrowly circumscribed exceptions – take part in the services of a neighbouring parish priest.[3] The significance of this quite strictly enforced and in course of time also expanded parochial organization was that virtually all important departments of life became ecclesiastical matters within a confined and closely defined territorial unit. This arrangement might well be seen as the forerunner of a modern registration and as an enrolment in a parish register. The full benefits (and duties) in an ecclesiastical and public respect were contingent upon this kind of 'registration' which somewhat resembles the modern electoral register of a municipality or borough. Moreover, the parish priest acted within this organizational arrangement not unlike a Ruler, for it

experience in preaching; they contained, as it were, model sermons which could suitably be expanded, paraphrased and rendered in German or Romance. In the later M.A. the sermon ceased to be a medium of instruction and confined itself to castigating the evil mores of society.

[1] 'Artium ars est regimen animarum' according to Gregory I in his *Reg. Pastoralis*, I. 1.
[2] See the Council of Riesbach in Archbishop Arno's instructions: *Conc.* 198, c. 4.
[3] *Cap.* 81, c. 8, p. 178.

was he who was held responsible for the parishioners in his trust and care.[1] Here at the grass roots of Frankish society the transformation or rebirth was not ineffectively undertaken from the cradle to the grave. The spatial centre of ecclesiastical life was the parish whose priest exercised control and supervision over 'his subjects'.[2] What in the higher regions of royal government the bishops and abbots were, were in the lower the parish priests: from the top to the bottom of society the ecclesiastics had a veritable monopoly as far as the ingredients of social and public life went. Again I cannot refrain from drawing your attention to the differences between this organization and the haphazard arrangement of less than a generation earlier.

That no pluralistic membership was tolerated and that everyone could be, and had to be, a member of one parish only, had also quite realistic economic reasons. For the royally imposed duty to pay the tenth made the closely circumscribed delineation of the parochial unit necessary, because it was royal officers who executed this duty, and their task would have been immeasurably more difficult in the case of multiple membership of parishioners.[3] The effect was that next to purely ideological reasons there was also a strong economic one for the incorporation of all freeholders into the organization of the parish church. Immobile property was what might be called the reified ground for the incorporation of the owner: he therefore 'belonged' to the parochial church.[4] In fact, as the ninth century wore on, there was increasing need for a careful geographical delineation of individual churches, because of the quite rapid proliferation of parochial churches – in the East-Frankish domains alone there were by 847 some 3,500 parish churches and in the West-Frankish still more.[5] For the sake of better

---

[1] See esp. the Council of Aachen in 836, c. 5 in *Conc.* p. 711: '. . . de omnibus hominibus, qui ad eorum (*scil.* presbyterorum) ecclesiam pertinent, per omnia curam gerant, scientes se pro certo reddituros rationem pro ipsis in die iudicii . . . quapropter *ab ortu nativitatis* cuiusque ad se . . . *curam* habeant.'

[2] Cf. *Conc.* p. 195, c. 13, lines 7–8: 'Nos autem, qui sacerdotes vocamur, debemus *populum nobis subiectum* et praedicando verbis . . . et faciendo . . . instruere'; Council of Arles, p. 251, c. 10.

[3] Cf., e.g., *Cap.* 20, c. 7, p. 48; *Cap.* 24, c. 11, p. 65; *Cap.* 34, c. 17, p. 101; *Cap.* 78, cc. 7, 12, p. 174; etc.

[4] Cf., e.g., the terminology chosen by the Council of Aachen in 836, c. 5, p. 712. There was, naturally enough, a strong temptation on the part of some parish priests to persuade wealthy owners of property situated in a neighbouring parish, to transfer it to their own; this prompted the explicit prohibition of such a transfer: *Cap.* 249, c. 17, p. 190 (anno 852); the sanction with which the priest was threatened was deprivation of his office or imprisonment 'longo tempore'.

[5] Cf. the Council of Mainz in *Cap.* 248, p. 173, lines 30 ff. In the diocese of Chur in 823

control and in order to prevent any further mushroom growth of churches, the Council of Tribur in 895 finally laid down that at least five miles must be between an existing parish church and one to be newly erected.[1]

Sermon and parochial organization complemented each other rather effectively. In the agricultural sections public and social order was represented by the parish priest, not by the count, not by royal officers or the *missus*, nor by the far-away local diocesan. It was the parish priest with whom the ordinary folk were in daily contact, and it was he – and not the bishop – who somehow represented *in persona* the ecclesiastical law and the Christian norm and doctrine. He was supposed to stand, in a literal sense, above his parishioners, differing from 'the people entrusted to him' not only in the special charisma he possessed, but also in his special attire as well as by his abode which was close to his church, in order to symbolize the symbiosis of the institution and his person.[2]

In fact, all the major presuppositions existed, or were created specifically, to make the transformation of Frankish society into an ecclesiological unit, to effect the Renaissance of this society in the ecclesiastical sense: literary, doctrinal, personal presuppositions combined with the ecclesiastical and royal law and an organization which implemented the rebirth in the lowest reaches of the rural population, bereft as it still was of any sort of schools. Taking together all the channels which I have tried to indicate, it seems to me that all the potent media were brought into play to secure the intended metamorphosis of a naturally grown and developed concrete Germanic society with its Germanic laws, customs and habituations into a conceptually different society, into one that had its roots in a divine act, that lived and prospered and grew not in accordance with the laws of a natural order, but with those set by

---

there were more than 230 parish churches, cf. Bishop Victor to Louis I in *MGH. Epp.* v. 309, no. 7, lines 35 f.

[1] *Cap.* 252, c. 14a, p. 221. No doubt, here too economic considerations were at work. It was apparently the custom for parish priests to deliver one quarter of the tenth received by them to the local diocesan (cf. A. Hauck, *Kirchengeschichte Deutschlands*, 4th ed. (Leipzig, 1922), II. 232 n. 6), hence episcopal control would have been much more difficult, if parishes had been allowed to proliferate. According to Alcuin the bishop of Limoges demanded annually from his priests $1\frac{1}{2}$ bushels of bread; 1 barrel of wine; 4 bushels of oats; 6 cakes of cheese; 100 eggs; and adequate amount of fish, vegetables and other garden produce: *MGH, Epp.* iv. 457, no. 298, lines 9 ff. If one multiplies these sums by four, one gets quite a respectable amount.

[2] See Regino of Prüm, *De eccl. disc.*, I. 63 in *PL* 132. 190; also c. 16: his 'cella' to be 'iuxta ecclesiam'.

divinity: consequently, this 'new society' pursued aims and ends which were radically different from that society which it was intended to supplant. A problem that of necessity came to the fore in this *nova creatura*, in this reborn society, was, how far was the structure of public power and government affected by the change brought about? For it stands to reason that public power, its function, its authority, its scope and end, was to be different in a society that had grown naturally and one that was held in conception at least, to have been a divine institution. To this problem I hope to turn in my next lecture.

Ecclesiology and Carolingian Rulership

I

The ecclesiological theme, embraced as it was by the Carolingians as a governmental programme, may be said to be an amalgam of ancient Christian, patristic and early medieval doctrines relative to the idea of the Church. As such the theme itself constituted a firm and secure link with not only the Rome of Christian persuasion, but above all with the more distant past, notably with that portrayed in the Bible. In order to understand the remarkable changes and repercussions which the application of the ecclesiological theme entailed, it is as well to bear in mind that the first impetus originated in the royal quarter. But the earlier development in Christian Gaul and the more recent development north of the Alps, engendered as they were by the missionary and subsequent organizational work of St Boniface, provided a highly suitable framework for the deployment of ecclesiological principles in Frankish society. The idea of the Franks as the *populus Dei* or as *Christianitas* greatly facilitated the correlative adoption of the idea of the city of God which for the Carolingians was nothing else but the concrete manifestation of the Church.

The doctrinal amalgam against which the progress of the ecclesiological transformation must be seen, makes a number of otherwise hardly comprehensible features accessible to the understanding. One of these concerned the basic idea of government to be exercised in an ecclesiologically conceived society. Here a great many streams combined to yield the conception of a Ruler that was in several respects different from that of his ancestors.[1] He was *qua* Ruler structurally incorporated in the organism of the Church, but it is the idea of the rebirth of the Ruler himself which, as we shall see in the next lecture, constitutes the focal point of the ecclesiological substance of Rulership. Having been created king (as well as patrician of the Romans) the papacy maintained that Pippin as Ruler appeared reborn as a new

---

[1] Cf. W. Mohr, *Die karol. Reichsidee* (Münster, 1962), 17, pointing out that Merovingian kingship was based on pagan ideas.

Moses or a new David.[1] In no wise different was Charlemagne's Rulership conceived as a rebirth of the Old Testament Jewish kingship symbolized by the very name of David which he bore:[2] his throne in Aachen was modelled on Solomon's throne: Aachen had become another Jerusalem.[3] But this same Ruler could, as indeed he did, appear as a 'new Constantine',[4] and the combination of these two powerful prototypes of Rulership produced the Ruler with monarchic powers the extent of which had hitherto hardly been envisaged. This rapid escalation of the monarchic idea itself was a response to the ecclesiological theme in the sense in which Charlemagne understood it, for his whole concept of government presupposed a firm and undisputed control over the higher clergy, especially the bishops and abbots.[5] It was precisely in this context that the appellation of Charlemagne as the new Constantine assumed added significance, for this prototype of Ruler was not only a monarch in every sense of the term, but was also believed to have been a renovator, a rebuilder of the Roman empire in a Christian garb: this latter consideration was especially important for the Carolingian idea of Renaissance,[6] since this designation was to indicate that a new era had arisen, one that in significance and import could be juxtaposed to that of the true Constantine.

It is therefore of considerable moment to keep in mind that the adoption of the ecclesiological theme by Charlemagne also promoted

[1] Stephen II to Pippin in 757: 'What else are you but a new Moses and a shining King David?' in *Cod. Car.* no. 11, p. 505, lines 5–6; Paul I told the Franks that Pippin was both a new Moses and a new David, ibid., no. 39, p. 552, line 9; also no. 42, p. 554, line 29; for Pope Constantine II Pippin was only a new Moses, ibid., no. 98, p. 649, line 18. We should take note that according to Eusebius Constantine was a new Moses (for this see O. Treitinger, *Die oström. Kaiser- und Reichsidee* (2nd ed., Darmstadt, 1956), 131 at note 5), though whether there were lines of communication between Eusebius and the papal designations, is in need of further investigation. In the tenth-century Book of Ceremonies at Byzantium the emperor was acclaimed as David, see Treitinger, 130, n. 2. But at Byzantium there was no anointing nor had the ecclesiastical coronation any constitutive effects. See also below 73.

[2] This was rightly recognized by E. H. Kantorowicz, *Laudes regiae* (repr. Berkeley, 1958), 56 ('revival of the biblical kingship of David'). For the biblical background of Carolingian kingship see now especially M. Wallace-Hadrill, 'The via regia . . .' in *Trends*, cit. 23 ff.

[3] For this cf. H. Fichtenau, *Das karol. Imperium*, cit. 76–7.

[4] Adrian I to Charlemagne, *Cod. Car.* no. 60, p. 587, line 17: the divine help implored by the pope with the words of Ps. 19. 10, was especially necessary, because 'now a new most christian emperor Constantine has arisen in our days'. For the link with the Donation of Constantine cf. *PG* 92–3.

[5] For full details see F. L. Ganshof, 'L'église et le pouvoir royal . . .' in *Settimana Spoleto*, 7 (1960), 95 ff.

[6] Cf. E. Ewig, 'Das Bild Konstantins d. Gr. . . .' in *HJb* 75 (1955), 20 ff.

the monarchic aspirations of the Ruler to an extent that was unknown in the Germanic societies of early medieval Europe. What provides a fascinating background to this escalation of monarchic powers[1] is the utilization of the thoroughly Germanic governmental concept of the *Munt*. Now the *Munt* had been operative as an integral element of kingship since the ancient Teutonic age and its composite parts did not need any radical change as a result of the infusion of Christian ideas. One could go so far as to say that from one angle the government of Charlemagne might well be described as a conspicuous application of the idea of *Munt*. The feature which stares the observer in the face is that the *Munt* conceived as protection, was quite particularly apt to bring the monarchic form of government into the clearest possible relief: for this old Germanic concept lent itself easily to the theocratic idea of Rulership, according to which divinity entrusted the kingdom to the Ruler so that he could protect it and guard it by appropriate governmental measures. Or to express this Germanic idea in Latin terms: *protectio trahit subiectionem*. The harnessing of the *Munt* to the ecclesiological theme by Charlemagne was a step which suggested itself: thereby the *Munt* became a central tenet of Rulership[2] and proved itself a vital ingredient of the newly aroused monarchic function of the Ruler. Hence also the avowal on the Ruler's part of his responsibility for the salvation of his subjects – *salvatio subditorum*.[3]

The other limb of the Ruler's monarchic strength was provided by the ecclesiological theme itself: the adroitness with which Charlemagne utilized an indigenous ecclesiastical Christian idea, is indeed a testimony to his wisdom and sagacity as a Ruler. By consistently adopting the royal intitulation of 'King by the grace of God' he applied not only profound Pauline ideas, but at the same time advanced, certainly within the precincts of the ecclesiological theme, the very idea of Rulership in a Christian body public, such as he meant the Frankish kingdom to be. By combining the two fundamental Pauline principles – 'all power comes from God' and 'What I am I am by the grace of God' – and shaping them into a governmental principle of the first order by means

[1] One is here reminded of a dictum by E. Rosenstock-Huessey, *Die europ. Revolutionen u. der Charakter d. Nationen*, 3rd ed. (Stuttgart, 1962), 236: 'Monarchie ist immer die einfachste Denkform für das Individuum.'

[2] For numerous examples of the *Munt* (= *mundeburdium*) appearing in Charles' *Capitularia* – and of course in those of his successors – cf. *Cap.* 35, c. 54, p. 104; *Cap* 69, c. 3, p. 158: '. . . ut *minus potentes* sub Dei defensione et *nostro mundeburdio* pacem habeant'; etc. See also below 122 f.

[3] Lothar I in *MGH. Urkunden Lothars I.* (1966), no. 32, p. 109. There is a strong hint at this in Smaragdus, *Via regia*, pref. in *PL* 102. 934 D.

of the adoption of the royal grace formula, Charlemagne by a single brilliant stroke made concrete in the realm of government what had hitherto been a rarefied abstract concept. It seems impossible to exaggerate the consequences of this Caroline step: not by clever speculation, not by the issuing of a tomos, not by wearying debates in ecclesiastical councils, but by the matter-of-fact 'simple' act of assuming a role – that of the recipient of divine grace for purposes of government – which none of his predecessors had assumed, he showed an alacrity and an appreciation of essential things which must always stand out as one of the greatest amongst his other great achievements. Let us be quite clear: no one else in the vast Frankish realms had at that period – that is, from the seventies onwards – the singular and unique distinction which he unostentatiously claimed for himself. In harnessing both the Germanic element – the *Munt* – and a crucial feature of the ecclesiological theme – that is, divinity conferring the grace (or benefit) of Rulership – he took indeed the perhaps most effective step to bring the ecclesiological transformation of the Frankish people nearer to realization. The monarchical handling of the process of transformation appeared to him a guarantee of its success. And in this connexion at least a passing mention should be made of the immediate legacy of Charlemagne. That the royal grace formula was adopted in the Western portions of the realm, is easily explicable by the already very deep roots which on purely historical grounds the ecclesiastics and the ecclesiological theme itself had struck there. But in view of the far thinner spread of Christianity – also historically conditioned – in the Eastern portions it is all the more significant that we can witness exactly the same adoption of the royal grace formula in the Eastern regions. Louis the German began from 830 onwards to call himself 'divina favente gratia rex'.[1]

Legislation was at all times one of the most appropriate means by which a kingdom as a body public was governed. The effective assumption of comprehensive powers by Charlemagne was accompanied by the royal creation of the law, notably in the *Capitularia* which either modified already existing law – *legibus addenda* – or created new (royal) law. In either case the material ingredient was the autonomous will of the Ruler.[2] But nothing illustrates the awareness of monarchic aspirations better than the realization of Pippin, the Italian king, that the multiplicity and ubiquitousness of customary law may well be a hindrance to the full deployment of monarchic law-creative powers:

[1] See BM 1339a and 1352a.   [2] For some details cf. *PGP* 123-4.

hence what would appear to me a statement of considerable jurisprudential value and insight, which also reveals the sensitivity of a monarchic-royal government towards customary law, deserves special
attention. For according to the *Capitulare* of 790, enacted law may do
away with customary law, but the reverse was not to be tolerated.[1]
There is no evidence to show that the very similar legislative enactment
by Constantine the Great, issued for exactly the same reasons of preserving monarchic-governmental legislation, was known to the king.[2]
The deeper significance of this legislative step lay in the desire to dis-
countenance the thesis that the king as monarchic Ruler could be bound
by those customs and practices which originated not in any exercise of
the Ruler's will, but in the people itself.

It is beyond doubt, therefore, that the early Carolingians were perfectly aware of the essential ingredient of monarchic-royal power, that
is, the monarch's will that resulted in the legislative command (*iussio*).
Hence not only the rapidly increasing law-creative activity, but also the
very effective use of the machinery of the royal *missi*: they were, in a
way, the personal counterpart of the impersonal *Capitularia*, because they
were the personified bearers and transmitters or mediators of the royal
will. To quote just one statement out of many: the function of the *missi*
was to announce 'our will to the people'.[3] Hand in hand with these
manifestations of monarchic power went others, such as the distribu-
tion of royal grace to, and its withholding from, the king's subjects,[4]

---

[1] *Cap.* 95, c. 10, p. 201: 'Placuit nobis inserere: ubi lex est, praecellat consuetudinem,
et nulla consuetudo superponatur legi.'   [2] Cf. *PGP* 281.

[3] *Cap.* 187, p. 8, lines 11 f.; also *Cap.* 25, c. 5, p. 67 and c. 6; *Cap.* 32, c. 8, p. 83, line
39; etc.

[4] Cf., e.g., *Cap.* 29, p. 79, line 44; *Cap.* 33, c. 28, p. 96, line 29; *Cap.* 75, p. 168, line
38; *Cap.* 76, p. 169, line 36; *Cap.* 130, p. 357, line 35; *Cap.* 161, c. 9, p. 324 (bracketing
together God's and the king's grace); etc. Royal grace began to make its appearance in
the greeting formula of charters – *gratiam et salutem in Christo* – see, e.g., E. J. Dronke,
Cod. dipl. Fuldensis (repr. Aalen, 1962), no. 556, p. 249 = D.52 in *MGH Urkunden der
deutschen Karolinger*, ed. P. F. Kehr (1934). I have chosen this example from the Eastern
part of the Frankish realms to show that although properly organized ecclesiastically
only recently, they lagged in no wise behind the much more developed Western parts.
In general cf. K. Beyerle, *Von der Gnade im deutschen Recht* (Göttingen, 1910), 8: 'In
diesem theokratischen Ideenkreise verschmilzt die Gnade Gottes mit der Gnade des
Königs ... Die Königsvasallen heissen "Dei et nostri fideles".' For the most recent
treatment of the whole subject see the magisterial exposition by F. L. Ganshof, 'La
"gratia" des monarques francs' in *Anuario de estudios medievales*, 3 (1966), 9 ff., who
established that the royal grace formula was used by the Merovingian kings in the sixth
century; here also (25–6) a most useful conspectus of the employment of the term in the
Theodosian Code. In parenthesis it may be noted that the idea, though not the term, of
gratia in the shape of *favor* was already in the Edict of Milan (313) ('divinus iuxta nos
favor' and similar terminology throughout), see C. Mirbt, *Quellen*, 4th ed. (1924), 39–40.

the principle of royal concession,[1] the power of reinstating a subject who had fallen into royal disgrace by the process of regracing him[2] and many other related items.[3]

There is one more manifestation of royal monarchic functions so powerfully engendered by, and exercised in the interests of, the ecclesiological theme, to which I must devote a few brief remarks, and that is the idea of the Ruler's personal sovereignty, his standing outside and above the kingdom (or empire) and indeed above every mortal. And the Ruler considered himself distinguished in this way, because he alone was, as he avowed, in receipt of divine grace that conferred on him the title-deed to rule. It is not without interest that some of the first documentary witnesses of this heightened status of the Ruler came from the Eastern region of the Frankish realm in the thirties of the ninth century. Louis the German in an apparent routine charter declared in 834:

> It is evident that by virtue of divine grace we are set above all other mortals.[4]

This highly characteristic expression of personal *superioritas* (= sovereignty) was not to disappear again until the late Middle Ages and constituted one of the many bequests of the Carolingian era to later ages.[5] What needs pointing out is that this idea of personal sovereignty did not admit of anyone else's sharing in the Ruler's power: he formed what on another occasion I have termed an estate of his own, lonely maybe, but one which was symbolically expressed by his position of elevation on the throne. The king stood outside and above the society or community or kingdom entrusted to him by divinity.

This brief sketch of the rapid development of monarchic aspirations by the early Carolingians should have shown how much these were stimulated by the ecclesiological theme. My witnesses are official docu-

---

[1] Cf. *PGP* 120 ff.

[2] See, e.g., the report on the Council of Frankfurt in 794, *Cap.* 28, c. 3, and c. 9, p. 75; etc.

[3] About which I have reported in a different context and into which I need not now enter, cf. above n. 1. It may be noted that the threat of a withdrawal of the king's grace may have roots in the fifth century, cf. P. Classen in *AD* 2 (1956), at 36 n. 180.

[4] 'Constat nos divina dispensante gratia ceteris mortalibus supereminere' (*Cod. dipl. Fuld.*, cit. no. 486, p. 214; no. 22, p. 27 = *Urkunden*, cit. no. 15, p. 18). The model is not older than the so-called imperial formulae from Louis I's chancery, see *MGH. Form.* no. 16, p. 298.

[5] For variants of the same idea, cf., e.g., *DD.* of Louis the German, in *Urkunden*, cit. nos. 101, 102, 115, pp. 145, 147, 163; for a later age cf. Conrad I in *MGH. DD.* i. 7, no. 6; Henry I, no. 1, p. 39; no. 15, p. 51; Otto I, no. 239, p. 333; etc.

ments and legislative acts. To these testimonies we may append some literary points of view which, needless to say, came exclusively from the ecclesiastical camp and from the chronological standpoint coincided roughly with the period of the other witnesses quoted. Indeed, when reading these literary sources advocating as they do exactly the kind of monarchic government which the early Carolingians postulated and exercised, one is inevitably reminded of the attitude of the ecclesiastics at the time of Constantine the Great: and the appellation of Charlemagne as a new Constantine may not have appeared a hyperbole at all to contemporaries, for in both cases it was the clergy who benefited most directly by the old and the new Constantine;[1] and in each instance there was an initially strong support for the Ruler's monarchic theme. Again, merely a few examples need be cited, if only to bring into clearer relief the subsequent development. One may go further and say that the very ingredients of the monarchic theme as set forth in the late eighth and early ninth centuries spurred the ecclesiastics on to back up this royal theme by their own scholarship and learning, however recently acquired it might have been. To them Charlemagne did not appear as anything else but God's chosen Ruler and the body over which he ruled, the *populus Dei*. The papacy itself had nurtured this notion of the king as God's inspired or instituted or illuminated Ruler.[2] What the Frankish ecclesiastics did was to supply the technical equipment in the shape of verbal expressions, allegories, nomenclatures, which enveloped the bare official bones with doctrinal and ideological flesh.

In one of the embryonic *Fürstenspiegel* of the Middle Ages in the seventies of the eighth century, the priest Cathwulf apostrophized Charlemagne as 'the Ruler of the kingdom of Europe' – a highly significant term for the time – calling the Frankish king 'the vicar of God' whilst the bishops were merely 'vicars of Christ'.[3] Quite in consonance with ecclesiastical thought Cathwulf wished to show the hierarchy of functions at work and quite especially to demonstrate that power

---

[1] Cf. E. Caspar, *Gesch. d. Papsttums* (Tübingen, 1930), i. 123 ff. and Ch. Dupont 'Les privilèges des clercs sous Constantine' in *RHE* 62 (1967), 729 ff. with relevant earlier literature. Cf. also J. Vogt in *RAC* iii (1960), 343 ff. and H. Hürten in *HJb* 82 (1963), 22 ff.

[2] Cf., e.g., *Cod. Car.* no. 11, p. 504, line 35; no. 13, p. 509; no. 53, p. 575, line 3. For other examples cf. E. Ewig in *Das Königtum*, ed. Th. Mayer (Darmstadt 1965), 51 notes 200 and 201.

[3] *MGH. Epp.* iv. 502–3; the passages are quoted in *PG* 106 nn. 1 and 6. Cf. the probable model, Ps. Augustine's *Quaestiones veteris et novi testamenti*, ed. A. Souter in *CSEL* 50 (1908), qu. 35, p. 62 ('Dei imaginem habere rex sicut episcopus Christi').

descended from God through the king to the bishops, whilst effective power over what he called the *populus Dei* was at all times retained in the hands of the kings: the members of the kingdom were, for Cathwulf, 'members of God'[1] who were to be ruled according to the law of God issued by the king in his function as the vice-gerent of God.[2] What Cathwulf wished to stress was that what he termed the 'lex totius christianitatis' should be established by the king in accordance with the mandate of God.[3] These were by no means isolated views. Shortly afterward, Theodulf of Orleans raised Charlemagne to the pinnacle of St Peter's vicar,[4] whereas in the first decade of the ninth century, one of the earliest authors of a proper *Fürstenspiegel*, Smaragdus, designated the king's function as that of a vicar of Christ.[5]

These literary expressions and points of view could easily be multiplied: they all make abundantly clear that the ecclesiastics, learned as they were in biblical and patristic exegesis, used their equipment in the service and interests of the king: this powerful assistance is comprehensible if due consideration is given to the actual situation at the turn of the century on the one hand, and the aim of Charlemagne on the other. Seen from the point of view of a contemporary the situation itself was not dissimilar to that in the age of Constantine. There is plentiful evidence that the Frankish ecclesiastical littérateurs – quite apart from the inner circle surrounding Charlemagne – supplied the technical material, if one may so call their doctrinal support, by underpinning and underpropping the monarchic-royal system with the help of ecclesiological principles. What the king did in practice, the ecclesiastical writers supplemented in theory: it was a powerful team, of which the practical and theoretical results were to reverberate throughout the following centuries.

But there is more to it. It was also the ecclesiastical littérateurs who drew the consequences from the king's monarchic function and position, consequences which may well have been endemic in the monarchic theme itself as practised, but which nevertheless were clearly and cogently set forth in literary productions only. You may recall that I

---

[1] *Epp.*, cit. p. 503, line 4.

[2] Ibid. line 7: 'cuius vices tenes', also referring to Ps. 2. 10 ff.

[3] Ibid. lines 10 f.

[4] Cit. in *PG* 106 n. 4.

[5] Smaragdus, *Via regia*, c. 18 in *PL* 102. 958 B: 'Fac quicquid potes, pro persona quam portas, pro ministerio regali, quod portas, pro nomine christiani, quod habes, pro *vice Christi*, qua fungeris.' The threefold division should be noted: the personal, the ministerial and the functional sides of the king. For Smaragdus cf. W.L., ed. H. Löwe, 3 (1957), 308 ff.; also J. Scharf in *DA* 17 (1961), 344 ff.

have just mentioned the concept of personal sovereignty in the Ruler, a concept that evidently emerged from the ideas underlying the monarchic form of government itself, but it was a concept which harboured many implications and was capable of numerous deductions. For where there is a superior, there must logically also be an inferior, and the ideological correlate is that the inferior becomes a subject of the Ruler, in whose creation he did not play any role and could not play any role, because the Ruler was what he was not by the will, consent or agreement of the people or of any of its members, but by the grace of God. Here the ecclesiological theme opened up great potentialities in the public sphere, and the synodists assembled at Paris in 829, intellectually guided by Jonas of Orleans, specifically dealt with one of the necessary implications of the relationship of the inferior (subject) to the superior (Ruler): Jonas and the synodists stipulated that the overriding public duty of the subject was obedience to the Ruler, in whose care and protection he found himself. And the reason for this emphatic insistence on the subject's duty of obedience was the divine establishment of the Ruler himself. We meet here the logical extension of the theocratic concept of Rulership in a descending order, down to the level of the last villein. 'Cuncti' – everyone – had the duty of obeying and carrying out the decrees issued by the Ruler: if, as the synodists declared, the subjects acted in this manner, they fulfilled a divine precept, and at once a whole galaxy of Old and New Testament passages came readily to hand to buttress this standpoint.[1]

From now on the element of obedience to a superior's law, decree or command was to become an integral part of monarchic rule, which is the same as saying that the personal sovereign had the right to demand obedience within the precincts of the public-royal law. Indeed, this quite unqualified support for the monarchic theme by the ecclesiastics and its most direct public consequence – obedience – is easily understandable, because the aims of their contemporary Rulers were wholly conform to their own, so much so that without them the intended rebirth of the Frankish people by the Rulers would have been stillborn.

[1] See Paris Council (829), in *MGH. Conc.* p. 659 f. and its significant heading; Jonas of Orléans, *De institutione regia*, ed. J. Reviron (Paris, 1930), c. 8, pp. 157 ff.; the main biblical passages adduced were: Matt. 22. 21; I Pet. 2. 13 ff.; Rom. 13. 1–2; Tit. 3. 1; I Tim. 2. 1 ff.; Jer. 29. 7. Jonas was greatly influenced by the Ps. Cyprianic tract *De XII abusivis saeculi* (of ca. 700), ed. S. Hellmann in *T.U.* (1909), see esp. Jonas c. 3, pp. 138 ff. The Ps. Augustinian *Quaestiones* (above 49 n. 3) may also have served as a model, see qu. 35, ed. cit. p. 63, lines 14 ff. ('licet ipse indignus sit'). For particulars of Jonas, see W.L. 311 f., and J. Scharf in *DA* 17 (1961), 353 ff., also 373 ff. (as conciliar mentor).

E

Let us be quite clear: the actions and laws of the Rulers were seen as distillations of Christian doctrine, as concrete expressions of an abstract theory. But the keepers, guardians and expositors of this doctrine and this theory were the ecclesiastics, not the kings, and the sonorous and reiterated ecclesiastical insistence on the duty of obedience to the king's laws finds therefore its effortless explanation. Differently expressed: the reason why the ecclesiastics were so emphatic on obedience was the king's appointment by divinity as the *minister Dei* and, functionally, as we have seen, the vicar of God or of Christ. In this the ecclesiastics saw the *ultima ratio* for obeying the king's law. The legal element of obedience to the Ruler was therefore strongly suffused with religious ingredients, but we shall also have to look at some social implications of this religiously buttressed view on obedience.[1] In brief, the Ruler was a divine appointee who had received a special commission in the shape of a *theokratische Amtsauftrag*.[2]

In promoting the royal programme which was their own, the ecclesiastics allowed the laws of logic their full play. An excellent example of this mode of argument is provided by Hrabanus Maurus, the great abbot of Fulda (situated in the Eastern part of the Frankish realms). Hrabanus Maurus sent a veritable *Fürstenspiegel* to Louis I. Hrabanus was one of the most learned and best equipped ecclesiastics at the time, and in his *speculum regis* he devoted a lengthy chapter to obedience and its denial, but went considerably further than Jonas and the Paris synodists had done five years earlier. What was only implicit in the latter, becomes explicit in Hrabanus. For to the *maiores* the *subditi* (the subjects) owed unconditional obedience, he declared, and this, because divinity had instituted the *maiores* as superior authority, with the consequence that disobedience constituted rebellion or sedition against divinity itself.[3] On the not too distant horizon appears the concept of *maioritas = maiestas* as an operational and constitutional notion which technically expressed the personal sovereignty of the Ruler.[4] Even in the East-Frankish portion the ancient Germanic right of resistance was

---

[1] See below 113 f., 117 f. For the utilization of biblical *exempla* (patterns) in these Frankish synodal decrees see now L. Buisson in *Adel u. Kirche* (Freiburg, 1968), at 466.

[2] In this sense rightly W. Schlesinger in *Karl d. Gr.*, cit. i. 842. See also E. Buschmann, 'Ministerium Dei' in *HJb* 82 (1963), 70 ff.

[3] Hrabanus Maurus, *MGH. Epp.* v. 404, *Ep.* 15, c. 3, at 406 ff. He was here, as the heading shows, concerned with Louis' royal, not imperial, authority. On this see also M. Wallace-Hadrill, 'The via regia . . .' in *Trends*, cit. 25 f.

[4] The concept of *reus maiestatis* appears in connexion with desertion from the army in 801, see *Cap.* 98, c. 3, p. 205, that is whoever goes home without the order or licence of the king. On the concept see E. Ewig in *Das Königtum*, cit. 65 f. and note 269.

now driven out and replaced by unconditional obedience to the Ruler who was designated by Hrabanus in the same place as the Lord's anointed (*christus domini*): disobedience was rebellion against the Lord's anointed. In order to appreciate this point of view we ought to realize that by the time of writing (834) royal anointing had not yet been given a place in the Frankish kingdom, but this statement was a portent of things to come. It was therefore all the more significant that he invoked the Old Testament statement – 'Who shall stretch forth his hand against the Lord's anointed and shall remain innocent?'[1]

Just as obedience was strongly soaked with religious contents, in the same way its negation came to be considered a substantially religious offence: indeed, this was the view which was enacted in the first synod held by Hrabanus as archbishop of Mainz in 847: rebellion or conspiracy against the king or ecclesiastical dignitaries or public officers was visited with anathema.[2] We find exactly the same theme pursued in the West-Frankish kingdom: here in fact a few years earlier (843) the synodists assembled at Lauriac (near Angers) had taken the first concrete legislative measures to protect the king by threatening anathema against anyone who proved himself to be acting against royalty in a treacherous, crafty or pernicious manner; similarly, anathema was decreed for disobeying just and reasonable orders of the king whose power, they insisted, comes from God.[3] These synodal decrees appear to be preparatory to the full elaboration of the crime of *lèse majesté*. The right of resistance was rapidly fading into the background. As Hincmar was to say shortly afterwards, disobedience to, or non-conformity with royal commands amounted to rebellion against the power that had set the king over the people.[4] The ecclesiastical writers enveloped the Ruler with the aura and the mythos of an Old Testament kingly figure, and thus in the prevailing conditions afforded him the greatest possible protection. By elevating the Ruler to this exalted status they elevated themselves.

The potentialities of the Ruler raised to the level of an Old Testament king, were great indeed. Here in this context I would like to invite your attention to the substitution of Rulership based on blood and the kindred – the *Geblütsrecht* – by a Rulership based on divine intervention and grace. The one was Germanic, the other Christian, and the

---

[1] I Kgs. 26. 9, cit. at p. 407, line 43, and p. 408, lines 2 ff.

[2] *Cap.* 248, c. 5, p. 177.

[3] These sanctions were re-enacted in the Council of Meaux-Paris in 845; *Cap.* 293, cc. 14, 15, p. 402.

[4] Hincmar, *De fide Carolo servanda* in *PL* 125. 979–80, quoting the famous passage from Gregory I's *Regula pastoralis*, III. 5.

substitution epitomizes quite neatly the essence of the idea of Christianity and the state of affairs it was supposed to replace: it epitomizes the conquest of natural-biological forces by the forces inherent in the Christian idea wherein the accent lies on the idea as the emanation of the spirit. In different terminology one may possibly hold that the substitution signified the victory of the spirit over matter.[1] The Germanic Ruler embodied a sacred and magical mythos because of his blood kinship with distant ancestors; this was now replaced by an equally sacred mythos that was derived from divine sanction and grace.[2] Kingship ceased to be a matter of blood and became a matter of divine intervention: the blood charisma gave way to a charisma sustained by grace.

The actual beginning of this process of substitution or replacement can, fortunately, be dated quite precisely: the first impetus in this direction came, not from the Franks, but from the papal quarter, in the highly important matter of replacing an established dynasty by a new ruling family, the Arnulfings, who, it so happened, were usurpers from the strictly constitutional point of view. Obviously, the reference is to the replacement of the Merovingian line by the Carolingian, the substitution of Pippin the Short for Childeric III, based on the anointing administered by the pope. The anointing was the instrument by which the charisma of blood was replaced by the charisma derived from divine grace that was transmitted through the mediation of the pope: it was the pope who on the very same occasion issued the injunction that henceforth no one should rule the Franks except those elected from Pippin's family. We take notice that Rulership was still tied to a particular family, though one which was hallowed in the person of its head, Pippin.[3]

The adoption of the ecclesiological theme of necessity forced both littérateurs and councils to declare themselves on the traditional kind of Rulership. The point of view expressed by the already mentioned Jonas of Orléans and the Council of Paris (829) may well be viewed as the classic ecclesiastical standpoint and took up that position which a generation earlier the papacy felt it could not yet take. For to these Frankish

---

[1] Cf. also below 57 n. 3.

[2] For a refreshing view and trenchant observations concerning the essence of Germanic kingship based on blood, see M. Wallace-Hadrill, *The Long-Haired Kings*, cit. 202 ff.; cf. also 184; see also W. Mohr, *Die karol. Reichsidee*, cit. 7 ff.

[3] See the *Clausula de unctione Pippini* in *MGH. SS. RR. Mer.* i. 465 f.: '. . . omnes interdictu et excommunicationis lege constrinxit, ut numquam de alterius lumbis regem in aevo praesumant eligere, sed ex ipsorum, quos et *divina pietas* exaltare dignata est et sanctorum apostolorum intercessionibus *per manus* vicarii ipsorum b. *pontificis confirmare* et *consecrare* disposuit.'

ecclesiastics of the twenties of the ninth century Rulership was a gift of God, and no king should therefore believe that his kingdom had come from his ancestors. Men, in other words, could not dispose of kingdoms: whoever ruled, did so because God had given the right to rule. Not only were Old Testament passages easily at hand to support this standpoint which, I must emphasize again, was the only one consonant with the basic ecclesiological theme, but these ecclesiastics could go even so far as to say that if any king were to believe that he succeeded his ancestors, the statement expressed in Hosea would then be directly applicable to him.[1] Here on the basis of the ecclesiological theme the whole institution of hereditary kingship was thrown out as incompatible with the fundamental ecclesiological premises – a point of view which was to remain a firm ecclesiastical dogma throughout the Middle Ages and was to give the theocratic conception of Rulership its firm biblical and doctrinal backing. We may also express this idea thus: the concept of Rulership itself underwent a Renaissance, underwent the same kind of rebirth which Frankish society itself was undergoing. The biology of blood charisma came to be reborn or renewed through the theology of divine grace and its charisma: the Ruler himself became *qua* Ruler a *nova creatura*.[2]

II

It is against this background that we may attempt to sketch the rise of the ecclesiastics from the role of consultant experts of the Ruler to that of determinant organs in Frankish society. The understanding of the course which this development took, no less than its correct assessment, presupposes the appreciation of the indispensable and dynamic initiative taken by Charlemagne. In order to carry out the aim he had set himself, he was forced to employ the higher ecclesiastics in the construction of the new society that was to consist of the people of God: no other section or group of contemporary society would have been fitted or equipped to perform the numerous tasks which the plan of rebirth or regeneration demanded – educationally, organizationally,

---

[1] Os., 8. 4. The whole passage is to be found in Jonas, *De instr. reg.*, ed. cit. c. 7, p. 155 f.; in Paris Council (829) ii. 5, p. 655. The main OT passages cit. were : Prov. 8. 15; Dan. 5. 21; Jer. 27. 4–5.

[2] And yet, the magic arising out of the charisma of blood, took an inordinately long time to die, cf. K. Hauck, 'Geblütsheiligkeit' in *Liber Floridus*, ed. B. Bischoff et al. (St Ottilien, 1950), 187 ff. This would seem to be paralleled by the difficulty of doing away with the 'animalic man' in the individual Christian. A good illustration of the continuing efficacy of the *Geblütsrecht* is provided by Thietmar, cf. A. Schneider in *AKG* 44 (1962), 34 ff., at 50 ff.

institutionally, legislatively; in a word he had no other choice, even if he had wished, but to rely on the ecclesiastics who became thus, in a personal and impersonal respect, the veritable pillars and architects of this new edifice. It was assuredly no hyperbole on the part of Charlemagne that, to select just one example, he called the bishops the *clarissima mundi luminaria*.[1] Indeed, seen from the point of view of his eventual aim, they were the most eminent luminaries of the world, because they alone possessed the intellectual qualifications to say what was to be done to bring the plan of a rebirth to fruition. When we further try to realize that in most developing societies the Ruler's chief function was to dispense justice and equity, it will be all the more comprehensible that in the Christian society which the Carolingian government envisaged, this function of the Ruler was not only to be paramount, but also to be exclusively seen from the Christian standpoint. The higher ecclesiastics were obviously credited by Charlemagne with the unique knowledge of the abstract principles relative to this function of the Ruler, and it was they who not so long afterwards claimed to be the public guardians, the custodians of 'the people of God'. The point I wish to make is that the ecclesiological theme itself sufficiently explains the mutually increasing status, if not elevation and enhancement: the king, as in Constantinean times, was exalted by the ecclesiastics with all the doctrinal and biblical ammunition at their disposal; the bishops and other higher ecclesiastics were enhanced by the Ruler in their status by his governmental measures.

The effects of the exclusive royal reliance on the bishops were faithfully reflected in the conciliar decrees of the first half of the ninth century, to which I have already had occasion to refer.[2] Only one or two examples need be given to show how quickly the bishops seized upon the situation. At the Council of Paris (829) the synodists enunciated with great solemnity the principle that it was the bishops who were charged with pronouncing and formulating those matters which belonging as they did to Christian religion affected princes and peoples, the reason being that the empire of Louis I was simply part of the universal Church, with the ecclesiological consequence that the sacerdotal order was to play the dominant part.[3] Hence, simply carry-

[1] *Cap.* 22, p. 53, line 32.
[2] For a detailed examination of all Frankish councils and assemblies see the successive studies by Ch. de Clercq in *Rev. de droit canonique*, 4 (1954) – 8 (1958); conclusion ibid. 149 ff.
[3] This is also emphasized by W. Mohr, 'Die kirchl. Einheitspartei' in *ZKG* 72 (1961), 1 ff. at 21, and id., *Die karol. Reichsidee*, cit. 91–2.

ing out the convocation edict,[1] it was for the bishops to tell both Rulers and their peoples authoritatively what should, and should not, be done from a Christian point of view. The bishops were the vicars of the apostles and therefore had been given the power to lay down on earth what was relevant for salvation. This was nothing less than the claim to fix, with final authority, the basic law for 'the people of God', since the bishops considered themselves uniquely qualified to know the law of God. For, as they also announced, the fundamental task of the ecclesiastic is to know this law – 'sacerdotis est scire legem Dei'. They found support for this advanced point of view – advanced, I mean, in comparison with less than a generation earlier – in Haggai's prophecy and quite especially in St Jerome's commentary on that passage which they took great pains to quote at length. And the same patristic authority enabled them to stake their claim as messengers of God and hence as mediators between God and man. They were charged, they avowed, with transmitting God's will to the people.[2] Their standpoint was little else but a concrete demonstration of St Augustine's view that 'God rules the mind, the mind commands the body, and there cannot be anything more orderly than this arrangement'.[3]

The practical conclusion which the synodists reached was that it was the bishops who had to legislate for the whole Church, laity and clergy alike, because

> the law of Christ was not laid down for the clerics alone, but for all the faithful,[4]

the presupposition being that the enunciation of the law by the ecclesiastics had reference to the basic fabric of society. Is it in these circumstances surprising that the bishops came to call themselves 'the janitors of the celestial palace'[5] because they were 'the key-bearers of the celestial kingdom'?[6] They went even further and applied to themselves a statement by Julianus Pomerius, a Gallic writer of the fifth century, when they claimed that they were 'the pillars and leaders of the people

---

[1] See above 26.

[2] *MGH. Conc.* ii. 607–8. Biblical passages adduced were: Matt. 18. 18 f.; Acts 2. 11. For Jerome see editorial apparatus.

[3] Augustine in *Misc. Agostiniana: sermones* (Rome, 1930), i. 633, lines 17 ff. A similar statement, n. 18.

[4] *MGH. Conc.* p. 657, lines 6–7; Jonas, op. cit. c. 11, ed. cit. p. 164.

[5] *Conc.* p. 612, lines 8 f. The papacy had referred only to St Peter as a janitor of the kingdom of heaven, see, e.g., *Cod. Car.* nos. 14, 53, pp. 511, 575; etc.

[6] *Cap.* 197, p. 51, line 39.

who make known the divine will': for they were 'the officers of the eternal king in whose court the ranks and functions of individuals are fixed'.[1] What these easily multipliable expressions make clear is the leading function which the higher ecclesiastics claim for themselves both as collective legislators in council and as individual administrators of synodal laws. And the tenor of these claims corresponded to the Christian character of contemporary society. These statements have also added significance in so far as through the invocation of the episcopal binding and loosening power the bishops almost naturally came to adopt papal theses as well as nomenclatures:[2] becoming aware of their virtually monopolistic status within Frankish society, they showed little hesitation in adopting papal manners if not arrogating them outright, thus presenting themselves at least as the equals, if not the superiors, of the pope,[3] for although the popes had designated themselves as the unworthy heirs of St Peter since the fifth century, they were not until the twelfth century to claim the vicariate of Christ: but in the case of the Frankish bishops this claim was already put forward in the forties of the ninth century.

Whilst the ecclesiastical points of view still moved on the periphery, so to speak, of governmental thought – however vital for the implementation of the ecclesiological theme – the subject, if not also the problem, of Rulership in this renewed or reborn Christian body formed quite evidently the central topic of all discussions and thought. This again was not a topic that emerged for the first time in the Carolingian age, but one that was endemic in any society in which Christianity was organized on more or less stable lines: it was in fact the first serious problem that confronted the Roman Church in the fifth century when the (first) solution of the problem was to stand the test of time. Here the Frankish ecclesiastics had a prototype that was, moreover, enriched by a respectable amount of patristic material. The principle that a Ruler should govern with justice and equity was linked with the equally Christian tenet that all power came from God: and both premisses were seen from the teleological point of view. The result of this doctrinal operation was this: the government of the people of God

---

[1] Julianus Pomerius, *De vita contemplativa* in *PL* 59. 415 f., cit. in *Cap.* 196, c. 22, p. 36, lines 12 ff. and in Paris Council of 829, *Conc.* p. 673, c. 9, lines 29 ff. and repeated in Aachen Council of 836, *Conc.* p. 717, c. 45, lines 16 ff.

[2] They stressed as much Matt. 18. 18 as the papacy stressed Matt. 16. 18.

[3] Cf., e.g., *Cap.* 293, p. 397, line 32: 'Nos omnes, *licet indigni, Christi* tamen *vicarii . . .*' Cf. further the expression used by the Aachen synodists of 836: 'nobis indignis apostolica vice fungentibus' (in the synodal letter discovered by G. Laehr in *NA* 50 (1935), at 127).

was entrusted by divinity to the Ruler's special charge so that he should 'gubernare et regere cum equitate'.[1] Indeed, there were three distinct concepts in this pregnant statement: (1) the people of God having replaced the Frankish people were to be governed by someone who was appointed by divinity (2), for the purpose of (3) governing them with justice and equity. None of these three concepts had much in common with the earlier – Germanic – thought-pattern. The origin of the Ruler's power was divinity, hence theocratic Rulership; the body over which government had to be exercised: the people of God having clearly enough shed its earlier biological cohesive force and had become a body held together by the element of the (Christian) faith; and thirdly the purpose of divinity in handing over government to one Ruler, that is, the exercising of justice and equity which – and this is one more crucial point – were (and are) relative concepts: they received their particular contents and substance from the source and object of government. It is not necessary for me to offer any further comments upon this simple and yet most pregnant expression of the Frankish ecclesiastics.

The theme which they tried to drive home in the first half of the ninth century was what they called the *salubritas et stabilitas populi*: in other words, they held themselves responsible for the kind of government which furnished the presuppositions for the health and stability of the people – health and stability once more being relative concepts, received in this context their special physiognomy through the infusion of purely religious elements. The *salus*, the well-being of the Frankish people, was given greater precision by the twin concept of health and stability. Not only can one now better understand, I think, the claim of the bishops to be the guardians and custodians of 'the people of God', but also one more theme which was to become crucial in course of time was the elaboration of the idea of the incorporation of the Ruler *qua* Ruler and in his official capacity into the body of the people of God, into the Church itself. This incorporation of the Ruler brought the application of the ecclesiological theme to its logical conclusion. There seem to have been two main streams which contributed to this theme, and each had a distinguished intellectual ancestry. Whilst previously the king stood outside and above the *populus*, he now through the full operation of the ecclesiological theme became, *qua* Ruler, incorporated into the *populus Dei*.

The one stream was the view that Christian Rulership to deserve the

[1]Paris Council (829), *Conc.* p. 651; also Aachen, *Conc.* p. 716, c. 3.

name, presupposed its subordination to the demands of religion, a point of view explicitly expressed at the turn of the fifth and sixth centuries by the noted Augustinian teacher, the North African Fulgentius.[1] As so much else at the time, this view too was a mere abstract postulate, but now in the ninth century the Frankish ecclesiastics avidly seized upon it when it became almost at once a matter of grave practical concern: the synodists assembled at Paris in 829 incorporated this statement word for word into one of their decrees.[2] The implication appeared obvious: if pressed to its logical conclusion the postulate of the subjection of the Ruler to the demands of religion precluded any sort of autonomous monarchic government by a secular Ruler. And this implication had all the more practical relevance, since according to the intentions of the Frankish Rulers the body over which government was to be exercised, was not so much the Frankish people as the people of God, or *christianitas* itself. The implication became explicit barely a dozen years later when the archbishop of Sens and the Count of Vienne jointly declared as a firm and basic principle that what the bishops taught should be carried out by the kings.[3] But Fulgentius and his ninth-century disciples went one step further: they asserted as a general principle that the government of a Christian empire was to prove itself all the more salubrious, if provision were made to consult, and give a hearing to, the ecclesiastical estate itself,[4] because this was likely to contribute to greater safety than the fight 'pro temporali securitate'.

The thesis of Pope Gelasius I, a contemporary of Fulgentius, perfectly supplemented this point of view, and may be considered the other stream which contributed to the incorporation of the secular Ruler into the body of the Church. Once again the synodists at Paris were thoroughly conversant with Gelasius' doctrines, and quite especially the synodal mentor, Jonas of Orléans. The Gelasian thesis was

[1] Fulgentius, *De veritate*, ii. 38 in *PL* 65. 647. About Fulgentius see B. Altaner, *Patrologie*, 5th ed. (Freiburg, 1958), 453 f. For similar ideas expressed by Gelasius I, see *PG* 21 ff., and his successor, Anastasius II, who exhorted the emperor at Constantinople in 496, 'ut, sicut decet, et spiritus sanctus dictat, monitis nostris obaedientia praebeatur', in A. Thiel, *Epp. Roman. pont. genuinae* (Brunsberg, 1868), 620.

[2] Paris Council, II. 1, in *Conc.* pp. 650 f.; also Aachen, ibid. p. 715, c. 2.

[3] *MGH. Epp.* vi. 73, lines 6–10.

[4] Paris Council, *Conc.* p. 651, lines 6 ff.: 'Magis enim christianum regitur atque propagatur imperium, dum ecclesiastico statui per omnem terram consulitur.' Some 300 years later the same viewpoint, but in much more accentuated form, was made by John of Salisbury and, following him, by the bishop of Lincoln, Rob. Grosseteste, though it may safely be assumed that neither knew of the ninth-century statements, see the passages cit. in *PG* 424 and n. 6.

nothing else but the ecclesiological point of view expressed in taut, succinct Roman language. According to him and his Frankish followers, the Ruler not only as a Christian, but also in his capacity as a Ruler formed an integral and indispensable part of the Church itself: he was part of the *corpus Christi* within which there were, to quote the synodists, two prominent persons – *eximiae personae* – that is, the sacerdotal and the royal.[1] Once this fundamental position was taken up, it was no great effort to advance one more step and to argue that, within the *corpus Christi*, within the Church or the people of God, a residual controlling power remained in the hands of the ecclesiastics, because it was after all they who were vocationally qualified to know the law of Christ, the only law that mattered as far as the fabric of this society was concerned. Moreover, they considered it their duty 'to admonish the king vigilantly' to pay heed to the will of God of which they were the proper guardians.[2] Here, too, the implication was conspicuous – and in course of time the conclusion was to be drawn conspicuously – that within the *corpus Christi* there was no room for monarchic Rulership, since the Ruler both as a private person and as bearer of a divinely conferred office, did not stand outside and above the people committed to his government, but very much formed an essential part of them. This incorporation created a severe and unresolvable tension between him as a Christian and as a Ruler in the traditional sense. Exactly the same point of view is represented in the influential *Fürstenspiegel* of the forties, significantly enough entitled *On Christian Rulers* by Sedulius Scotus, who considered that there was nothing autogenous and autonomous in a Christian Ruler: he was set up by divinity for the sake of the common good or as he expressed it: 'ad utilitatem reipublicae'. Moreover, the Christian Ruler is distinguished by what he called a *religiosa sapientia*, that is, wisdom informed by religion.[3] For what made a Christian a Ruler was divine grace which enabled him to grasp the full implications and the full meaning of the will of God, so that he was in a position to put divine counsel as proffered by those who were qualified to do so, before any human consideration.[4]

This survey will have shown that within an astonishingly short

---

[1] See Jonas of Orléans, *De. inst. reg.*, ed. cit. c. 1, p. 134.

[2] Ibid., p. 135.

[3] See Sedulius Scotus, *De rectoribus christianis*, ed. S. Hellmann in *Quellen & Unters. z. lat. Phil. des M.A.* (Munich, 1916), c. 4, pp. 30–1.

[4] Ibid., c. 6, p. 38. For the consequences with regard to the king's sovereignty, see below 119, 133.

period there began to emerge two conceptions concerning Rulership. On the one hand, there was the royal theme, thoroughly monarchic, which was also applied in practice, and which held that for the rebirth of the Frankish people as a Christian body the monarchic government of the king was necessary, assisted as he was in his task by the ecclesiastics as the repositories of all matters relating to the ecclesiological theme. The presupposition was the conferment of divine grace as the title-deed for the monarchic form of the king's government.

Although the ecclesiastics potently supported the scheme of Charlemagne, they nevertheless began to clarify their own concept of Rulership: the more they steeped themselves in the source material, the more their thesis emerged, initially not so much antagonistic to, as rectifying and supplementing, the original royal theme, which, to be sure, soon began to suffer considerable inroads. This was not at all surprising since the ecclesiastics had a monopoly of the intellectual equipment which enabled them eventually to construct a theme which in all its essential features not merely modified or supplemented, but replaced the royal theme. As we shall presently see, the actuality of the situation in the late twenties and early thirties of the ninth century greatly helped the ecclesiastics to put some of their themes to a practical test.

Here, at this juncture, it may be worth while to point out how much the Carolingian experiment of a rebirth rested on purely intellectual and doctrinal, if not dogmatic, foundations. Is it then surprising that the unadulterated original royal monarchic theme became so much diluted that in the end very little remained of it? The history of the Middle Ages was set on its course by the turn of the eighth and ninth centuries: or rather the naturally evolved Germanic character of society was exposed to the relentless force and overpowering might of the intellect. The antithesis of nature and grace, with which the high Middle Ages are said to reverberate, first appeared on the historical landscape in the Carolingian age, and in no less a matter than that of the problem of public government.

What I would like to stress in this connexion is that, during the first half of the ninth century, both the royal theme and its ecclesiastical counterpart suffered from severe shortcomings. However insistent Charlemagne or for that matter his immediate successors were in their emphasis on divinity as the source of their power, the question obtruded itself, what proof was there that divinity had in fact conferred its grace upon the king? One can go further and ask: did not royal ideology by its very insistence on the theme of grace, virtually invite ecclesiastical intervention? And this, I would like to stress, quite particularly in the matter of grace which had always been considered, at any rate since the fourth century, the special métier of the learned ecclesiastics. How did the king obtain divine grace, after all the most vital and fundamental of all the ingredients of theocratic kingship, was a question which loomed large. The question was all the more pertinent as the Ruler distributed his royal power 'downwards' and thus gave very practical meaning to the descending theme. I am sure I need not elaborate upon this conspicuous weakness any further.

On the other hand, the ecclesiastical theme was far from being free from weaknesses. It is true, the ecclesiastics could call upon an impressive array of arguments which in effect deprived the Ruler of his monarchic status; it is also true they conceived of Rulership as a *ministerium*,[1] as an office, as a *munus*, with more or less well-circumscribed rights and duties, with a more or less well-defined scope and purpose; it is true, furthermore, that the ecclesiastics had taken a great step forward by declaring Rulership a divine trust and the Ruler a trustee, with the consequence that the ecclesiological theme had indeed come full circle, since the kingdom itself as the object of the divine trust, was laid up in heaven and merely temporarily entrusted to the king; it is true, lastly, that the ecclesiastics were – or at least held themselves to be – the custodians of all matters divine and that they therefore claimed some residual control over the Ruler in the interests of *salubritas* and *stabilitas*. All this was true, but at least two weak points showed themselves. The first was almost the same as in the royal camp, only seen from a different angle: how could the ecclesiastical assertion of trusteeship and of the ministerial nature of the royal office be proved in concrete terms? How could this assertion be demonstrated in reality, that is, by sensual means, by visible and audible media? The second weakness, as the ecclesiastics indubitably were aware, concerned the very core of any kind of government. The ecclesiastics claimed, as we have seen, the control of basic matters relative to the fabric of society, but the pertinent question was: how can this claim be substantiated? To assert a claim is one thing, however well buttressed in literature and in theory it is; to prove it by concrete means, is an entirely different matter. This had special relevance in the present context, since the ecclesiastics alone had the charisma and

---

[1] One of the basic statements was in Wisd. 6. 4–5, quoted in the episcopal *Relatio* to Louis I in 829 (*Cap.* 196, p. 48, lines 4 ff.). See also St John 19. 11.

by virtue of its operation stood in intimate contact with the divine; it was therefore all the more pertinent to supply tangible evidence that there was in fact a well-founded claim to exercise the control claimed. For the charge handed to the king was not a human, but a divine matter: a pregnant statement[1] which in prevailing circumstances was in need of sensual, concrete demonstration, one that by virtue of its visual and audible character was unambiguous and inaccessible to divers interpretations. Both these weaknesses as well as the related one in the royal field were to be resolved by one act, and one act alone: unction. Both the ritual and the symbolism of unction as well as its theory were to furnish the appropriate answers to the questions, which I have asked. Unction was to become the central element of theocratic kingship, but thereby, at least as far as doctrine went, the fate of the royal monarchy within the ecclesiological framework of the *corpus Christi*, was sealed. It was, in brief, the unction which visibly and tangibly brought about the rebirth of the Ruler.

III

This sketch of the accelerated development of certain governmental ideas within an ecclesiologically conceived unit should be supplemented by a brief analysis of the events of the year 833. For the steps taken by the bishops in the matter of Louis I's loss of ruling powers would seem to be a significant application of at least some of the ideas which we have just surveyed. However much our present-day moral standards and inclinations may be in revolt against this sort of ecclesiastical intervention, from the purely historical angle the episcopal measures may be considered under the heading of a trial run of a prototype engine. And in actual fact far more was at stake than just the rebellion against the father by the sons, notably Lothar, for what the year 833 demonstrated was the dynamic, purposeful and well-prepared intervention by the higher ecclesiastics in a concrete situation, and this with the help of doctrines hitherto understood in a purely abstract sense.

It was less than two decades after Charlemagne's death that in dealing with his son and successor, the pious Louis I, the bishops

---

[1] Cf. *Conc.* ii. 652, lines 5 ff.: 'Scire enim (rex) debet, quod causa quam iuxta ministerium sibi commissum aministrat, non hominum, sed Dei causa existit, cui pro ministerio, quod suscepit, in examinis tremendi die rationem redditurus est.'

referred to themselves as 'spiritual doctors',[1] and in their medical capacity considered themselves justified in raising severe charges against the descendant of the 'rector totius Europae': in October 833 they asserted that he unworthily handled the trust conferred on him by divinity; that he had scandalized the Church and offended God by his governmental measures, and gravely perturbed the people by his negligence.[2] These failings of Louis I amounted in the opinion of the bishops to the endangering of the safety of the kingdom and to a defamation of the royal office.[3] They declared that a just divine judgment had deprived him of ruling power.[4] Now we should take due notice that this was not an episcopal judgment or verdict, but a merely declaratory statement which was to make known the judgment of divinity. We shall see in a moment that this episcopal declaration was nothing more nor less than an interpretation which was put on the preceding events of June 833. And because Louis was declared to be without ruling power, he was treated by the bishops as a mere private person upon whom they imposed quite severe penal measures. In parenthesis we should also point out that Louis I owed both his royal and imperial position first and foremost to his father, Charlemagne, who, within a wholly secular framework, had raised him to the imperial function in 813, and secondly to the pope who three years later had crowned (and anointed) him at Rheims.

There is not a shred of evidence nor any assertion in the episcopal quarter to the effect that the bishops had taken any part in the creation of Louis as king or emperor. Nevertheless, the charges which they raised against him, made them indeed appear as 'spiritual experts': they claimed to pronounce authoritatively on the way in which Louis had discharged the divine trust: and in these matters of divine trust and grace they claimed a unique expertise.[5] At the same time we note that they waited some three months before they proceeded to subject Louis as a private penitent to ecclesiastical censures. The importance of this step lies in that no penitent could ever claim to exercise any ruling power (let alone imperial functions) which divinity had, understandably enough, conferred only on suitable persons: a penitent was unsuitable to (possess and) exercise ruling powers. Lastly we note that although they did not depose or dethrone Louis, by the infliction of

---

[1] *Cap.* 197, p. 53, lines 36 f. (A).
[2] Ibid. p. 52, lines 45 ff.
[3] Ibid. c. 8, p. 55: 'et regni periclitatio et regis dehonestatio'.
[4] Ibid. p. 53, line 3.
[5] See also Agobard's *Cartula* in *Cap.* 198, p. 56, lines 29 ff.

penalties they achieved exactly the same result: they asserted that a just divine judgment had intervened and *therefore* the divine grace (which, let us be clear about this, was not conferred on him by them) was withdrawn. It is therefore of some considerable importance that the rebellious Lothar I, although having 'succeeded', i.e. usurped his father's government in late June 833, did not change his title until 7 October 833, that is, after the bishops had pronounced on the withdrawal of his father's grace: from then on Lothar's title ran: 'divina ordinante providentia imperator augustus'.[1] Accordingly, when in 835 the bishops maintained that Louis had expiated for his crimes and was re-instated, he most significantly used this formula: 'Emperor by the grace which God has restored.'[2]

Evidently, the abstract theme of the Ruler's incorporation into the Church approached its practical implementation and was on the way to becoming an operational theme. In order to bring some of the ideological features into better relief, it is advisable to go into a few more details. After the events in June 833, to which I will turn presently, Louis declared himself guilty in October 833 on those charges which the bishops had raised against him: they delivered a detailed charge sheet which contained a number of grave accusations.[3] After pleading guilty to the charges in the church of St Médard at Soissons, Louis took off the belt of his sword and deposited it next to the charge sheet on the altar. There is ample evidence to prove that Louis divested himself of the 'cingulum militiae', the symbol of armed virility, because the bishops had, if not exactly forced him to do so, at any rate strongly urged him to this (humiliating) action.[4] Thereupon Louis was vested with the special garments of a penitent: the purpose of this, as the acting bishops themselves tell us, was to make it impossible for Louis to resume a ruling position again.[5] Now it should be understood that

---

[1] See *MGH. Urkunden Lothar I.* cit. nos. 13 ff., pp. 79 ff. Until then his title (as co-emperor since 823) was: 'Hlotharius augustus invictissimi domini imperatoris Hludowici filius.' The meetings started on 1 Oct. 833, see L. Halphen, *Charlemagne et l'empire Carolingien*, 2nd ed. (Paris, 1949), 291.

[2] Charter of 4 February 836 in *Cod. dipl. Fuld.*, cit. no. 489, p. 216, further no. 523, p. 230; both charters in favour of Fulda.

[3] For sources see BM 926a–b; further Kern–Buchner, 343. For the deplorable part which Pope Gregory IV through his personal presence played, cf. H. Fichtenau, *Das karol. Imperium*, cit. 277 ff.

[4] See, for instance, *Vita Hludowici* in *MGH. SS.* ii. 637; the episcopal *Exauctoratio* (*Cap.* 197, p. 55, lines 28 ff.) merely states the fact of Louis' laying down his arms.

[5] *Exauctoratio*, in *Cap.* 197, p. 55: '. . . habitu saeculi se exuens habitum poenitentis per impositionem manuum episcoporum suscepit: ut post tantam talemque poenitentiam nemo ultra ad militiam saecularem redeat.'

the (voluntary or enforced) abandonment of arms signified at the time that the man was no longer fit to do public service, let alone to act as a Ruler, the underlying reason being that he had no longer the means to afford protection;[1] quite especially he could not fulfil the role of a defender of the Church; the bearing of arms was in fact made the focal point for him to act in this capacity. Lastly, since Louis was a public penitent, nobody could have any contact with him: the close arrest in which he had been kept upon episcopal order since 30 June 833 in the church of St Médard (Soissons), was thus retrospectively and formally ratified by the bishops in October.[2] Let us be quite clear about one point: for the first time in European history an ecclesiastical hierarchy had acted within the framework of existing canonical rules and had declared a king to be unfit for government. This was how the bishops themselves viewed their role: 'We as bishops having been set up *over* the empire of the most glorious prince and emperor Lothar, have convened a general meeting.'[3]

In order to assess the significance of these canonical and legalizing measures more adequately, we should bear one further point in mind: at no time before October 833 (nor for that matter in October 833) had Louis been formally deposed. There never was at any time any kind of formal judgment decreeing his deposition or dethronement. For what had happened in June 833 near Colmar was no more nor less than the withdrawal of obedience and loyalty from Louis by the forces who, in a word, deserted him. This was an action which everyone at the time understood and which was entirely in keeping with very old Germanic customs: an army which left his leader or king was held to have deprived him of ruling powers.[4] No formal judgment was in fact necessary nor even contemplated: the fact of withdrawal amounted to an act of deposition and was a specific application of the Germanic right of resistance: withdrawal by the troops was a mere fact, and did not constitute any moral evaluation of crimes or offences.[5] It was a *de facto* deposition. The interesting point now is that in October 833

---

[1] Cf., e.g., *Cap.* 196, c. 35, p. 39; also the synod of Pavia, *Cap.* 228, c. 12, p. 120; Jonas of Orléans, *De inst. reg.*, c. 2, ed. cit. p. 137.

[2] Cf. *Ann. Bertiniani*, ed. *MGH. SS. RR. GG.*, 7: '. . . ita ut nullus loqui cum eo auderet, nisi illi qui ad hoc fuerant deputati'; *Vita Hludowici*, ed. cit. c. 51, p. 638. For part of this church see the reproduction in D. Bullough, *The Age of Charlemagne*, cit., fig. 14, p. 46.

[3] *Exauctoratio*, cit. p. 52, lines 22 ff.

[4] Cf., e.g., *Ann. Bertiniani*, 6–7; *Ann. Fuldenses*, ed. *MGH. SS. RR. GG.* 26: 'imperator . . . a suis desertus et proditus . . .'

[5] See especially Kern–Buchner, 341. Here also further literature.

F

the bishops maintained that the army's defection was a divine judgment upon Louis' crimes and therefore that 'according to divine counsel and ecclesiastical authority' he had lost his ruling power.[1] And it was this interpretation by the bishops of Germanic customs in an ecclesiastical sense which changed the whole situation: Louis was formally pronounced a public penitent who therefore was unable to govern. The *de facto* deposition of June 833 was, so to speak, ecclesiastically legitimized by the bishops in October 833, that is, they treated it in accordance with their own canonical and ecclesiastical standards. That, it may be remarked in parenthesis, Louis I was therefore punished twice for the same thing – first by the army and then by the bishops – was indeed pointed out at the time, though without avail – a startling antecedent to the reproach of double punishment made some 300 years later by Archbishop Thomas Becket.[2]

In order to reinstate him when circumstances changed, it was necessary to put the same process into reverse gear. In fact, Louis himself first insisted upon the bishops restoring him to communion with the Church,[3] which was solemnly done, whereupon he was reinvested with his sword and other royal garments – by the bishops themselves.[4] This was followed by the diet, which was also a synod, at Diedenhofen on Candlemasday 835, according to which the canonical measures imposed on Louis in October 833 were solemnly declared uncanonical, hence null and void,[5] and four weeks later on 28 February in the cathedral of St Stephen at Metz the last act of the reversing procedure took place: the re-crowning of Louis, so that he was now fully reinstated (*plenaria restitutio*).[6] An illuminating sidelight is thrown on the self-confidence of the Frankish bishops in their assumption of the role of coronators: Louis had never been crowned by them, but first by his father and then by the pope, and in any case as emperor, but these were probably considered by the bishops as trifling details or as negligible blemishes in the *modus procedendi*.

There is no need to underline before this forum the revolutionary nature of these actions, all taken within a span of less than two years

---

[1] *Exauctoratio*, cit. p. 53, line 7.

[2] See *Vita Hludowici*, cit. c. 49, p. 636, lines 42 ff.: some bishops used the argument that 'et leges forenses non contra unam culpam semel commissam bis invehant et nostra lex habeat non iudicare Deum bis in idipsum'. Cf. also Kern–Buchner, 195 n. 416a.

[3] *Vita Hludowici*, c. 51, p. 638.

[4] Nithard, *Historiarum libri quatuor*, ed. in *MGH. SS. RR. GG.* I. 4, p. 6, line 24. See further BM 926p.

[5] By the same bishops who had in the first place decreed them: cf. BM 938a.

[6] For details of sources see BM 926p and 938a–c.

and within twenty years of the great Charles's death. Had the ecclesiastical intervention not taken place, the whole affair would have lacked its dramatic complexion and would probably have been viewed by the chroniclers as a minor matter. By interpreting the defection of Louis' army in a wholly ecclesiastical-religious sense the Frankish ecclesiastics created a new situation. True enough, the active part played by the bishops confined itself to the formal declaration that Louis was a penitent wherefrom followed his inability to govern. But this ecclesiastical intervention was wholly conditioned by the development in the secular sphere of law and fact, that is, the army's withdrawal in June 833. In utilizing this situation in an ecclesiastical sense the bishops took a mighty step towards replacing the non-ecclesiastical contingency by ecclesiastical measures: in the thirties they still needed this secular or military contingency, but the time was not so far off when this was no longer necessary, so that the making and un-making of a king became a wholly ecclesiastical matter. For let me stress one point again: the bishops indisputably emerged in this historic episode as the final judges of any issue concerned with divine grace, with which the defection of the army had nothing even remotely to do. To have linked these two wholly unrelated matters – divine grace and desertion by the troops – was the great ideological advance made by the bishops. Louis was pronounced to have lost divine grace, hence rulership, which could be regained only by a formal reconciliation between him and the rest of the Church – only then was he capable of receiving divine grace again and of becoming 'emperor' once more: *divina clementia repropriante imperator augustus*. The bishops were the sole instruments in withholding divine grace and, what is of even greater import for the future, in restoring it. Nobody can convey better what the bishops thought about their newly asserted power than they themselves. The following statement may well be taken as a landmark in the practical implementation of the ecclesiological theme:

> We have taken (the bishops say in October 833) great care to make clear to him (Lothar) and his barons as well as to the whole people how great the strength and power and the office of the bishops is and what sort of damning punishment awaits him who is unwilling to obey sacerdotal admonitions.[1]

[1] *Exauctoratio*, cit. p. 52, lines 26 ff.: '. . . qualis sit *vigor* et *potestas* sive ministerium sacerdotale et quali mereatur damnari sententia, qui *monitis sacerdotalibus oboedire noluerit*.' Cf. Anastasius II, above 60 n. 1. The resemblance between the measures taken against Louis and those which culminated in the removal of the Visigothic king, Wamba, in October

If any particular action or measure had been needed to make the contemporary world realize how far the ecclesiological theme had developed by the thirties of the ninth century, it would have been provided by the interpretation of the events of 833 at the hands of the Frankish bishops. What strikes the observer and what assuredly must have struck the bishops themselves is that the ecclesiastical measures, however far-reaching and revolutionary, were still contingent upon a fact which strictly speaking was outside the scope of intervention by the bishops: this fact was of ancient Germanic origin and tradition. All therefore that remained to the bishops to do was to interpret this fact in the purely ecclesiastical sense, backed as this interpretation was by an array of doctrinal arguments. If, however, the ecclesiological theme was to be brought to its fruition, this remnant of the Germanic past was to be removed. So far the bishops were only able to display their authority and power in regard to Louis as a private person; what was needed in order to close the circle, was that they should be able to deal with the king in his capacity as a Ruler – only when that requirement was fulfilled, could the thesis of the Ruler's incorporation be said to be practically and concretely realized. In brief, the actual making of the Ruler, the concrete conveyance or transmission of the divine grace of Rulership, was to be shown in episcopal hands; then, and only then, the idea of the Ruler as a *homo renatus* – as a reborn man *qua* Ruler – could become fully operational in the ecclesiological sense. To the rebirth of Frankish society was to be added the rebirth of its Ruler. This will be the subject of my next lecture.

680, is so close that, in common with many others, I am inclined to think that the records for the latter had been available to the Frankish ecclesiastics. For some of the sources dealing with Wamba's removal and his replacement by Erwig cf., e.g., Toledo Council XII, in *PL* 84. 470 ff.; *Epitome Ovetensis*, in *MGH. AA.* xi. 374; *Laterculus regum Visigothorum*, nos. 44–6, in *MGH. AA.* xiii. 468; further F. Dahn, *Die Könige d. Germanen*, 2nd ed. (Leipzig, 1885), VI. 463 ff. also V. 215–17; H. v. Schubert, *Gesch. d. Kirche im frühen M.A.* (Tübingen, 1921), 254; R. Menendez Pidal, *Historia de Espana* (Madrid, 1940), iii. 127; Kern–Buchner, app. XXVI; J. O. Rovira in *Settimana Spoleto*, 7 (1960), 349 ff., here also additional literature. The parallels are too close to be merely coincidental: the only difference was that the Frankish ecclesiastics did not have recourse to such reprehensible means as the Visigoths had when they drugged Wamba in the middle of the night. Cf. also below 81 f.

The Rebirth of the Ruler

I

Since in the Frankish period as now society and government were complementary, the Renaissance of society necessarily effected, if indeed it did not presuppose, a change in the structure and concept of Rulership: and since the social Renaissance was to be brought about by the application of the ecclesiological theme, the standing and function of the Ruler was inextricably involved in most material respects. For, as I have tried to point out, by virtue of the ecclesiological theme 'the people of the Franks' were held to be 'the people of God' in close resemblance to biblical doctrine; and 'the people of God' were nothing less than the Church, seen corporately as a divine institution, and not one that had its roots in ordinary humanity and in the ordinary laws of nature, an institution over which the king was set by divine volition, by the working of the divine grace. There was, however, the great question: how could the Ruler actually prove that he was in possession of divine grace?

It is at this juncture that the exegesis of the Bible so powerfully promoted by Charlemagne, bore fruit. If I am not mistaken, there are two different and yet closely related constituents which when seen together, yielded a well-nigh perfect answer to the question in form of the liturgical act of regal anointing. To begin with, the Old Testament provided a superabundance of instances in which Jewish kings were anointed: two points emerge immediately from a perusal of the relevant Old Testament passages. First, that it was priests or prophets who, obviously by virtue of their special charismatic qualifications, administered the unction on the Ruler's head; and secondly, the administrators of unction appeared to act as organs mediating between divinity and the king to be anointed: this becomes clear if one attends to the actual formula of benediction: 'Behold, the Lord hath anointed thee to be prince over his inheritance.'[1] The administrators of unction were, so to speak, executive agents of divinity, acting as mediators and conferring the unction vicariously. They spoke the formula as if God Himself had performed the anointing. The effect of this Old Testament

[1] Cf., e.g., I Kgs. 10. 1; II Kgs. 2. 4; 5. 3; III Kgs. 1. 34 and 39; IV Kgs. 9. 6; etc.

anointing was clearly constitutive, for without it the Ruler was not established legitimate king. Through it he had received the special charisma of Rulership, having now been set *over* Israel, the Lord's inheritance,[1] and stood in a specially close relationship to divinity. This had the crucial consequence of his being endowed with sacrosanctity, that is, he was removed from ordinary membership of the Jewish community and raised onto a different plane altogether, with the further consequence of his enjoying a very special protection: since through unction he had become a *christus Domini* – the Lord's anointed – and been sanctified, he was inviolable. Offences against him amounted to sacrilege deserving the most severe punishment.[2] The anointed king became the *dux populi Domini*, the leader of God's own people.[3]

The other basic characteristic of Old Testament anointings and the one of special concern in the present context related to the transformation of the king's whole being. He was transformed into a being fundamentally different from that which he was before the unction. He was, literally speaking, turned into another man, as the Old Testament concretely depicted the rebirth of the anointed king.[4] And a relationship between father and son was established as a result of the close kinship with divinity.[5] By becoming an anointed king, the Old Testament Ruler lost whatever he had before, since 'God gave him another heart'.[6] This renewal or rebirth as the Lord's anointed explains why the Old Testament king also possessed certain charismatic qualities which amongst other things transformed him into a prophet.[7] I would like to emphasize that this Old Testament rebirth of the Ruler was perfectly clearly understood in patristic literature, where the change of name was sometimes seen as evidence of this rebirth, as in the case of Joshuas changing into Jesus.[8]

In brief, the Old Testament conception of the anointed king conspicuously demonstrated a rebirth of the Ruler: this Old Testament idea of the Ruler seems to me crucial to the understanding of the

---

[1] See especially the expression in I Kgs. 10. 1.

[2] I Kgs. 24. 7 and 11; 26. 9, 11; but also II Kgs. 1. 14, 16.

[3] Cf. I Kgs. 9. 16; II Kgs. 6. 21; etc.

[4] I Kgs. 10. 6. Cf. in this context J. Funkenstein, 'Unction of the Ruler' in *Adel & Kirche: Festschrift f. Gerd Tellenbach* (Freiburg, 1968), 6 ff., at 10: 'Unction (in the OT) constitutes a kind of rebirth, the ruler being regarded as having been reborn on the day of his inauguration as God's son.'

[5] Cf., e.g., II Kgs. 7. 14.

[6] I Kgs. 10. 9; cf. also ibid. 11. 14, Samuel saying 'Let us renew (*innovare*) kingship.'

[7] I Kgs. 10. 6, 10.

[8] Cf., e.g., St Augustine, *De civ. Dei*, 16. 43.

meaning and liturgy of unction, however little prominence is accorded to this phenomenon by modern historical authorities. Here indeed the hitherto unrecognized meaning of the benediction which the crowning and anointing pope spoke over Louis I in October 816 at Rheims, deserves at least a passing mentioning: slightly altering the Old Testament text the pope uttered these benedictory words: 'Blessed be our Lord who has granted us to see the second David.'[1] This is a highly significant prayer text, because the idea of the Ruler's rebirth now even formed part of papal doxology. Could there be better proof for the efficacy of this rebirth of the Ruler? In the West the actual administration of the unction with real oil played an important part in drawing a clear line of demarcation between the East and the West, for in Constantinople there was no unction, therefore no oil was used and there was of course no chrismation, consequently the ecclesiastical coronation of the Ruler never displayed constitutive effects, but was merely declaratory.[2] The more the Ruler's rebirth was understood in its intended spiritual sense, the more the Old Testament nomenclatures for the king faded away.

In view of this rebirth of the king, it is not therefore surprising to find that the anointing of Old Testament kings was considered a sacrament in the strict sense in which the concept was taken in the early Middle Ages. There is the testimony of Gregory the Great which warrants a few remarks. To Gregory it was self-evident that the unction administered to the Old Testament king was a sacrament because it itself contained divine grace.[3] The essential point in this Gregorian doctrine seems to be that the royal unction was inextricably linked with the concept of divine grace (and indeed in this sense he speaks of a *plenitudo unctionis*).[4] One of the reasons for the combination of unction and grace[5] appears to lie in the handing over of the inheritance of God to the king, for this metaphorical 'inheritance' was nothing

---

[1] See Thegan, *Vita Hlud. imp.*, in *MGH. SS.* ii. 594, lines 10–11: 'Benedictus sit Dominus Deus noster, qui tribuit oculis nostris videre *secundum David*.' The original passage is in III Kgs. 1. 48. Cf. also Amalarius of Metz, in his *Ep.* 7 (*MGH. Epp.* v. 259, line 1): Louis I as *novus David* (about 820). The idea of the king's rebirth has not been recognized by W. Mohr, *Die karol. Reichsidee*, cit. although he frequently comes near to seeing it, cf., e.g., 51.

[2] There was only an allegorical anointing ('bildliche Salbung'), see O. Treitinger, op. cit. 29; here also literature concerning the declaratory character of the ecclesiastical coronation. See also below 91, 164 (A).

[3] Cf. Gregory I, *In I Regum Expos.*, iv. 5. 1 in *PL* 79. 278 A: '. . . ipsa unctio sacramentum est . . .'

[4] Ibid. col. 278 D; also v. 3. 18, col. 457 D: unctions of kings as 'sublimia sacramenta'.

[5] Cf. also ibid. v. 3. 21, cols. 459–60, esp. B.

less than the totality of God's people, of the *multitudo fidelium*, as Gregory I terms it. The purpose of conferring governmental powers on the king was the defence of this inheritance against enemies. Moreover, all mundane ambitions of the king were said to be removed when once he was anointed and thereby reborn as a king. The effect which unction achieved according to Gregory was that the king exclusively served the needs of 'the divine inheritance', in other words, occupied a ministerial office.[1] Here in this Gregorian exposition a great many ingredients of the later theocratic conception of kingship can be detected, which quite specifically concern the present topic; his writings could not fail to strengthen the view of the sacramental character of royal unction.

It should not, however, be assumed that Gregory I's doctrine was an isolated or idiosyncratic one: his contemporary, Isidore of Seville, propounded exactly the same thesis apparently without any knowledge of the papal views. To him, too, the unction administered to the Ruler was a sacrament.[2] What makes the views of both these writers so remarkable is that they referred exclusively to the Old Testament anointings of kings, since at the time of their writings there had been no anointing of a contemporary king. This needs to be stressed, since the Old Testament always remained the pattern of royal anointings of kings, and the sacramental character attributed to it by these two outstanding sources of medieval theology, could all the more easily be absorbed. In fact, right down to the twelfth century (Otto of Freising and Peter of Blois) and the thirteenth century (Robert Grosseteste), the royal anointing was reckoned amongst the sacraments proper,[3] although by that time the great majority of theological writers had adhered to the fixed number of sacraments which excluded royal unction.

The other constituent powerfully reinforcing the Old Testament practice of unction, was supplied by the New Testament. This second

---

[1] *In I Reg. Exp.* col. 279 C, c. 2: '. . . Haereditas enim multitudo fidelium est . . . unctionis ergo fructus est cultus divinae haereditatis.' For the ministerial conception see also v. 3. 18, col. 458 A.

[2] Isidore of Seville, *Quaest. in Vet. Test.: in Gen.* 29. 8 in *PL* 83. 269: 'sacramentum mysticae unctionis.'

[3] See Otto of Freising speaking of the *sacramentum unctionis* on the occasion of Frederick's royal coronation, *Gesta Fred.* in *MGH. SS. RR. GG.*, ii. 3, p. 104, line 28; Peter of Blois, in his *Ep.* 10, in *PL* 207. 28 B ('magna est enim huius efficacia sacramenti' and immediately afterwards (col. 29) he speaks of the transformation of him who was anointed); see also in the thirteenth century Robert Grosseteste's letter to Henry III in L. Wickham Legg, *Engl. Coronation Records* (London, 1901), 67 (A).

channel or root concerned baptismal anointing[1] (although there were in actual fact two baptismal anointings of which one was reckoned to belong to the baptismal rite proper, whereas the other (post-baptismal) was reckoned to belong to confirmation, but the matter remained controversial and is of no real interest to us here), which was continuously practised down to the early Middle Ages and beyond. The oil used was chrism, as Pope Siricius' statement made clear, and the effect of its administration on the head was that thereby grace was imparted to the whole body: the significance of this statement is that unction was intimately and inextricably linked with the conferment of grace—in fact a view based on the Old Testament unction.[2] There are two further witnesses of the late fourth century whose testimonies are of direct relevance, and they are all the more valuable as the one comes from the West, the other from the East. St Ambrose in his tract *On the Sacraments* declared that through unction man was made an athlete of Christ,[3] and came to be, allegorically speaking, crowned – the suggestive force of this point of view for royal matters need no comment. At virtually the same time St John Chrysostom in the East expressed a view which was hardly distinguishable from that of Ambrose: the unction of baptized man signified him an athlete entering the arena: man was baptized in order to enable him to fight.[4]

That (baptismal or post-baptismal) unction was also administered in the Frankish realms of the eighth century – and hence had been done so continuously since the introduction of Christian rites in the Merovingian Church – is evidenced by the interest which Charlemagne took in the subject. In his questionnaire which he addressed to the bishops he concerned himself with the meaning of baptismal rites and his especial curiosity gave rise to the question 'Why is the breast anointed with oil?' as well as the question 'Why is the head anointed with holy chrism?'[5] The answers to this rather lengthy and formidable examination paper are of little concern to us in the present context;[6] what is

---

[1] For details see A. Stenzel, *Die Taufe* (Innsbruck, 1958). See further P. E. Schramm in *Sav. Z. KA* 68 (1951) (review of De Pange), at 395: 'Mit der Taufe konnte sich die Salbung verbinden, weil Christus, der mit dem hl. Geist Gesalbte (Apg. 10. 38), die Seelen der Gläubigen salbt . . . Die Taufsalbung ist also eine spirituelle Königssalbung.'

[2] Siricius, in his *Ep.* 10, c. 11, in *PL* 13. 1189 A to the Gallican bishops.

[3] St Ambrose, *De sacramentis*, i. 2. 4 in *CSEL* 73. 17 (A).

[4] St John Chrysostom, *In Ep. Ad Coloss.*, c. 2, hom. 6, c. 4 in *PGr* 64. 342.

[5] *Cap.* 125, pp. 246–7: 'Quare pectus unguatur oleo. Cur sacro crismate caput inungitur.'

[6] Cf., e.g., Odilbert of Milan, *Lib. de baptismo*, ed. F. Wiegand in *Erzbischof Odilbert über die Taufe* (Würzburg, 1879): Theodulf of Orléans in *PL* 105. 223–40; Amalarius,

of concern is that baptismal and post-baptismal rites presupposed anointing on the head and that the rite was linked to what was indisputably conceived to be a sacrament.

Now it had been from the beginnings of an embryonic theology one of the incontestable doctrinal points that only bishops (or priests) could validly confer sacraments. The valid administration of sacraments presupposed that they were conferred by those specially qualified by virtue of being divinely instituted for this purpose. In other words, sacramental theology from its infancy provided one of the most powerful reasons for the sharp cleavage between the (unqualified, because unordained) layman and the (qualified, because ordained) priest or bishop, whose specific *raison d'être* in a Christian society was precisely that he alone could provide the means of salvation by the vehicle of sacraments. At the same time this point of view gave rise to what was called the mediatory role of the priests (or bishops): they mediated the sacraments between divinity and man. This thesis was expressed often enough, and it must suffice if I refer to only two statements in our (Carolingian) period. Agobard of Lyons, one of the great luminaries of the time, said in his tract *On the privileges and rights of the priesthood*, that

> Although the just laymen are worthier to merit eternal salvation than unjust priests, nevertheless sacraments through which and in which salvation lies, can never be administered by just laymen, but only by priests, however unjust they may be.[1]

Here we have not only the unambiguous and unqualified expression concerning the mediatory role of the priests in regard to the sacraments, but also the equally unambiguous and sharp distinction between the office of the priest and his person: what mattered for purposes of salvation was the office, and not the personal merits or demerits of the man himself: and it was the office which enabled the man to confer sacraments. It is in this context that the otherwise extravagantly sounding expression of the bishops as 'janitors of the kingdom of heaven' and as 'the discoverers of the divine will through the grace of God'

Opera liturgica omnia, ed. J. M. Hanssens (= *Studi e Testi*, 1948), i. 236; Magnus of Sens in *PL* 102. 981 ff. (through baptism man 'in melius mutatur' (col. 981 C), so that a *nova regeneratio* comes about (col. 983 B)).

[1] Agobard, *De privilegiis et iure sacerdotii*, c. 7, in *PL* 104. 134 B. This is one of the chapters omitted in the ed. in *MGH. Epp.* V. 203 f., no. 11. For Agobard's views cf. also *PG* 135–7. His views, too, may be derived from the Ps.–Augustinian *Quaestiones*, ed. *CSEL* 50, qu. 35, p. 63, which had made the same point in regard to obedience (A).

assume their full significance.[1] It is important to keep these considerations in mind, if one wishes to understand the role which the episcopacy was to play in the clericalization of the royal office.

For what was lacking in the thesis that the Rulers were set up not through any human agency, but were Rulers 'by the grace of God', was the concrete, firm proof. It was no more than an assertion, and an assertion that concerned what is perhaps the most vital point in any Christian society: where did royal power originally come from? It stands to reason that the very idea of divine grace as the focal origin of royal power and the royal office opened up the way to the intervention of the bishops, and this quite especially when we give due consideration to the – by the Carolingian time – traditional view that regal anointings were sacraments. The more the kings themselves stressed the divine origin of their power and office, the more they invited, at least by implication, episcopal intervention, if for no other reason than to supply the concrete evidence that their ministry was a divinely conferred office. And what better proof could there be than by visible, sensual and realistic imitation of the models which the Old Testament supplied in abundance? In these models the priest administered the oil, but acted as the instrument of divinity: It was a concrete action which by virtue of its simplicity and clarity, was not open to misunderstanding. The priestly action was constitutive: the king was not king before.

II

It is difficult to say whether the royal anointings in the second half of the eighth century served as precedents for the historically much more influential unctions of exactly a century later.[2] The reason for administering unction on Pippin seems clear enough: a substitute had to be found for his lack of blood charisma, and that substitute was to legitimize the *coup d'état*. Consequently, this legitimization – the unction conferring a charisma of grace – was credited with at least as much authority, force and efficacy as the replaced blood charisma had displayed. Nevertheless – and this is an essential point – he was anointed

---

[1] *MGH. Conc.* ii. 611, lines 31 ff.: 'indices divinae voluntatis per Dei gratiam'. See also above 57.

[2] M. Wallace-Hadrill, 'The via regia . . .' in *Trends*, cit. 27, rightly points out that 'the Western clergy had never taken any interest or part in king-making before 751'. In this context cf. also R. Kottje, *Studien zum Einfluss des A.T. auf Recht und Liturgie des frühen M.A.* (Bonn, 1964), 94 ff., at 104, stressing how rarely reference was made to the OT before the ninth century.

by St Boniface (751) in his capacity as papal legate and was thus created king of the Franks. The administration of the unction by the pope little more than two years later in 754 was teleologically conditioned: Pippin was (not only now papally created a king, but much more importantly and) above all constituted and consecrated as a patrician of the Romans, that is, a special defender of the Roman Church.[1] This particular orientation of the eighth-century kingly anointings towards the Roman Church is significant, because all of them, including the imperial unction conferred on Louis I in October 816, were so intimately related to and linked with the papacy that whenever after 754 an original anointing took place, it was performed by the pope.[2] Both the consecrator and the purpose of all these unctions would seem to make it unlikely that they could have served as precedents or direct models for those in the ninth century. It should also be borne in mind that the papally administered unction on Louis I was not even mentioned as an impediment to his 'deposition' by the Frankish episcopacy: it was as if Louis had not been anointed at all. The furthest one can go, I think, is that West-Frankish ecclesiastics might have been inspired by the eighth-century anointings[3] and moved to imitate them when actual conditions and circumstances proved propitious. Then in taking up the papal cue the sense of novelty, at least within Frankish lands, was also greatly diminished.

There is one point which is worth mentioning, and this is the institution of a co-regent during the lifetime of the Ruler. In all likelihood this was borrowed from Byzantium, where, in any case, all ecclesiastical coronations were declaratory only. Now I believe it is of some interest to note that with the progress of the idea of the Ruler's rebirth through unction the institution of a co-regent created in a purely secular manner by the living Ruler himself, was completely abandoned. Charlemagne made, within a secular 'rite', Louis I his co-regent as emperor in September 813; Louis I again made his son Lothar I his co-regent in July 817; Louis also raised Charles the Bald to kingship in 838. In each of these instances the secular creation was followed by an ecclesiastical one: Stephen IV anointed and crowned Louis I emperor at Rheims in October 816; Lothar I was anointed and

---

[1] For this see *PG* 67–74.

[2] For some remarks on this topic see also C. Brühl, 'Fränkischer Königsbrauch' in *HZ* 194 (1962), at 305 f., and the as yet unpublished Cambridge dissertation by my pupil, Mrs J. L. Nelson.

[3] Including also the coronation and unction of Louis II as *king* of Italy at St Peter's by Sergius II on 15 June 844, see *Lib. Pontificalis*, ed. L. Duchesne (Paris, 1886), ii. 89.

crowned emperor by the pope in St Peter's at Easter 823; to Charles the Bald we will turn presently. The important point is that in the course of the tenth century both in France and Germany this institution of a co-regent was revived, with the important qualification however that it was from now on an exclusively ecclesiastical matter and followed all the norms and rites of the orders as they had meantime developed. The last secular creation of a Ruler in medieval Europe appears to have been that by Louis I of Charles the Bald.[1]

Before reviewing the stages of the Ruler's rebirth it may be profitable to draw attention to a feature which has been barely touched upon in the present context. It is adoptionism which warrants a few words, though not the theological thesis, but what one might well term the royal species of adoptionism. We may recall that the papacy in the second half of the eighth century had often enough apostrophized Pippin (and his sons) as the adopted sons of St Peter[2] and in one of the most influential *Fürstenspiegel* of the time, that by Smaragdus, to select just one more example, this idea of the king as a divinely adopted son is made one of the points central to kingship: God, Smaragdus said, had adopted the king as His son through administering on him the unction.[3] Although even this concept of regal adoptionism soon faded out of sight (as far as the royal side was concerned)[4] it is nevertheless of interest, because it clearly portrayed at the time when it was current, the idea of a particular distinction conferred on the anointed king, a distinction which no other living mortal could claim – in no wise different from that of his possessing the divine grace (of Rulership) which he also was the only one to enjoy. In brief, the conception of the king's being God's adopted son, manifested the idea of the Ruler's rebirth.

When Charles the Bald – the *fons et origo* of most of Louis I's

---

[1] I omit the creation of sub-kings, such as Charles the Bald's making his son sub-king of Aquitaine in 855; P. E. Schramm, *Kaiser*, cit. ii. 98 n. 145, rightly calls attention to the later creation of a prince of Wales by the king which had the same purpose as the earlier creation of a sub-king.

[2] Cf. *PG* p. 68 n. 5.

[3] Smaragdus, *Via regia*, pref. in *PL* 102. 933 B: 'Deus omnipotens te, o clarissime rex . . . caput tuum oleo sacri chrismatis linivit et dignanter in filium adoptavit.' The preface in *MGH. Epp.* iv. 533, no. 23, is the beginning of the first book; cf. also the edit. by D. de Bruyne in *Rev. Bénédictine*, 12 (1924), at 15. According to H. Fichtenau, this statement of Smaragdus was mere flattery (*Das karol. Imperium*, cit. 64 n. 47), though I think it was a direct application of the OT view concerning unction which created the sonship of the king (cf. II Kgs. 7. 14; Ps. 2. 7; 89. 26 f.; and above 71 ff.).

[4] In the imperial coronations the principle of adoption by the pope of the king remained, though clearly it had undergone some change of meaning. Cf. the statement of John VIII in regard to Boso, cit. in *PG* 164 n. 6; here also further literature and at 257.

troubles – wished to assume final control of Aquitaine, he had to dis-
lodge his nephew Pippin II (of Aquitaine); his territory was part of
the portion allocated to Charles by the treaty of Verdun, but it was an
apportionment which the nephew was willing to recognize to a limited
extent only. He, moreover, was deserted by a number of his nobles
because of his inability to raise appropriate defences against the
Normans.[1] The essential point here is that Charles had been crowned as
king by his father, Louis I, in September 838, in a wholly secular
manner.[2] He had become king of Neustria, but not of Aquitaine
against which, in 848, he now employed force. This created a new
situation as far as his constitutional position went. Certainly he had
been king, though not of Aquitaine: one way out of this impasse was
some sort of election by the secular and ecclesiastical princes of
Aquitaine[3] but leaving aside the accompanying circumstances, was
this – in the forties of the ninth century – a sufficiently strong enough
title-deed for Rulership? Moreover, through becoming 'king' of
Aquitaine the kingship which his father had conferred on him ten
years before, was clearly bound to be affected by this new addition.

It is at this juncture that the episcopal hierarchy emerged in a new
role. Led by the archbishop of Sens,[4] Wenilo, they proceeded immediately after the 'election' to anoint (and crown) the king and thus
brought to bear upon a constitutionally hardly definable situation an
unambiguously sacral-theocratic element. This initiative now taken by
the episcopacy was the potent step by which was effected the visible
and concrete sacralization of the kingly office: a step the potentialities
of which could not be foreseen by the acting personalities themselves,
and which also showed the readiness with which the ecclesiastics seized
the initiative presented as they were by this unique opportunity in the
face of the legal and constitutional entanglements of Charles the Bald.
For through their action the bishops quietly but rather efficiently set

---

[1] For factual details see L. Auzias, *L'Aquitaine carolingienne 778–987* (Paris, 1937),
218 ff.; and L. Halphen, *Charlemagne et l'empire Carolingien*, 2nd ed. (Paris, 1949), 338 f.;
now also Th. Schieffer in *Festschrift f. A. Stohr* (Mainz, 1960), 43 ff.

[2] BM 982a for sources. For Charles the Bald in general see F. Lot, *Naissance de la
France*, 16th ed. (Paris, 1948), 419 ff. and in particular F. Lot and L. Halphen, *Le règne
de Charles le Chauve* (Paris, 1909), 186 ff.

[3] See *Ann. Bertiniani*, ed. cit. 36. See on this also W. Schlesinger, 'Karlingische Königs-
wahlen' in *Festgabe f. H. Herzfeld* (Berlin, 1958), 207 ff., at 231 f.; and P. E. Schramm,
Der König von Frankreich, 2nd ed. (Darmstadt, 1960), 15 f.

[4] Sens had been a metropolitan see since Merovingian times with seven suffragans,
including Paris; John VIII conferred on the archbishop the title of 'Vicarius apostolicae
sedis per Galliam et Germaniam' (see *LThK* s. v. Sens).

aside the antecedent difficulties. The episcopal initiative was to remedy and restore a situation that was irremediable by other contemporary means. Clearly, the secular creation of Charles by his father was, so to speak, absorbed through this unction and coronation. Not only was this the first royal unction administered by bishops on their own, but it was also the first time that a royal symbol – the sceptre – was handed over by them, and also the first time that a Ruler was crowned a king by the officiating ecclesiastics.[1] All three ingredients from then on belonged to the ecclesiastical province only: no longer did a layman crown a king. It was the West-Frankish ecclesiastics who substituted the ecclesiastical unction and coronation as king-creating agencies in place of conquest and election. The unction and coronation of Charles the Bald at Orléans in 848 marked the birth of the fully-fledged sacral-theocratic kingship in Western realms. The military conqueror had become legitimized, sanctified as an athlete of Christ: it was a veritable Renaissance of the warrior who was reborn as a divinely chosen instrument of power. The ecclesiastical rite was from the very beginning a collective act of the episcopacy, not an act performed by a single ecclesiastic: and the focal point of the rite was the unction, a liturgical act which unquestionably was, by virtue of the sacramental character imputed to it, the prerogative of the ecclesiastics to perform.

One point requires a few remarks. Was this episcopal action at Orléans wholly unaided or can the possibility of an actual model at least be envisaged? I am inclined to think that there is considerable justification for holding that the Wamba–Erwig affair served here too as a pattern, and perhaps even more directly than it did on the occasion of Louis I's penance.[2] This assumption is not only justified by the influence which Visigothic literary vehicles exercised on the ever alert Carolingian writers and thinkers but also by the influence which, behind

---

[1] See also below 95, 106. Yet it is noteworthy that Charles's creation as king of Aquitaine did not change his dating of charters; dating of regnal years from the day of unction (coronation) began, as far as I can see, in the tenth century. As emperor Charles kept the regnal years apart from his imperial years, see *Recueil des actes de Charles II*, ed. A. Giry et al., ii (Paris, 1952), no. 400, p. 392. For charters commemorating his unction as king cf., e.g., no. 355, p. 290, lines 26, 34; 364, p. 315, line 3.

[2] Above 69 n. 1. Some of the arguments adduced in favour of Theodulf as chief redactor of the *Libri Car.* (A. Freeman in *Speculum*, 40 (1965), 203 ff., at 223 ff., esp. 273, 275 ff.) would seem to me further strong support for Frankish knowledge of these Visigothic matters. Even at a later date, in 878, a copy of the Visigothic laws was produced at the Council of Troyes, see Ch. de Clercq, 'La législation . . .' in *Rev. de droit can.*, 7 (1957), 276. For Visigothic influence (mainly on the unction administered on Pippin) see E. Müller, 'Die Anfänge d. Königssalbung' in *HJb* 58 (1938), 317 ff., at 343 ff.; also R. Kottje, op. cit. 95 n. 10. Cf. Toledo XII, in *PL* 84. 471 B.

the scenes, Hincmar himself had upon the king as his trusted counsellor. He, of all the outstanding ecclesiastics, was the one most likely to have realized the potentialities of the Wamba–Erwig affair. In both instances there is a kind of election – in the case of Erwig his predecessor Wamba was said to have 'pre-elected' him; in the case of Charles it was the nobility which 'elected' him, a procedure which a long time ago was called 'une élection simulée'.[1] In neither case was the 'election' which was much more likely a designation of the successor, considered strong enough to provide a firm and irremovable title-deed, at any rate within the ambit of the prevalent religious conceptions; and in each case it was the unction which legitimized the otherwise illegitimate accession.[2] That the unction of Erwig was constitutive, cannot be disputed:[3] it was the sacral-liturgical act that constituted, so to speak, a *sanatio in radice*; whatever had gone before, was made lawful – and what stronger title-deed could anyone ask for than the visible conferment of divine grace?

There can be little doubt that exactly the same considerations applied in the case of Charles the Bald and, if anything, with still greater force. Conquest and election as merely human agencies were eliminated by the sacral act of unction. The naturalness of Charles's status – first as king made solely by the father, then by conquest and by some sort of election as Ruler of Aquitaine – was washed away by the ecclesiastical unction which changed the status of the king altogether: he had undergone a true transformation. The idea of a Renaissance could hardly have been better demonstrated than in this episcopal transaction at Orléans. We might well recall one of the passages in the Old Testament which deals with royal anointing: after receiving unction he was turned into another man.[4] As far as Frankish royal inauguration ceremonies went unction and coronation were joined together for the first time in the rite performed at Orléans. Orléans had assumed the same significance in regard to Frankish kingship as Rheims had thirty-five years earlier in regard to Roman emperorship.[5] But in one respect Orléans was of greater import in so far as on the same occasion the

[1] F. Lot cited by L. Levillain in *Bibl. de l'école des chartes* 64 (1903), 47.

[2] We should also note that in the same year 848 the king of the Brettons, Nomenoi, also a usurper, had himself anointed, see Levillain, art. cit., pp. 42–3; Schramm, *König*, cit. 25.

[3] For this see J. O. Rovira, in *Settimana Spoleto*, 7 (1960), 351.

[4] I Kgs. 10. 6.

[5] Cf. *PG* 143 ff. The fusion of unction and coronation may have been modelled on the papal unction and coronation in 844, see above 78 n. 3.

ecclesiastics began to implement the symbolic enthronement of the king – it was the reappearance of a secular-mundane symbolism in an ecclesiastical garb and setting – the baptism, so to speak, of an old tradition.[1]

The importance of all these novel features surrounding the rebirth of the king as a Christian Ruler, was to emerge with impressive clarity exactly ten years later when Louis the German had invaded the kingdom of Charles the Bald. A number of Frankish barons as well as Charles's own coronator, Archbishop Wenilo of Sens, had joined the invader's side.[2] The incident produced two very pregnant documents which are of direct relevance to us; and in both of them the hand and spirit of Hincmar are detectable. The question which stood in the forefront was, what was the status and position of an anointed king when confronted by rebellion and sedition. The document entitled *A proclamation against Wenilo* issued under the name of Charles the Bald, contains a number of highly interesting points: first, the 'election' of 848 is here seen for what it was, that is, as an episcopally managed arrangement.[3] Accordingly, it was Wenilo and the other bishops who had 'elected' Charles to which election the other 'faithful' had expressed their agreement, consent and acclamation. The reduction of the non-episcopal participants of the 'election' to a merely consenting and acclaiming role is, in view of the subsequent development, very noteworthy,[4] for here we have the first tangible step towards the later conception of the election as a mere designation of a candidate to a (vacant) office.[5]

The second decisive point emerging from the *Proclamation* is that because Charles was consecrated and enthroned, he was removed from any jurisdiction and subjected only to the judgment of those through whose service he had obtained his kingdom: it is they – the bishops – who were called the thrones of God in which God Himself resides and who were the instruments of pronouncing the divine will and

---

[1] See also below 107 f.

[2] For sources see BM 1435a–n. For the constitutional background concerning the West–Frankish region see the fundamental study by P. Classen, 'Die Verträge von Verdun und Coulaines 843 als polit. Grundlagen d. westfränk. Reiches' in *HZ* 196 (1963), 1 ff., esp. 20 ff.

[3] See *Cap.* 300, c. 3, p. 451.

[4] Shortly afterwards but probably independently Stephen V adhered to the same standpoint: *MGH. Epp.* VII. 352, no. 32: 'sacerdotum quippe est electio et fidelis populi consensus adhibendus, quia docendus non sequendus est populus'. Cf. also *PGP* 134, on Celestine I and Alcuin employing the same mode of argument.

[5] See below 104, 109.

G

judgment, and Charles went so far as to declare his readiness to subject himself to their (the bishops') 'paternal corrections' and 'castigatory judgments'.[1] These statements of Charles (Hincmar) leave nothing to be desired either in clarity or in intention: having received unction from the bishops, the king had but to translate ecclesiastical teaching into practice and, above all, became subjected to episcopal judgment only. The powers of the king were of divine origin, and the 'electors' had nothing to do with any conferment of these: this was the special prerogative of the ecclesiastics uniquely qualified as they were to transmit divine grace to the king. And it was this episcopally conveyed grace of God which gave proper shape and contours to the royal office as a ministry in the service of God. In a roundabout way Pauline doctrine could be said to have asserted itself: 'What I am, I am by the grace of God', but the actual organs of conferring this distinction on the king, were the bishops – and they at once presented their bill for their 'services'.

The other document of which Hincmar declared himself the author[2] was the formal protest of the synod of Quiercey of 858 against the attempted invasion by Louis the German and addressed to him personally. The sagacity, skill, elegance of diction and bitter irony of Hincmar make the document a first-class literary testimonial. Here we can only touch upon some points of direct relevance to us. The first part contains a small *Fürstenspiegel* in the guise of barely concealed recriminations against the invader. Here it is of some interest to note the role allocated to the ecclesiastics: they were to be treated by the king as his 'patres et Christi vicarii',[3] and the king (Louis the German) is reminded of the duties imposed upon him in the recent councils, notably those of Meaux and Paris (845); he is told that if he wishes to be a Christian king and an alumnus of the Church, he must oppose customs not in conformity with conciliar views. All this seems to be little more than a paraphrase of Isidorian views, with the consequence that the

---

[1] *Cap.* 300, c. 3, p. 451: '. . . a qua consecratione vel regni sublimitate subplantari vel proici a nullo debueram, saltem sine audientia et iudicio episcoporum, quorum ministerio in regem sum consecratus et qui throni Dei sunt dicti, in quibus Deus sedet . . . me subdere fui paratus et in praesenti sum subditus.' The same argument was also employed by Hincmar against the Roman Church: when arguing against his nephew Hincmar of Laon there is exactly the same line of reasoning: the younger Hincmar had declared that he was subjected only to the Roman Church, but Hincmar would have none of this: 'ipsis subditus es et ab his potes iudicari, a quibus potuisti ordinari', in *PL* 126. 378 D.

[2] *Cap.* 297, p. 428, lines 1 ff.

[3] Ibid., c. 7, p. 432, supported by the appropriate OT passages: Ecclus. 7. 31 and 4. 7.

theme of the secular Ruler's auxiliary function within the Church itself was given practical and tangible expression.

To this theme was now added the new doctrinal conception based upon the liturgical act of unction. Here Hincmar is perhaps still more explicit than he was in the *Proclamation*. To begin with, there is no more talk of an election, but merely of a consent of the people (to the episcopal decision concerning Charles's appointment); and all the greater is the emphasis upon the king as the Lord's anointed.[1] On behalf of the synodists Hincmar reminds the invader and his counsellors of the Old Testament kings, notably of Saul and David, prototypes of anointed kings. In other words, the bishops assembled at Quiercey under the presidency of Hincmar declared their adherence to Charles, not because he was elected by the people, not so much because he was the king by the grace of God, but because he was in receipt of the sacrament of unction which had been administered by them and which had changed his being and status. The pivot of the coronation proceedings ten years earlier was the unction. Let us be clear about the great advance of the ecclesiastical theme: the king is to be obeyed and honoured because of the episcopally administered unction which alone transmitted divine grace; vice versa, a king without receipt of unction cannot claim to possess divine grace – and Louis the German was not anointed. But anyone raising his hand against the anointed king however incompetent or inefficient he may in actual fact be, raises his hand against Christ Himself and will perish at least spiritually. To proclaim this principle aloud, Hincmar avows, was the duty inherent in his office.[2] In brief, the king as the Lord's anointed stood on a level fundamentally different from that of the Ruler in his natural state.

The importance of these strong Hincmarian words is only heightened by the views expressed on the relative position of bishops and lay people in public matters. For church property was property dedicated to God and must not be treated in any manner similar to that of fiefs or feudal goods. And 'we bishops consecrated as we are to God are not like ordinary men such as lay people who can enter into a relationship of a vassal or can take a (feudal) oath which is forbidden to us by evangelical, apostolic and canonical authority'.[3] Here indeed we may

---

[1] *Cap.* cit., c. 15, p. 439, lines 1 ff.

[2] Ibid., p. 439, lines 18 ff. As Smaragdus had already declared: because the king was reborn, the *via regia* was *sancta* (*Via regia*, pref., *PL* 102. 834 D, referring to Is. 35. 8).

[3] *Cap.* cit. lines 28 ff.

not only hear faint echoings of Pseudo-Isidore, but are also taken right into the central theatre of conflict: church property and its subjection to ordinary civil laws. But apart from this, since at this time the oath of fealty played a crucial role in the public field, it was a step of some considerable magnitude when Hincmar here declared that the hand which was anointed with holy chrism and which mixed sacramentally the body and blood of Christ, would be polluted by the taking of an oath.[1] After all, 'the word of a bishop was, by the grace of God, the gateway to heaven'.[2] It is hardly possible to exaggerate the significance and the tenor of passages of this kind. They certainly indicate the formidable advance which ecclesiastical views had made in regard to Rulership; and they also demonstrate with all desirable clarity the leading position which the bishops and ecclesiastics in general felt equipped to assume – in no lesser an undertaking than in bringing the Renaissance of society and its Ruler to fruition. For a number of reasons Hincmar's statement deserves full quotation:

> We do not fight for a terrestrial king, but on behalf of the celestial Ruler for our own well-being as well as for that of the terrestrial king and of the whole people entrusted to us.[3]

Nothing appears more revealing than that the whole people was committed to the bishops – 'totus populus nobis commissus'. The mighty advance of the ecclesiological point of view, the resultant episcopal-hierocratic form of government and the reduction of royal-monarchic power manifested themselves with a clarity which leaves nothing to be desired.

No comment is called for on the character of these actions and statements as precedents.[4] Barely ten years later Charles the Bald stood in the centre of things, once more, when the intellectually towering superiority of a Hincmar as the main ideological mentor proved itself abundantly again, both vis-à-vis the king himself, and the pope. And with the unction and coronation as well as the preliminaries to the act of Metz on 9 September 869 a very definite stage was reached in regard

---

[1] Cf. also the respective enactment in the Council of Tribur (895), c. 21 in *Cap.* 252, p. 224.

[2] *Cap.* 297, p. 439, lines 40 f.: 'Lingua episcopi (quae) facta est per Dei gratiam clavis coeli.'

[3] Ibid. p. 440, lines 29 f.

[4] Since the anointings (and coronations) of Lothar II as king of Lotharingia in 856 and the coronation of Judith, Charles's daughter (*Cap.* 296, see C. Brühl, art. cit. 289 f.) and of Irmintrud, the wife of Charles, in 866 (*Cap.* 301, see Brühl, 286), do not materially add to the ideological substance, I have not dealt with them.

to ecclesiastical ideology concerning Rulership and the indispensable role of the ecclesiastics in the process of transforming a 'natural' Ruler into the fully-fledged Lord's anointed – the very process of rebirth of the king as a Christian Ruler. Seen from another angle, the coronation at Metz signifies in practice the withering away of even the shadowy remnants of what one might perhaps euphemistically call royal election.

The issue itself was quite simple.[1] King Lothar II of Lotharingia died on 8 August 869 at Piacenza: his kingdom was orphaned, since he left no heirs other than the children of his 'concubine' Waldrada, and they were, by contemporary standards, not considered suitable to succeed. The kingdom became an easy prey to the ambitions of the neighbouring Charles the Bald and his spiritual adviser, the archbishop of Rheims who, perhaps more so than his royal protégé, saw in the acquisition of Lotharingia the culmination of his aspirations in regard to the province of Rheims. The speed with which events took place is indeed remarkable, and this speed would also indicate how ready and well-planned both the design and its execution were. The initiative lay entirely in the hands of Hincmar, ably assisted as he was by Hincmar of Laon and Adventius of Metz, Hatto of Verdun, Odo of Beauvaix and other high and geographically suitably placed ecclesiastics. Letters were dispatched with the order to meet the king, Charles the Bald, at Metz, where indeed he arrived on 5 September: the reason given for the haste was that swift action was imperative 'for the good of holy Church and the peace of the Christian people',[2] a strategy which from any objective standpoint indicates – like similar devices in modern times – that the swiftness of the intended action was to create a *fait accompli*, which it would be very difficult to undo.[3]

Only four days after the arrival of the king, Charles the Bald, and exactly a month after the death of King Lothar II whose kingdom was

---

[1] For factual details see R. Parisot, *Le royaume de Lorraine sous les Carolingiens 843–923* (Paris, 1899); L. Halphen, op. cit. 405 ff.; for Waldrada (called a concubine by contemporary standards) see E. Hlawitschka, *Lotharingien und das Reich an der Schwelle d. deutschen Geschichte* (Stuttgart, 1968), 17 f.; here also further literature.

[2] See Hincmar's letter in *PL* 126. 534 A; here also is the reminder to the younger Hincmar that he had been given the grace of God through the imposition of the uncle's hands: '. . . (gratia Dei) quae data est tibi per manuum mearum impositionem.' See also BM 1473f for sources, of which the *Ann. Fuld.* assess the situation correctly: 'Karolus . . . regnum Hlotarii invasit et secundum suum libitum disposuit . . .'

[3] This strategy worked particularly well against the pope (Adrian II) who on the very same day, 5 Sept. 869, when the stage was prepared at Metz, dispatched a number of letters to the bishops, magnates and Hincmar himself urging them to desist from invading Lorraine, which by hereditary right was to go to the Emperor Louis II: *MGH. Epp.* vi. 717 ff., nos. 17–20.

to be the subject of the swift transaction, the stage was reached which signified, on the one hand, the collapse (and it was nothing else) of any popular or even aristocratic role in the making of the king, and on the other hand, the entrenchment of the ecclesiological theme: doxological, liturgical, symbolic instruments were now ready to play their full and exclusive part in the creation of the Ruler. What happened at Metz on 9 September 869 was not merely the ecclesiastically sanctioned incorporation of a kingdom (the legality of which was gravely in doubt) or the constituting of a new king, that is, of Charles the Bald as king of Lorraine, but above all the symbolic and incontrovertible ending of a long tradition which had already been exposed to serious corrosion for the last twenty years. Metz marked the symbolic beginning of a new era in the ideology of Rulership which was to be overwhelmingly ecclesiastical in its making, theocratic in its substance, symbolic in its execution, an ideology which was to set the tone in regard to the creation of Rulers for the subsequent medieval period in Western Europe, and also beyond. The coronation at Metz in 869 was as much a caesura as the imperial coronation of Charlemagne in 800 or of his son in 816 had been, with this difference, however, that the *royal* coronations never lost their earthiness and strong link with reality, whilst in imperial coronations a streak of unreality and wishful thinking was always detectable. Naturally, the speed of the transaction proved not only how ready the programme was to be executed, but also how carefully this ideology had been nurtured and absorbed for the last two and a half decades, so much so that there was not the slightest ideological protest anywhere.

It is a fortunate contingency that we have the transaction recorded in two substantial documents, the one giving the speeches and the responses of some of 'the thrones of God' in the persons and shapes of Bishop Adventius of Metz and Archbishop Hincmar of Rheims as well as of the king; the other document records the actual prayer texts and benedictions spoken on the occasion of the coronation. It is regrettable that the latter document has no rubrics, but the kind of information which they usually purvey, can be gathered to a great extent from the speeches and responses.

Let us briefly review the proceedings which in structure and arrangement reveal throughout the master-hand of Hincmar of Rheims. Bishop Adventius of Metz opened the ceremonies on 9 September before the beginning of the mass at St Stephen's cathedral with an address which contained a number of points relevant to our enquiry. In the first place, he began by citing a great many biblical passages about kingship and invoked God's mercy so 'that He may give us a king and Ruler according to His own wishes, who should govern after His will'.[1] This invocation of God's mercy was the preliminary to the immediately following statement which studiously avoided all reference to any kind of election: Adventius declared that 'we (that is, the bishops) recognize God's will in our unanimous concord and see in the present King Charles the legitimate heir of this (Lotharingian) kingdom',[2] and it was to him that they committed themselves spontaneously. No doubt, the bold statement that Lorraine was Charles's inheritance when backed up with a reference to the will of God[3] should not be taken in the literal sense, but in the biblical-ecclesiastical one. How else was he to get round even a semblance of a formal election? This indeed seems to me the real significance of the bishops spontaneously entrusting themselves to Charles's government, because it was God's will that he should succeed to his 'inheritance'. In other words, the bishops had discovered and made known God's will.

This brings me to the second crucial point in the speech of Adventius. He announced that Charles the Bald was God's elect through unction: this was for Adventius *signum certissimum* that God had in fact chosen the king. And for such good deeds, the bishop goes on to say, borrowing from Gelasius I, one should not show oneself ungrateful.[4] The pronouncement by Adventius that the episcopally administered unction was 'the surest sign' that God's grace had been transmitted to the king, seems to me the core of his speech. The creation of this king as king of a country to which he had – despite episcopal assurances – no claim, had become an exclusively ecclesiastical matter: the lay princes present left no record in the extant proceedings.[5]

The second speech, called a response, by Charles the Bald himself, in no less skilful a manner evaded the delicate issue of election. He expressed his satisfaction, not at having been elected, but at the unanimous acclamation of the bishops by which they had announced to the world that for the sake of everyone's salvation he had been elected by

---

[1] *Cap.* 276, p. 338, lines 42 ff.

[2] *Cap.* 276, p. 339, lines 5 ff.

[3] Ibid. line 4.

[4] Ibid. lines 9 ff. For the Gelasian background see *PG* 22 f.

[5] In a very imaginative and ingenious way Schramm, *König*, cit. 27, plausibly suggests that the proceedings in the cathedral were modelled on the usual synodal procedure to which the ecclesiastics were accustomed. Elections formed part of this synodal procedure.

God to the government.[1] What is of particular concern in this very context is that Hincmar made the king repeat in slightly shortened form the affirmations[2] which he had made in regard to his own West-Frankish kingdom in July of the same year 869 at Pîtres but which had no connexions whatsoever with the Lotharingian matter. These affirmations were now extended to cover also the kingdom of Lotharingia, because they were embodied in the formal response which the king made at Metz. They were as yet no formal promises, but merely the expression of the king's volition[3] to govern well and with justice, and concerned in particular the protection of the ecclesiastical orders and dignities and the preservation of ecclesiastical and mundane laws: what Hincmar inserted here was the assertion that the kingdom of Lothar was given by God to Charles the Bald: 'regnum mihi a Deo datum'.[4] It was, as far as one can see, the first time that the king made some more or less solemn affirmation before unction was administered. This what has once rightly been called 'juristic-liturgical drama'[5] embodied features and elements of different orders and fused them into one continuous action – indubitably the achievement of the ecclesiastical master mind Hincmar, an achievement which was to constitute the medieval norm *par excellence*.

The lion's share of the proceedings belonged to this master mind. He as the 'organizer' of the day had reserved to himself the longest and most important speech which can conveniently be divided into two parts. In order to assess the importance of this address we should keep in mind that the archbishop of Rheims had not as yet emerged as a king maker liturgically. Hence some sort of explanation appeared advisable as to why now and without any ostensible reasons, the archbishop of Rheims was to function as the principal actor in a ceremony which, moreover, was not even performed in his own church, but in that of a neighbouring diocese. It is to this point that Hincmar refers in the first part when he puts forward a mock apology for his leading participation: nobody should think, he deferentially remarked, that he was presumptuous to interfere in the affairs of another province since Metz belonged after all to the province of Trier. Nevertheless, his

---

[1] *Cap.* cit. p. 339, lines 19 ff.: *Karoli Responsio ad populum:* '. . . vos acclamatis *me De electione* ad vestram salvationem et profectum atque regimen et gubernationem huc venisse, sciatis . . .'

[2] *Cap.* 275.

[3] The essential verb is *velle*: *Cap.* 276, p. 339, line 24.

[4] Ibid. p. 339, line 7.

[5] Schramm, *König*, cit. p. 28.

participation, he avowed, could be explained by the two provinces of Rheims and Trier having always acted as 'comprovincial' sisters and having always conceded to each other priority of status according to priority of ordination and consecration. It was mere coincidence that another slight advantage emerged in that Trier was at that moment vacant: he, Hincmar, had therefore been requested by the suffragans of Trier to act as their metropolitan.[1] But to make sure that his intervention was really approved by the suffragans, he asked them: 'Is that not so, brothers?' And the response was, as no doubt expected, in the affirmative: 'It is.'[2]

There was, however, an additional reason why Hincmar of all other metropolitans should become the chief actor in the making of the king. After the Trier suffragans had expressed their approval, he continued by referring to the statement of Bishop Adventius, according to whom 'you could see at work the will of God in this business'; 'after all this king had come to this place (Metz) having been guided by the Lord, and you yourself have flocked here by the Lord's inspiration and by whose instinct ("cuius instinctu") all living creatures had come together, without any compulsion, in this arc of Noah, thus signifying the unity of the Church'.[3] The climax of Hincmar's speech lay, however, in that the ancestors of the king (Charles) who so obviously was chosen by the Lord, had always been linked to the church of Rheims in a rather special way: his own father, the emperor Louis I, had been anointed and crowned as emperor at Rheims by the pope, and it was there at Rheims that Clovis was baptized and anointed with the holy oil of celestial origin. Here with all desirable clarity the ecclesiastical coronation was declared solely constitutive: Charlemagne's coronation of Louis I three years earlier was not even mentioned. This was a mighty step forward in the direction of the royal coronation becoming as constitutive as imperial coronations. And once more the difference with Byzantium where the ecclesiastical coronation was merely declaratory, emerges clearly. To all this should be added, Hincmar went on, the evidence of the Old Testament, according to which kings were crowned when they acquired additional kingdoms. Hence it appeared right and proper, Hincmar concluded, that 'this king should now through the sacerdotal ministry be anointed, crowned before this altar and consecrated to the service of the Lord. If this pleases you, make

---

[1] *Cap.* cit. pp. 339–40, esp. nos. 1 and 3 of Hincmar's speech.
[2] 'Est ita, domini fratres? et responderunt ipsi episcopi: Ita est.'
[3] *Cap.* cit. pp. 339–40.

your will known by appropriate shouts.' The answer was as expected: 'Let us thus act,' and they all unanimously intoned the *Te Deum*.[1]

Hincmar's speech marked not only the emergence of the archbishop of Rheims as France's (future) coronator, but also the first step towards the formalization of the Recognition,[2] as well as the first public announcement of the Clovis oil in connexion with royal anointing, that very oil which, according to Hincmar himself, had effected the rebirth of King Clovis as a *novus Constantinus*.[3] That Hincmar could, as in fact he did, rely for the Clovis oil on certain liturgical practices in the church of Rheims, has been proved,[4] but it was he who linked these practices with the conferment of divine grace upon a king through the medium of this self-same holy oil; and as Adventius had remarked in his opening address this anointing was to be the surest sign of God's grace shining upon the king. The significance of these proceedings – and we should take notice that they took place before mass had begun – may be summarized thus: firstly, the implicit dropping of any formal election or even a pretence to an election procedure, and the reduction of the non-episcopal participants to a mere assenting role: all they did was to acclaim the choice of God made known to them by the bishops. Secondly, since the unction was asserted as the surest sign of God's grace, the mediatory role of the higher ecclesiastics came into full play. It was these two points which from now on were to give every medieval creation of a king its particular complexion: the sacrality of the king as elected and 'graced' by God, now finally supplanted the Ruler's purely mundane creation, of which until then a good many ingredients had survived. Thirdly, and this applies to France only, it was the archbishop of Rheims who was to become the officiating, that is, mediating and crowning organ in the rites of king making; and though it was not until the third decade of the twelfth century that the holy Clovis oil was in actual fact used in the royal anointings, it is nevertheless worth while drawing attention to the initiating broadcast of the legend by Hincmar. In brief, the significance of all this is that the Clovis oil – originally used at Clovis' baptism – was henceforward to be used in royal coronations, and in each case, that of baptism and that of coronation, the essential idea was that of a

---

[1] *Cap.* cit. pp. 340–1.

[2] See below 108.

[3] See his *Vita Remigii*, c. 39 in *PL* 125. 1160.

[4] Cf. Schramm, *König*, cit. 146; and especially M. Wallace-Hadrill, *Long-haired kings*, cit. 102 ff., clarifying the origin of the 'holy oil'. F. Oppenheimer, *The Legend of the sainte Ampoule* (London, 1955), is of not much help here.

rebirth, a Renaissance of the king. That idea, I believe, explains why Hincmar disseminated the Clovis legend and harnessed it to the unction of a king at precisely the right moment – the coronation of Charles at Metz. But thereby also all doubt as to the meaning of a royal consecration was to be dispersed.

Some remarks on the actual doxology of what can now be called a proper coronation rite[1] are here in place. It should be noted that quite in contrast to episcopal consecrations the actual rite, including anointing, coronation and conferment of symbols, was still performed before mass had begun but within the cathedral and in front of the altar: it is a feature to which Hincmar obviously attached great importance, because despite the sacralization of kingship, and the clericalization of the royal office, the difference and the distance from the bishops were to be clearly demonstrated, but this could not be done better than by separating the highly liturgical, if not liturgicized, sacralization of the king and the mass itself. Although the benedictions said over the king by the seven bishops, again led by Adventius of Metz, were closely modelled on old sacramentaries, mainly the Gregorian one, they nevertheless contained the one or the other slight modification which is worth recording.[2] Thus in the very first benediction pronounced by Adventius in which he implored God to bestow upon the royal servant the spirit of wisdom, a heavy accent is laid on the exclusively divine origin of royal power:

> God, who providest for thy peoples by your mercy and rulest over them in love, grant this thine servant the spirit of wisdom, to whom thou hast given power to govern.[3]

By going beyond the model Hincmar, the likely redactor, managed to express the purpose of God's assistance which was none other than that the king should always remain suitable for the exercise of royal functions.[4] In other words, the principle of suitability was here incorporated in the liturgical formula: the day was not so far off when the full meaning of the king's suitability was to be brought home by those

---

[1] Its liturgical and ideological elements are analysed with great skill and acumen in the already mentioned dissertation by Dr J. L. Nelson. For additional material especially the sources on which Hincmar drew, see A. Sprenger, 'Die Gebete der Krönungsordines Hinkmars' in *ZKG* 63 (1951), 245 ff., esp. 248 ff.

[2] *Cap.* 302, pp. 456–8.

[3] This was clearly modelled on the Gregorian Sacramentary for the anniversary of the pope's election or consecration, see H. A. Wilson, *The Gregorian Sacramentary* (H.B.S. 49 (1915)), 119; also C. A. Bouman, *Sacring & Crowning* (Groningen, 1957), 103.

[4] '. . . ut tibi toto corde devotus et regni regimine maneat semper idoneus . . .'

who considered themselves qualified to pronounce upon it. In the benediction administered by Hincmar – which served as the introduction of the anointing itself – the prayer text may well be of older provenance, but makes its appearance here within the structure of coronation rites for the first time. The doxology culminates in imploring God to grant the king grace and mercy: that after all was the very essence of the unction, to the administration of which Hincmar at once proceeded.

The anointing has few features in need of special comment. As the record says, the king was anointed by the archbishop's applying the chrism from the right temple across the forehead to the left temple as well as on the vertex of the head. What is of special interest is that there was no anointing of the hands and that no biblical persons or allegories were here mentioned, as was apparently the custom in the East-Frankish realms later. All the anointing formula of Hincmar has is a general reference to the unction of priests, kings, prophets and martyrs; the prayer text explicitly links the governmental function of the king – the *regimen regni* – with the divine grace transmitted through the oil.[1] Nor does Hincmar omit to drive home once more that it was a divine decision to constitute Charles king over God's people. It is therefore all the more comprehensible why the king undertook to obey divine commands in the exercise of his governmental functions. The implication was clear enough: what these divine commands were could be made known only by those who had special qualification and knowledge, that is, those who had effected the change of the king's status, his rebirth. The essential significance of this anointing prayer was the emphasis on the invisible grace transmitted through the visible oil which was to make the recipient a participant in Christ's government of the heavenly kingdom. Whatever doubt there may still have lingered on concerning the origin of the king's power, was now set at rest through the unction and the accompanying text: it was purely and simply the episcopally revealed will of God that created the king.[2] What had gone before, was 'washed away' by the effects of divine grace: the king *qua* Ruler had become a 'new creature'. The unction was the central point of the ecclesiastical rites employed in the creation of the king. By virtue of the process of the Renaissance both society

---

[1] *Cap.* 302, p. 457.

[2] In a communication to Charles Hincmar tells him exactly this: 'episcopali unctione ac benedictione regiam dignitatem potius quam terrena potestate consecuti estis', *PL* 125. 1040 D, continuing with a clear implication of the king's subjection to those who had conferred unction on him.

and its Ruler were transposed on to a plane which was detached from their natural foundations. And it was the reborn status of the king alone which explains the otherwise hardly explicable coronation prayer text said by Hincmar on this very same occasion, namely that God should crown the king with the crown of glory and justice so that he might obtain the crown of the everlasting kingdom,[1] an allusion to the king's co-regency with Christ.[2]

The structure, doxology and liturgy of the coronation at Metz in 869 were to remain unchanged in subsequent ordines. If ever a man had been intent on erecting his own memorial, it was Hincmar. The coronation ordines were the most appropriate and persuasive vehicle by which the rebirth of the Ruler could be impressively and effectively demonstrated. They also showed how this Christian Ruler was now in practical terms and in his ruling capacity turned into an essential and outstanding member of the *populus Dei*. He was, and yet he was not, a layman. He was something of an amphibious creature, a creature which later doctrine was to call a *persona mixta* and which, as we shall presently see, was expressed by the intermediate position that was allocated to the king between the ordained and unordained members of the *populus Dei*, between clergy and laity, between *clerus* and *plebs*.[3] Hincmar's efforts, admittedly aided by very favourable circumstances which he knew how to exploit fully, culminated in the establishment of a Ruler who was seen to be the creation of the ecclesiastics. In other words, within two generations the process of regeneration or rebirth had engulfed both society and its Ruler: both had left behind the natural and human platform and had moved on to a level that was

[1] The 'crown of glory' is of OT provenance (Ecclus. 47. 7; Isai. 28. 5); the 'crown of justice' is Pauline: II Tim. 4. 8. This prayer text was still used in 1953. Summing up the development in the ninth century W. Schlesinger in *Karl d. Gr.*, cit. i. 841, rightly points out that the unction 'und nicht das Erbrecht oder die Wahl' had become the legal basis of royal power; in the same sense H. G. Richardson in *Traditio* 16 (1960), at 116: 'to the medieval mind a greater significance (than in the coronation oath) lay in the unction'. But cf. the cautious note sounded by M. Wallace-Hadrill in *Trends*, cit. 28 f. who however very aptly observes that 'the Carolingian Ruler was put directly in touch with the source of his power'.

[2] There is just a faint possibility that this idea of a co-regency was derived from the twelfth Toledan Council, see *PL* 84. 479–80, where the synodists in their prayer for the king (Erwig, who probably needed special prayers) implore God that 'post diuturna huius aevi curricula ad regnum aeternae vitae cum suis omnibus coronandus perveniat' (cf. Rev. 2. 10). The same term *perveniat* also in Hincmar's text: 'ad coronam pervenias perpetui regni.' The idea of the king's co-regency with Christ is now also touched upon by Schramm, *Kaiser*, cit. i. 79 ff., though he is unaware of the Visigothic source. Cf. also below 105 n. 4.

[3] See below 107.

devoid of all natural human features. Governmental ideology shaped by Frankish ecclesiastics had removed society and Ruler to the ecclesiological precincts.

Led by Hincmar the ecclesiastics had soon a further opportunity of developing the lines they had already mapped out: it was the death of Charles the Bald in 877, now also emperor of the Romans, which provided the occasion, and once more we can see how prepared the episcopacy was to take the initiative. Barely two months after Charles's death his son, Louis (II) the Stammerer, was consecrated and crowned at Compiègne by Hincmar. This coronation has an additional interest. By virtue of his being the son and therefore in direct succession, in other words by virtue of an indisputable hereditary right to succession, Louis would have had no need of any ecclesiastical approbation, still less of ecclesiastical intervention to make him king of West-Francia. Apart from this, whatever doubts there may have been eight years earlier about the reasons which made Hincmar assume a leading role, apparently no such doubts were raised at Compiègne on 8 December 877, which was another great day in Hincmar's career as a king maker.

By now it is possible to separate the constitutional or juristic from the liturgical matter. That these two can in fact be divided goes a long way to show the maturity of Hincmar's thought and his awareness of what a proper ecclesiastical ideology required. As to the constitutional part, it neatly contains two distinctive segments: the first is the declaration of Louis the Stammerer – in the transmitted text headed a *Professio*[1] – according to which he promises the ecclesiastical orders to keep the ecclesiastical 'rules', and he promises the people to observe the laws and statutes according to the common counsel of his faithful. In themselves these pledges were somewhat modelled on those which his father, Charles the Bald, had made in 869,[2] but they may well show some reassertion on the part of the magnates: not only was the reference to the common counsel of our faithful new, but also the intitulation of the king himself was novel: 'Ego Hludowicus misericordia domini Dei nostri et electione populi rex constitutus.' It may well be a little difficult to reconcile the two irreconcilables – 'King by the grace of God and through election by the people' – but the intitulation would seem to reflect the unresolved tension between the ecclesiastical

---

[1] *Cap.* 283 A, p. 364. Schramm, *Kaiser*, cit. ii. 148–9, shows that this was thoroughly ecclesiastical terminology.

[2] *Cap.* 276, p. 339; W. Schlesinger in *Festgabe Herzfeld*, cit. 243–4 would seem to go a little too far.

hierarchy and the lay magnates who wished to preserve some of their functions in the creation of a king. That there was no formal election in the two months intervening between the death of Charles and the act at Compiègne, is evident: there were merely a number of informal meetings between Louis' legates and some magnates, but it would seem to go too far to see in them proper and formal electoral meetings.[1] This unusual formula was, I think, an emergency solution and coined in an attempt to find and fix a base of royal power in addition to divine grace. For Louis had been designated by his father and to this designation the magnates had assented.[2] The assumption may justifiably be made that in order to ingratiate himself with his magnates Louis expanded his intitulation and declared their assent to the paternal designation as a formal election. It was in any case a very short-lived royal title. What was far more important was the explicit declaration on the part of the (future) king that he would observe the rules, laws and statutes, a promise which he himself signed.

The novelty which formed the second segment of the constitutional part and which Hincmar introduced into the pre-liturgical proceedings, was the so-called *Petitio episcoporum*, the demand of the bishops concerning the king's solemn promise to observe the 'canonical privilege' and the laws as far as they related to each and every bishop in his kingdom and to each and every church.[3] Louis most solemnly gave a promise to this effect.[4] In substance however the promises demanded and given did not materially differ from those which the father, Charles the Bald, had on various occasions given between 843 and as recently as June 877,[5] and which considered in themselves, had greatly assisted the ascendancy of the ecclesiastical hierarchy. But – and this is the crucial point – these promises which strictly speaking had originally been no more than mere concessions or affirmations on the part of the young Charles, were now utilized as a (preliminary) condition for his

---

[1] As W. Schlesinger, art. cit. 242–3, would appear to do. See Schramm, *König*, cit. 56, with reference to the royal title of Louis the Stammerer: 'Das ist umso auffallender als gar keine Wahlversammlung stattgefunden hatte.'

[2] Here I entirely agree with W. Schlesinger, 242 at n. 193; it is what Hincmar himself also declared: *PL* 125. 986.

[3] *Cap.* 283 B, p. 364.

[4] Ibid. C, p. 365. For the ideological roots of these promises reference should be made once for all to M. David, *Le serment du sacre du IXe siècle au XVe siècle* (Strasbourg, 1951), 24 ff., 39 ff., specifically 97 ff.

[5] See *Capp.* 254, p. 255, c. 1; 292, cc. 1, 3, 5–7, p. 388; 281, c. 1, p. 355; 282, c. 1, p. 362; see also Hincmar himself, *PL* 125. 1041–2. For the importance of Coulaines (*Cap.* 254), see P. Classen again, *HZ* cit. 20 ff.

receiving the sacrament of unction and herewith of kingship. In other words, what originally was an affirmation or concession, was now wrung from the (future) king as a solemn promise; and what was no more than hinted at eight years earlier at Metz, was now built as a preamble into the coronation rite itself. The point which deserves special attention is that of the time lag between the declaration (headed the *Professio*) on the one hand and the episcopal Petition with its promises on the other hand: the former was given on 30 November 877, whilst the latter were made on 8 December 877. In fact, a whole week lay between the declaration and the demand of the bishops for a solemn promise: this can hardly be coincidence. Just as the short-lived royal title of Louis was an apparent means to ingratiate himself with the magnates, in the same way the pre-coronation promises (the declaration of 30 November) were an attempt to ingratiate himself with the hierarchy, notably with Hincmar. Can we be surprised that the immediately succeeding coronation order constructed a decade or so afterwards, began, not with the declaration, but with the episcopal Petition and the royal promises?[1] In any case, the Petition and promises belonged, from December 877 onwards, to the basic structure of most subsequent royal coronation ordines.

Turning now to the liturgical part proper, we can be brief: after all, the main points of its structure had been fully worked out for the coronation at Metz eight years before. Only one or two remarks are necessary. The doxology at the actual anointing was greatly expanded on the lines already indicated in 869: this prayer was now incorporated into the much fuller text of 877 which gave the proper Old Testament passages and personages concerned with the anointing of kings. This text too remained the basic anointing text throughout the medieval period and, in shortened form. was used in 1953. Secondly, in 877 the prayer said on the occasion of putting on the crown had a very significant addition which was obviously intended to underline the mediatory role of the officiating bishops: the text of 869[2] was amplified by the words: 'per officium nostrae benedictionis', the meaning of which was clear enough. The king was, as in 869, to enjoy the co-regency with Christ, but now in 877, he achieved this distinction through the service (or office) of episcopal commendations.[3] The third observation concerns the text spoken when the sceptre was conferred. This was new, both in its wording and its substance. It too went into virtually every other medieval coronation ordo. The sceptre was here

---

[1] See below 102.   [2] See above 95.   [3] *Cap.* 304, p. 461.

seen as the royal symbol *par excellence*, that is, of just and good government and proper defence of 'holy church, that is, of the Christian people committed to your care'.[1] And the purpose of the king's using the sceptre was 'that from the temporal kingdom he may advance to the eternal kingdom with the help of Him whose kingdom is everlasting'. Here the idea of the king's eventual co-regency with Christ is particularly stressed, which can be comprehended only under the presupposition of the rebirth of the king *qua* king.

Louis the Stammerer's short reign – barely eighteen months – was punctuated by one more significant episode, which symbolized the ideological union between Rome and Rheims in the liturgical field and in fact completed, liturgically, what had begun intellectually and doctrinally less than three decades before in the Pseudo-Isidorian productions. Moreover, there was a remarkable resemblance between the journey of Stephen II to Pippin the Short in 753–4, and this journey of John VIII (the pope who brought the papal theme in regard to emperorship to completion)[2] to Louis the Stammerer in 878; and there were to be in future several other episodes for which this papal journey may well have provided a model. In any case, the papal visit in 878 was prompted once again by the precarious situation in which the pope found himself in Rome and in Italy, and once more the king was bidden to come to the rescue in terms not at all dissimilar to those of 125 years earlier: Louis should come to Rome 'for the sake of defence, liberation and exaltation of the Roman Church'.[3] This was the motive for the pope's journey. But it may have been that Louis requested the pope to perform a royal coronation, although he had only the year before been anointed and crowned by Hincmar with all due pomp and ceremony. There is no evidence that if Louis did express this wish John VIII fulfilled it.[4] What there certainly was, was a papal benediction of the king:[5] the terms used by the pope leave no room for doubt that his intention was to confirm papally, that is, on behalf of

[1] Ibid.: 'Accipe sceptrum . . . qua teipsum bene regas, sanctam ecclesiam, populum videlicet christianum tibi a Deo commissum . . .'
[2] See *PG* 161 ff., 219 ff. The pope had made Charles the Bald 'another David' by virtue of his having been 'pre-elected' and 'elected by God', see his *Ep.* 22 in *MGH. Epp.* vii. 20, l. 34.
[3] *PL* 126. 961; also in Baronius, *Ann. eccles.*, ed. A. Theiner (Bar-le-Duc, 1868), 15. 294.
[4] Cf. C. A. Bouman, op. cit. 25 n. 2, pointing to the theological reasons militating against a second unction. For an explanation of the repeated anointings in the eighth century see C. Brühl, art. cit. 306.
[5] For the text see the ed. in Schramm, *Kaiser*, cit. ii. 210, no. 5; for comments, ibid., pp. 145 f. Baronius, loc. cit. 293, does not mention a second coronation or unction.

H

St Peter, the ideology enshrined in the liturgy of the coronation rite. In other words the opportunity was taken – Hincmar's hand appeared once more – to have the novelties introduced since 848 sanctioned by the highest ecclesiastical authority. The doxology of the benediction for the king would seem to have great significance, because it contained a train of thought not in evidence before, but one that was shortly afterwards to be raised to major importance.[1] Here the theme was only barely perceptible: it is still quite crudely expressed, no doubt due to the urgency which dictated its composition. What the pope wished to convey in this text was the desirability of a harmony between the king's external governmental power and his internal religious attitude and being. Here at Troyes in 878 this was only just audible, but a few years later an alert and most perceptive composer was to polish the text and perfect the theme in its full symphonic sonority.

As far as the ideological and liturgical framework went, the proceedings of 869 and 877 were to constitute the backbone of the future royal coronation rites.[2] The reason why I have given them some prominence is not because of their liturgical contents, but because of their ideological substance. What synodists tried to express in abstract words, or in legal terms, the coronation rite tried to convey in its rubrics, gestures, prayers and symbols, that is, by liturgical means. Words could have different significations, but liturgical vehicles should (and on the whole did) have only one unambiguous meaning: the intellectual effort which went into the making of the coronation rites must command the deepest respect. Far be it from me to belittle the achievements of writers, littérateurs, public speakers, or draftsmen of synodal or royal decrees, but these efforts cannot bear comparison with those which showed themselves in the rites, for these had not only to be crystal clear and unambiguous, but also and above all readily comprehensible to even the most dull-witted contemporary accustomed to thinking in only the crudest terms. But these observations do not exhaust the significance of these orders: concise, precise, succinct and economical as they were, they nevertheless left plenty of margin for expansion, precisely because they pursued one clearly defined theme that could be expressed in a variety of ways. Because they were thematic and programmatic, both theme and programme could be,

---

[1] See below 105.

[2] For the subsequent coronations beginning with (the first Capetian) Odo (888), see Schramm, *Kaiser*, ii. 151 ff.; texts 211 ff., and id. *König*, cit. 70 ff.

as indeed they were, developed by the elaboration and expansion of rubrics, prayer texts and symbols. And here a further consideration seems in place. There is no action, still less any evidence that Hincmar or any of the other leading ecclesiastics imposed, so to speak, a doctrine upon their contemporaries in the coronation ordines. What they did was to give explicit expression to an ideology that was already explicitly or at any rate implicitly accepted. True enough, this ideology was overwhelmingly the effect of ecclesiastical influence, but it was an influence that was exercised without specific regard to the initiation, inauguration and liturgical symbols, as manifested in the rites. The latter were a consequential, but not inevitable, development. In a most literal sense can one say here that ecclesiastics and kings were *ambulantes pari passu*, acting as a team, and as such had to observe the boundaries of what was immediately realizable.

III

Although the coronation orders had been tested in concrete situations and not found wanting, their framework was still little more than a skeleton; and in view of the rapidity of the development and the harsh reality nothing else could reasonably be expected. One might go further and say that the West-Frankish ecclesiastics had ventured as far as it was possible in the practical exploitation of the actual situation as it offered itself. But these restrictions and limitations did not apply to the privately working liturgists, to the *Privatgelehrten*, who were alert and intelligent enough to realize the potentialities offered by the coronation orders. And it is to two works of such anonymous redactors that I must now turn if the practical attainments of the Frankish ecclesiastics are to be put into a proper historical perspective. As private liturgists they had none of the inhibitions which might have impeded the efforts of, say, a Hincmar who had to come to terms with concrete situations. It was these anonymous composers who perfected the framework in precisely the direction which its originators had intended, and had they lived to see it, would have applauded. It was their work developing as it did the already applied orders, which came to constitute the norm of virtually all relevant medieval coronation proceedings, including the Anglo-Saxon, the Burgundian, German and Lombard orders. Here it is only necessary to point to the one or the other salient feature as far as it directly affects the theocratic theme of Rulership.

The one which most likely originated in or around Sens by the end of the ninth century, is designated as the West-Frankish Ordo in more recent literature,[1] and can be briefly dealt with. Obviously having the orders of 869 and 877 before him, the composer, somewhat timid in his close following of his models, nevertheless added and expanded and also expunged. The first feature that strikes the observer is that there is no longer any royal declaration as there was in 877,[2] and the whole proceedings have now become much more streamlined and professional. They began with the Petition of the bishops and the corresponding Response of the king relative to his conserving and preserving the canonical privilege and the law in regard to each and every bishop and his church.[3] The second feature of considerable ideological significance marks a definite advance towards the so-called Recognition which will engage us shortly. Here in the West-Frankish Ordo the rubric telescoped, so to speak, the lengthy addresses of the bishops in 869 into a mere question asked by two bishops, enquiring the will of the people.[4] It is clear that this was little more than a pure formality. And just as the model had no election in any juristic sense, so there was none in this ordo, and the anonymous composer ended his new rubric – itself a mighty step towards the full Recognition – in the same words as the earlier text. The anointing formulae were identical with those used at the coronation of 877. The private ordo, however, makes provision for a far greater number of symbols to be conferred than there was in any antecedent ordo. This redactor took great pains in trying to bring out the teleological element in the prayer texts which accompanied the conferment of these symbols. This is especially noteworthy in the sword formula which brings the Pauline and Petrine points of view[5] into clear relief: the text culminates with the view that the sword was conferred on the prince with God's blessings for the purpose of warding off his own enemies as well as all adversaries of the Church: as a symbol of the king as a tutor the sword was to serve for the protection of the kingdom which God had committed to the Ruler.[6]

---

[1] Ed. by P. E. Schramm in *Kaiser*, cit. ii. 217 ff.; see also id. *König*, 58 ff. Here again the hitherto unpublished dissertation by Dr J. L. Nelson should be consulted. But cf. also C. A. Bouman, op. cit. 155–7.

[2] See above 96.　　　　　　　[3] Ed. cit., §§ 1, 2.

[4] See above 88 ff. and also below 108 f. Cf. also M. David, op. cit. 105 at n. 27.

[5] Rom. 13. 3–4 and I Pet. 2. 14.

[6] Ed. cit., § 8, p. 218: 'Accipe hunc gladium cum Dei benedictione tibi collatum . . . regnumque tibi commissum *tutari* atque protegere castra Dei.' For the official German ordo see below 108.

The second private elaboration originated in the late ninth or in the very early years of the tenth century, and possibly in the province of Rheims. This product greatly expanded the West-Frankish tradition: the personality of the redactor is shrouded in mystery, but whoever he may have been, one thing is certain: he was a first-class liturgist as well as an exponent of governmental ideas in liturgical and doxological terms. There can be little doubt that this private work had one man as its author and that it was composed as one coherent and consistent piece: there is one idea running through this ordo, and that is to make the theocratic idea of kingship as crystal clear and unambiguous as liturgically possible. It is an ordo of central importance,[1] which modern research has given the name of 'Ordo of Seven Forms'. The influence of this ordo was incomparably greater than the just-mentioned West-Frankish one, upon which, indeed, this one greatly relied. It is marked by a maturity and a depth of ideological and liturgical penetration the like of which cannot be found anywhere in contemporary Europe: here indeed a master mind and master hand was at work completing what the great Hincmar had begun. That this ordo was so influential, is understandable.

Our author has taken the skeleton of the anointing texts from the ordo of 877 and the West-Frankish rite,[2] but he also makes a very significant addition. It may be recalled that Hincmar tried to reduce the participation of non-ecclesiastics and, correspondingly, to increase the role of the episcopal element in the creation of a Ruler; this idea is taken a step further in the West-Frankish ordo. Here in this second private work we find what Hincmar clearly had intended, but could not and did not put into an explicit liturgical formula, that is, that the election of the Ruler belonged to the officiating bishops, to those alone who functioned in a crucial and indispensable manner at the one and only ceremony which inaugurated the rebirth of the Ruler in a Christian society. In the consecratory prayer initiating the unction we read how God is beseeched to pour out the divine blessings upon this servant, the prince,

> whom in lowly devotion we do elect as king
> (quem supplici devotione in regem eligimus).

---

[1] Rediscovered and analysed by C. Erdmann, *Forschungen zur polit. Ideenwelt des Frühmittelalters* (Berlin, 1952), 87 ff., from which all my quotations in the texts are taken; cf. also Bouman, 21–2 and Schramm, *Herrschaftszeichen & Staatssymbolik* (Stuttgart, 1954), ii. 617 f. and id., *Kaiser*, ii. 166 f.

[2] See Bouman, op. cit., 114–15.

The doctrinally and juristically significant election of the king had become a matter exclusively belonging to the bishops. What had gone before, whatever 'electoral' proceedings may have preceded the coronation rite proper, was eliminated as juristically irrelevant and reduced to no more than a mere designation of the prince as a suitable king: as Hincmar in plainest possible language declared, the formal and proper election was conducted by the bishops within the ecclesiastical setting of the coronation rite[1] which culminated in the sacring of the king himself. This election by the officiating bishops is easily accessible to understanding: since it was through their services and their mediation of divine grace that the Ruler *qua* Ruler was reborn, it stood to reason that they must choose the man prior to administering the instrument of rebirth (unction). The formal election was therefore built into the sacramental-liturgical act of the coronation rite and became an essential part of it. And in order to underline the electoral right of the bishops the text employed the present tense.[2] The 'election' by the magnates preceding the coronation, had within the ambit of theocratic kingship no meaning other than designation.[3] That this text was copied in virtually all Western coronation orders with only minor modifications, is due to its linguistic, doxological and intellectual superiority: it brought out with great force and yet very subtly the reborn status and sacrality of the king and the indispensable and vital role of the bishops as the effective electors of the Ruler.[4]

No doubt vital in itself and revealing the distance which ecclesi-

---

[1] This indeed is the sense of the passage in Hincmar's letter to King Louis III in *PL* 126. 119 D: 'Non vos me elegistis in praelatione ecclesiae, sed *ego* cum collegis meis et ceteris Dei et progenitorum vestrorum fidelibus *vos elegi ad regimen regni*, sub conditione debitas leges servandi.' This is in part an adaptation of John 15. 16. Cf. also below 108 n. 3; see also Erdmann, *Forschungen*, 61.

[2] This was kept in all the subsequent royal coronation orders which adopted the formula. For some further remarks cf. W. Ullmann in *Festschrift f. P. E. Schramm* (Wiesbaden, 1964), I. 73 ff.

[3] About this cf. *PGP* 145 f. and especially H. Mitteis, cit. ibid. Hence also the fully developed coronation orders speak of the *princeps designatus* before the unction, see below 109. For the continued efficacy of the pure electoral principle in Burgundy in the ninth century, see the very informative study by L. Boehm, 'Rechtsformen . . . burgundische Königserhebungen' in *HJb* 80 (1961), 1 ff., esp. 18 ff., 33 ff.; now supplemented by Schramm, *Kaiser*, ii. 249 ff., at 257 ff. In parenthesis we should note that just as the ecclesiastical hierarchy was anxious to see the pre-coronation election reduced in significance, in the same way royalty itself was anxious to do away with elections through the continuous attempts at establishing hereditary monarchy.

[4] The English *Lib. Regalis* of the fourteenth century changed 'eligimus' into 'consecramus' and with this modification the text has been employed right down to the last coronation in 1953.

astical thought had traversed in the preceding half century, the novelty in the consecratory prayer is by no means an isolated one. Whilst the prayer accompanying the actual anointing refers in a – by now – customary manner to the king's co-regency with Christ and contains nothing new, the crown formula deserves some comment. The crown formula of the Order of Seven Forms substitutes a new and longer version for that hitherto employed. Here the full incorporation of the king into the ecclesiastical ordo is made the central point: the king is declared to be sharing in the bishops' ministry in so far as they are to be the pastors of internal matters and directors of souls, whilst the king is to appear in external matters as an ever ready husbandman of God fighting against all His enemies.[1] This very compressed text does not contain any Frankish revival of the alleged Constantinean statement that he was the *episkopos tōn ektos*, but represents a more satisfactory expression of the idea of the king's rebirth in his function as a Christian Ruler. Juristically considered, this text is nothing less than a refurbishing of Isidore of Seville's view of the function of royal power: what the word of the priests cannot achieve, the sword of the kings should.[2] Precisely because the king participated in the episcopal ministry, his functions in the external field correspond to the bishops' functions in the internal sphere: the functions of the one are complemented by those of the other. Episcopal and royal function are in so far complementary as each pursues the same end by different means and on different planes: and both have by now become the indispensable and integral organs of the ecclesiological entity, the Church itself.[3]

But the significance of the crown formula of the Ordo of Seven Forms is thereby not exhausted. In it the bishops remind the king that he had received the kingdom as a gift from God which was mediated by them, standing as they did in the place of the apostles. They further remind the king that he is set up by them as a defender of the kingdom entrusted to him who now bears the name and stamp of Christ Himself.[4]

---

[1] This military view was all the more easily adopted as the idea of the earthly *militia* and the *miles* was in any case current coinage, about which see E. Lesne, *Hist de la propriété ecclésiastique*, i (1922), 270 ff., ii (1926), 457 ff.

[2] For this cf. *PG* 29 n. 9.

[3] It was this theme, I believe, to which the prayer text of Pope John VIII strongly alluded at Troyes, above 100.

[4] 'Accipe coronam regni, quae licet ab indignis . . . capiti tuo imponitur . . . intelligas per hanc te participem ministerii nostri non ignores, ita ut, sicut nos in interioribus pastores rectoresque animarum intelligimur, tu quoque in exterioribus verus Dei cultor strenuusque contra omnes . . . coronatus cum redemptore ac salvatore Iesu Christo,

The Ruler has, in metaphorical language, lost his former naturalness and membership of a family, or tribe, or people, and has become a new creature in the role allocated to him by divinity: he becomes not only a participant in the episcopal ministry, but also as the Lord's anointed himself shows the mark of Christ – in a word his prime duty is that of acting as an *athleta* in the service of Christianity. But because of his rebirth he bears the name and office of the Saviour – 'cuius nomen vicemque gestare crederis' – and the crown which the bishops, 'however unworthy they are', put on the king's head, also bears a special significance: it is a crown of sanctity and glory.[1] The idea of the Ruler's rebirth could hardly have been better demonstrated than in this crowning formula.

These observations lead me to the sword formula which, we now know, had a very short history in the royal ordines, not going back further than the West-Frankish Ordo of the late ninth century. Both diction and substance of the sword formula in the Seven Forms was again on a higher level than in its immediate model. The purpose of conferring the sword by the bishops was here brought out in clearest possible terms. Once more the bishops emphasized their own mediatory role in handing over the sword, and at the same time they stressed that they acted on behalf and on the authority of the apostles. The sword was given to the king so that he could defend the Church, and this idea of defence was here conceived in the widest possible terms, including the destruction of the enemies of the Christian name and cause. If the king acted in the sense intended, he merited the co-regency of Christ whose stamp he bears in name: *cuius typum geris in nomine.* There does not seem any need to offer any further comments on this text. The frequently encountered view that the coronation texts of the early period adopt the idea of *mimesis*, does not seem to have much in its favour. The 'typology' here employed was little more than a paraphrastic circumlocution of the effects of the unction which resulted in

cuius nomen vicemque gestare crederis . . .' The whole cluster of ideas surrounding the co-regency of the king with Christ and his participation in the episcopal ministry, is very much in need of a close analysis. There is in the *Cod. Car.* no. 43, p. 557, lines 16–17, a statement by Paul I to Pippin which clearly contained similar ingredients, with the difference that Pippin was here made with King David a participant in the government of the heavenly kingdom. See also above 95 n. 2; this too was overlooked by Schramm, loc. cit. 95 n. 2.

[1] H. Beumann in *Das Königtum*, cit. 209, refers to Wipo's statement concerning Henry III's coronation in 1028: 'accepit *sanctam* regni *coronam*'. Beumann rightly remarks here that this crown symbolized the 'theokratischen Amtsauftrag'. Cf. also above 95 n. 1.

the rebirth of the king as a Christian Ruler who became the Lord's anointed and therefore bore His likeness and stamp: he had through his rebirth become the *typus Christi*.[1] What, however, deserves mentioning is that the sword formula of this ordo, adopted by virtually all other coronation rites, contained the element that facilitated the (later) emergence of the kingly function as a tutor.[2]

One of the most sonorous and memorable texts in all medieval royal ordines was the enthronement formula *Sta et retine*. This too made its first appearance in the Seven Forms ordo and may well be regarded as the piece which in a hitherto unsurpassed manner was to round off the whole series of texts. The bishops reiterated their own mediatory role by stressing that it was by the authority of almighty God that they now formally handed over the throne on which the king was to sit: *per presentem traditionem nostram*. Here the text in concise and unambiguous language linked the theocratic character of Rulership with the function of the king as the mediator between clergy and people: for the mediator between God and man, that is, Christ, was implored to confirm the king as His own mediator between clergy and people so that he might for ever be a co-regent of Christ.[3] The king had the unique distinction of standing midway between the ordained and unordained members of the Church: indeed he was a *persona mixta*, partly ecclesiastical, partly lay. By virtue of his unique position he was viewed as the mouthpiece of the bishops who through their offices had been instrumental in handing over the symbol of true sovereignty, the throne.[4] The assertion of the king's mediatory function brought to a final conclusion the whole complex structure of the king's rebirth, for the dual nature of Christ as both God and Man is here transferred to the king in his dual role as both an ecclesiastical and lay person: it

---

[1] Cf. Isidore, *Allegoriae quaedam scripturae*, c. 59, in *PL* 83. 109: 'Moyses typum Christi gestavit, qui populum Dei a iugo diabolicae servitutis eripuit . . .' See already St Augustine, *De civ. Dei*, 17. 10: 'unus verus Christus, cuius illi (i.e. the anointed kings of the OT) figuram prophetica unctione gestabant'. For the concept of *typus Christi* see W. Dürig, 'Der theol. Ausgangspunkt vom Herrscher als vicarius Dei' in *HJb* 77 (1958), 174 ff., esp. 176 ff. with numerous extracts from Carolingian writers who 'bringen mit der vicarius Dei Lehre nichts Neues'; the concept of *typus* goes back to the Ambrosiaster and eventually to the Bible, ibid. 179 ff., 182. Cf. also Odilbert's reply to Charlemagne, *Cap.* 126, p. 247, line 40: David as 'typus nostri redemptoris'.

[2] See below 123, 177 ff.

[3] 'Mediator Dei et hominum te mediatorem cleri et plebis in hoc regni solio confirmet et in regnum eternum secum regnare faciat.'

[4] For the symbolic meaning of the throne, cf. my remarks in *Individual and Society*, cit. 28 ff.; further H. Beumann, art. cit. 205 ff. and above all Schramm, *Herrschaftszeichen*, cit. I. 317 ff.

was this duality which distinguished him from all other mortals, raising him above his subjects, sitting high up on his elevated throne, 'so that he himself could see, and could be seen by, everyone' as the enthronement of Otto I in 936 was described.[1]

I have still to refer to one more Carolingian *Baustein* in the impressive coronation ritual. This one comes, not from the West-Frankish, but the East-Frankish kingdom, was contemporaneous with the one just discussed, and likewise a private work: it, too, however, was to become official by its incorporation in the so-called Roman German pontifical of the tenth century. This private ordo has been called the early German ordo of *ca.* 900,[2] and there is one item in it which especially calls for comment. In this early German ordo there is a most significant and important rubric: after asking 'the designated prince' – he became king only after receiving the unction – whether he was willing to defend the churches and the people committed to him (in so far there is no great difference between West-Frankish and East-Frankish rites) the coronator turns to the people to ask them whether they are willing to subject themselves to this prince and to obey his laws in accordance with the apostolic precept that everyone should be subject to the higher powers.[3] It is then that the people shout 'Fiat, fiat.'

This was the origin of what later became technically known as the Recognition in the coronation service which was the last pale remnant of the ancient right of the people to elect their own Ruler. And we note that the element of Recognition in its fully formalized shape made its début in the early German ordo, that is, in the East-Frankish realms which had been subjected to ecclesiastical influence far less than the West-Frankish domains. This Recognition was later built into most European coronation orders.[4] It could be, as indeed it was, combined with the 'election' by the bishops of the king,[5] and the very appellation

---

[1] Cited from H. Beumann, art. cit. 206 (Widukind of Corvey).

[2] By C. Erdmann who did so much to clarify these difficult matters, see his *Forschungen*, cit. 54 ff.; see also Bouman, op. cit. 27 ff. and now also Schramm, *Kaiser*, ii. 166 ff.

[3] Ed. C. Erdmann, op. cit. 84, no. 7: '. . . episcopus affatur populum, si tali principi ac rectori se subicere ipsiusque regnum firma fide stabilire atque iussionibus illius obtemperare velint iuxta apostolum: omnis anima . . .' Erdmann, 65, pointed out the similarities between this and the episcopal procedure: the words *eligere* and *electio* are altogether avoided, ibid. and 61.

[4] To begin with, in the *Pontificale Romano–Germanicum*, ed. C. Vogel and R. Elze (in *Studi e Testi*, 226–7 (1963)), lxxii. 7–9, pp. 248–50. For the place and date of this pontifical see introduction, pp. xvi f.

[5] See above 92.

of the future king as 'designatus princeps' in this early German ordo gained therefore all the greater significance. The election of the Ruler before the coronation service was nothing more than a mere designation: the juristically relevant election was carried out by the bishops within the coronation proceedings. It is no doubt of some interest to note in this context that the French were never enthusiastic about this populist-ascending element, however diluted it was in any case, and they were the first to excise it in the second half of the thirteenth century: no populist element was henceforth to mar the coronation of the theocratic king of France, *le roi très chrétien*.[1]

This brief sketch of the development of coronation rites will have conveyed what great ideological and liturgical advance was made within about half a century, an advance which was remarkable on any account, both in depth and penetration, beginning with the coronation of Charles the Bald at Orléans and ending with the private works of the Ordo of Seven Forms and the contemporary East-Frankish ordo: official, unofficial and private liturgical contributions combined and resulted in the coronation rites from the tenth century onwards. What followed, no longer touched fundamental or essential issues, amongst which the idea of the Ruler's rebirth seems to me predominant and to manifest itself in numerous variants throughout the doxology employed – whether as a co-regent of Christ, or as the Christ-like Ruler, or as a vice-gerent of Christ, or as the mediator between clergy and people, or as the eternal Ruler, and so on: all attributes of the rebirth of him who had been consecrated through the act of unction.

But I cannot end this lecture without once more referring to the man who figured so prominently in it as the chief architect of the coronation proceedings who, precisely because he had this profound grasp of the meaning and significance of the rites he devised, also made a vital contribution in the public constitutional sphere relating to the scope of the Ruler's sovereignty.[2] Hitherto unrecognized by modern scholarship, it was the sacrament of unction which performed an invaluable service in the process by which any kind of medieval royal absolutism was from now on effectively prevented. And it was the chief architect himself, Hincmar, who indicated how unction could serve the purpose of controlling secular Rulers. It was by an ingenious utilization of the

---

[1] For this cf. *PGP* 202–3, with further literature; on the Recognition itself, ibid. 145 ff.

[2] For an assessment of Hincmar as a builder of a kingdom outside the Carolingian unit, see Hlawitschka, op. cit. 237 ff.

ancient Gelasian doctrine that he managed to bring unction to bear upon the problem of a constitutional supervision of the Ruler.

You may recall that Gelasius had declared that sacerdotal authority had greater weight – 'gravius pondus' – than royal power because it had to render an account for the doings of kings on the day of judgment, that is, how the (Christian) Rulers had discharged the divine trust.[1] Now on what precise grounds Gelasius should have claimed this supervisory power of sacerdotal authority over Rulers, has never been quite clear, for in Gelasius' time there was no ecclesiastical intervention whatsoever in the creation of kings or the emperor in Constantinople – and to him this letter was addressed – and this wide gap, perhaps left open intentionally by Gelasius, Hincmar attempted to close with the help of his own theme of royal unction. And indeed this was a concrete, visible, easily comprehensible and indisputably ecclesiastical act, admitted on all sides to be the constitutive factor in the creation of a Christian king. The Gelasian theme was now rendered intelligible and became operational: nobody could now dispute that the divine grace of Rulership was transmitted by the ecclesiastics who thereby constituted the Ruler. But Hincmar went even further than this. In unambiguous and categorical terms in this very context he amplified the Gelasian 'gravius pondus' of the ecclesiastical authority into a 'maior dignitas' which was only another expression for superiority, 'since kings are consecrated as Rulers by the bishops but bishops cannot be consecrated by kings'.[2] What Hincmar wished to convey here clearly was that the essence of sovereignty belonged in a Christian society, not to the king, but to the ecclesiastical body. By virtue of having received the unction the king was shown to be dependent on those who conferred upon him divine grace, the very base of his Rulership. Indeed the king had no more than a stunted sovereignty,[3] the very bar to absolutism. With a few genial strokes Hincmar indicated the way towards the constitutionally very important concept of stunted sovereignty, of which I hope to give an outline in my next lecture.

---

[1] Gelasius I in his *Ep.* 12, c. 2; cit. in full in *PG* 22 n. 1.

[2] *PL* 125. 1009 A. See further Hincmar, *De ord. pal.*, c. 5 in *MGH. Capit.* ii. 519.

[3] We should note that the last synod Hincmar was able to attend and to chair, that of Fîmes in April 881, issued a decree on this very point – *PL* 125. 1071 – with interesting side-lights and OT illustrations, for instance, King Ozias.

LECTURE V

The King's Stunted Sovereignty

I

It will have become sufficiently clear by now that, at any rate in the West-Frankish portion of the Carolingian inheritance, king and hierarchy pursued similar aims; they met each other, so to speak, half-way – in some respects an almost ideal method of making progress. But this process of reaching accommodation between royalty and episcopacy was greatly accelerated by the concomitant emergence of the power of the nobility: the aristocrats, themselves claiming to have a special blood charisma and not owing their position to either king or bishop, had begun by the mid-ninth century to exercise an influence in public matters which was in scope larger than that which could be observed on any comparable scale before.[1] And this influence was largely based on their wealth. The nobility can be counted as a third force coming into the sphere of public life with rapidly increasing vigour. They were powerful, assertive and aggressive.

This articulated emergence of a third force in the shape of the Frankish nobility is of direct concern to my topic. For their target was both the king and the ecclesiastical hierarchy who saw their own interests challenged and threatened. It was the 'wachsende Verselbständigung' of the nobility[2] which led to a sharpening tension between aristocracy on the one hand and the high ecclesiastics (many of whom indeed came from the aristocratic stratum) and the king on the other

[1] W. Schlesinger in *Karl d. Gr.*, cit. i. 839, gives an excellent picture of the development; he speaks of an 'Adelsherrschaft' which resembled more an 'Adelsanarchie' (833). For a detailed social history and the influence of the higher West-Frankish aristocracy from the second half of the ninth century, see K. F. Werner, 'Untersuchungen z. Frühzeit d. franz. Fürstentums' in *Welt als Geschichte*, 18 (1958), 256 ff., 19 (1959), 146 ff., also 20 (1960), 87 ff. Cf. also W. Hessler in *AD* 7 (1961), 1 ff. for the first half of the ninth century and the East-Frankish realms.

[2] Of the numerous works of G. Tellenbach cf. his contributions to *Herrschaft & Staat m M.A.* (Darmstadt, 1960), at 200; id., in *Entstehung d. deutschen Reichs* (Darmstadt, 1956), 120 ff., with further literature; also id., in *Primo Congresso internaz. della soc. italiana di storia del diritto* (Florence, 1966), i. 353 ff., with plentiful references to recent literature. Detached observers at the very beginning of the tenth century, such as Regino of Prüm, were perfectly aware of the growth of aristocratic power, cf. H. Löwe in *Geschichtsdenken & Geschichtsbild im M.A.*, ed. W. Lammers (Darmstadt, 1965), 91 ff., at 109 ff.

hand.[1] The tension was aggravated by the wholly different outlook of the two camps and by their different aspirations. The bases from which these differences stemmed, had little in common. The aristocracy was exclusively tied to the soil, was therefore basically agrarian and military, whereas the hierarchy was, at least as a rule, unmilitary, highly intellectual and educated claiming not a charisma of blood but a charisma of allegedly divine provenance. Whilst the one was securely rooted in the native this-worldly Frankish soil, the other believed itself to be the transmitting representative of the omnipotent and omniscient divinity residing in the inaccessible regions of the heavens. And it was precisely this inaccessibility of divinity which had raised the ecclesiastics to the level of purveyors of the divine will – and herewith to the level of organs who in actual, visible and concrete manner conferred divinity's own grace upon the king. The interests, aims, aspirations and views on society, as understood by the hierarchy and the king on the one side and the magnates on the other, showed on closer inspection a divergence which in the last resort explains the growing social as well as governmental tension between the two groups.

It would seem that the identity of interests between king and hierarchy produced something of a common front against the aristocracy. Nevertheless, there can be no doubt that the king had exchanged one controlling body for another, had exchanged 'the people' – of whatever composition it may in fact have been – for the ecclesiastically organized body of the bishops. It was no doubt, at first sight, a loss on the part of the king; we have but to recall the theme of royal sovereignty as expressed by the kings before the implications of their theocratic kingship had become explicit. But in view of the rapidly growing strength of the secular aristocracy this – unlimited – royal sovereignty was in any case gravely threatened, and paradoxically enough the realization of the potentialities inherent in theocratic kingship made the Ruler considerably stronger, and this not despite of, but because of, the curtailed or stunted sovereignty which he now had. Compared with the often unpredictable support of the quickly shifting aristocratic factions, he now had the far more stable, far more resilient, intellectually superior and ideologically far better equipped ecclesiastical organism on which he could rely. As far as the basic and sustaining factors of society and its government came into question, the ecclesiastics had a programme, even if not a blueprint, and above

---

[1] For this see Schlesinger, art. cit.; M. Hellmann in *Entstehung*, cit. 292. Cf., further, H. Mitteis, *Staat des hohen M.A.* (Weimar, 1944), 105.

all a 'memory' that they held reached back to post-apostolic times. The exchange, therefore, of one controlling element for another was, from the king's angle, by no means all on the debit side: on the contrary taking into account the reality of the ninth century, there was considerable gain on the side of the king, in spite of the replacement of his unlimited sovereignty by a limited or stunted one. For however stunted his sovereignty was vis-à-vis the ecclesiastical hierarchy, he was given by them the tools with which he was enabled to claim effective control, that is, sovereignty over his non-ecclesiastical subjects.

In this context the protection of the king's status by virtue of his rebirth and sacrality assumes especial significance. The protective measures resulting from this changed status of the king *qua* king, were to become essential structural elements of all medieval kingship. Not the least important point to be made is that whilst the protective measures were to a large extent worked out in theory and partly also enacted in legislation throughout the West-Frankish kingdom, they were later applied to the East-Frankish portion with a frictionless ease which is indeed remarkable. The synod of Hohenaltheim in 916, which will engage us presently, transferred the West-Frankish principles to the Eastern kingdom.

One thing ought to be borne in mind: without the rebirth and the sacral status of the king, without in other words the central element of the unction, it would have been quite impossible to devise adequate protective measures for the Ruler, adequate, that is, by contemporary standards. It is comprehensible, therefore, why the actual protection was not only devised by the ecclesiastics, but also stemmed from the religious-sacramental armoury. To no one else but to the king applied the biblical 'You shall not curse the Rulers of the people';[1] none but the king was credited with the function of being the mediator between the ecclesiastics and the people; none had that dual role which the king had been accorded, *because* he was reborn and had emerged as a participant in the sacerdotal ministry, having been established in the Lord's likeness and as His stamp; to none other could be applied the Psalmist's words 'Do not touch mine anointed'[2] which meant an immunity on a scale barely comprehensible from the twentieth-century point of view;[3] none but the king reborn enjoyed so high a degree of commanding power and a corresponding right to obedience, underpinned

[1] Exod. 22. 28.
[2] Ps. 104. 15.   [3] Hincmar, *De fide Carolo servanda* in *PL* 125. 979 B.

as this was by the charge of high treason.[1] In precisely this respect, too, the filial relationship established between consecrator and king deployed its effects: by virtue of his unction the king had entered into a special kinship with both divinity and his consecrator.[2] The principle of royal inviolability was clearly formulated, and formulated it was by the ecclesiastics who by virtue of their common interest with the king had every reason to shield him from attacks: and in the ninth century what other means were considered more effective – or at least were thought to promise greater efficiency – than those originating in the religious-sacral quarter? But even so, reality was sometimes harsher than ecclesiastical doctrine could have provided for, or could have coped with.

It is evident that these protective measures were bound to influence society at large and to reflect upon the social structure itself. This topic is outside my examination, but a few remarks in addition to those already made on the subject of obedience to royal command[3] would seem in place. And these remarks are all the more justified as the respective statements could have practical meaning only in regard to the aristocracy. Certainly, doctrine had at its disposal powerful biblical models and, above all, the hitherto barely appreciated point of view of Gregory the Great relative to obedience: although the last of the great Doctors of the Church had said that by nature we were all equals, he nevertheless also insisted that there was 'an occult dispensation' according to which this natural equality gave way to subordination to a superior.[4] A man of Hincmar's calibre realized of course the potentialities of this Gregorian thesis. The availability of the fount of all hierarchical thinking in an intelligible Latin translation furthermore assisted Hincmar: Pseudo-Dionysius Areopagita had just been translated by John Scotus, and since then his works have populated the landscape of the Middle Ages for more than 600 years. Pseudo-Denis not only coined the very term *hierarchia* but also constructed a symmetrical thesis of the hierarchical ordering of society.[5] The combination

---

[1] See above 53.

[2] Cf. above 71 f.; probably on the basis of the baptismal and post-baptismal anointings (see above 74 f.), the relationship of father and son had established itself already in the fifth century, notably in the public field between pope and emperor, cf. *PG* 22 f.

[3] See above 51 ff.

[4] For this cf. *Individual & Society*, cit. 14 f.

[5] I have tried to draw attention to this in *PGP* 46 ff., though at the time I was unaware of the ninth-century use made of these works. It should be noted that interest in Pseudo-Denis was expressed earlier, cf. Hildwin's letter to Louis I, *Ep.* 20 in *MGH. Epp.* v. 327 ff. (anno 835); it was actually Hildwin who broadcast the identity of the author with

of the Gregorian and Pseudo-Dionysian thesis resulted in a powerful thematic alliance which, when joined to the biblical 'Be *subject* to every human creature for God's sake, be it the king or the princes sent by him'[1] yielded the possibly strongest doctrinal protection for the Ruler himself; it also yielded an important principle of government and was bound to affect views on the structure of society itself.[2]

For, structurally, society was given a cosmological setting and presented an emanation of the divine ordering. This would probably nowadays be called a sociological problem posed by the different classes, orders and layers of society and their mutual relations. It was on the tripod of Gregory I, Pseudo-Denis and the New Testament that Hincmar advanced the view according to which the various orders and ranks in society were copies of the heavenly dispositions.[3] If to this was added the Ruler as the Lord's anointed – that is, the 'king' of the Petrine text – it will not be difficult to appreciate that this Ruler had thereby been accorded the role of the pivot of that society over which divinity had set him. After all, this society, in concrete terms: the kingdom, was so to speak, laid up in heaven and was divinity's own. Consequently, the very theme of obedience – and let us call the thing by its proper name: the theme of subjection of the aristocracy to the king – had been endowed with such formidable strength, fibre and influence that other protective measures appeared pale in comparison. This doctrine found its legislative reflexion in the *Capitulare* issued by Charles the Bald in 862 at Pîtres. The ideological significance of this legislative act – most likely the work of Hincmar himself – has not been noticed, but the doctrine and its mirror, the law, would seem to deserve a few observations.

Denis of Paris, see B. Altaner, *Patrologie*, 5th ed., p. 467. For Charles the Bald's letter to John Scotus, see *MGH. Epp.* vi. 158–61, no. 14. Cf. also *Cod. Car.* no. 24 (Paul I), *MGH. Epp.* iii. 259. For literature cf. Manitius, iii. 1062. A thorough examination of the very great influence exercised by Ps. Denis throughout the ages, is long overdue; cf. as a modest beginning B. Vallentin, 'Der Engelstaat' in *Festschrift f. G. Schmoller* (Berlin, 1908), 40 ff. E. Delaruelle in *RHEF*. 38 (1952), 66, spoke of an 'aréopagitisme latin du IXe siècle' and remarked: 'Sur l'aréopagitisme latin au point de vue politique il n'existe malheureusement pas d'étude' – a remark which is still true. For the contemporary theological influence on John Scotus himself, see now R. Roques, 'Remarques sur la signification de Jean Scot Erigène' in *Misc. André Combes* (Rome–Paris, 1967), i. 245 ff., esp. 247 n. 8, 258 ff., 312 ff.

[1] I Pet. 2. 13.

[2] Hincmar, *Opusc.: n causa Hincmari Laudunensis*, cc. 12–14, in *PL* 126. 325–8, combines these points; here also, so far unnoticed, the reference to 'beatus Dionysius Areopagita, antiquus scil. et venerabilis pater, sicut, didicit ab apostolo Paulo, qui . . . duos libros de angelico et ecclesiastico principatu scripsit' (c. 12. col. 325 D).

[3] *PL* cit. col. 327.

I

Striking up all the sonorous chords of the duties incumbent upon him as king, Charles declared that he was forced to express himself on the vital theme of superiority and inferiority in society, on the theme of obedience and subordination, on the principle of the higher and the lower ranks in society: in pithy language he laid down as a principle that

> We can neither be all kings nor can we suffer a king set up above us by God.[1]

In a most economical way he enunciated the principle of the authority of one in a community, the principle of monarchy: vice versa, there was no such thing as an equality of those who govern and those who are governed. On the contrary, the monarch must, for governing purposes, be in a position to enforce his decrees and laws against anyone: the well-being of the social organism demanded this subjection of all to the divinely appointed Ruler. There can be hardly any doubt that here we have a practical application by Hincmar of Pseudo-Dionysian views, clothed in the language of the law and adjusted to the contingencies of the time; this application was in addition buttressed by the citation of the Pauline views.[2] Both the ordering of society and its government were emanations of the divine arrangement and it was also this arrangement which made the Ruler a participant of divine attributes of power and established him in the place of divinity as king on earth.[3] No further comment seems called for to point out the importance of this statement in relation to the theocratic-monarchic Rulership arrived at without any outside help, such as the Roman law: in reality this point of view was an amalgam of the already-mentioned triple alliance.

Whilst therefore there was nobody who could share the Ruler's estate in his governing capacity, there was, however, in the ranks below the Ruler's platform what this law designates with the new and exquisite term of a *parilis equalitas*, a like equality of all in relation to the governing king.[4] As regards the duty of obedience and subordination there was, in other words, no difference amongst the king's subjects. The decree goes so far as to say that those who refuse to be co-equals as subjects – 'pares vel coaequales in regno' – prove them-

---

[1] *Cap.* 272, c. 1, p. 305, lines 34 f.   [2] As expressed in Rom. 13. 1 ff.
[3] *Cap.* cit. referring to Ps. 65. 12: 'voluit et esse et vocari regem et dominum pro honore et *vice sua regem in terris*'.
[4] *Cap.* cit. pp. 305–6.

selves as the enemies of divinity and the allies of the devil. Although there is for understandable reasons no explicit reference to the magnates, it seems evident enough that the decree could receive its full topical meaning only in regard to them. They cannot refuse to obey and to subordinate themselves to royal power which was constituted by God Himself.[1] If the subjects of the king were not equals, he would not be in a position to act in the function of a *pater patriae* with which divinity had charged him.[2] He can discharge this function only when he renders justice and equity to all estates and states and social ranks or, as Hincmar himself also says, relying on Pseudo-Cyprian, that the king should treat all his subjects alike,[3] for in this equal dispensation of justice and equity consists the supreme vocation of the *regia maiestas*.[4] What apparently was in Hincmar's mind was that society itself was one whole in which there may be different social layers, ranks and estates, which have, however, from the point of view of government, no meaning or relevance: they assume relevance and importance only in a social respect. It is a thesis that was assuredly remarkable for the time in which it was propounded. It is, I am certain, no exaggeration to claim that here we are quite plainly presented with the doctrine of equality of all before the law, of all those who, at least in theory, were the king's subjects.

The thesis that the Ruler's supreme task was the equal dispensation of justice and equity looks innocuous enough, if not commonplace. Yet, a closer inspection easily reveals that this thesis is the Achilles heel of royal monarchy in a theocratic framework. Who determines what is just? and what is equitable? I may perhaps invite your attention to the development of the consultative role of the ecclesiastics into that of a determinative organ.[5] This process, for understandable reasons, greatly accelerated as the century wore on, and the claim to a controlling function on the part of the higher ecclesiastics became quite insistent. The very decree of the synod of Fîmes (2 April 881) combined the Gelasian point of view relative to the sacerdotal 'greater

---

[1] Ibid., exemplifying the fate of the archangel in Isai. 14. 12, the decree declares that those who refuse to acknowledge their subjection to the king and who do not suffer equals in the kingdom, turned themselves into subjects of the devil and enemies of God. The term *parilitas* was also used by Nicholas I, though not with the same connotation, see his *Ep.* 91, in *MGH. Epp.* vi. 518, line 8, and in his *Ep.* 120, ibid., p. 638, line 13.

[2] *Cap.* cit., c. 4, p. 310, line 9.

[3] Hincmar, *De ord. pal.*, c. 6, p. 520: 'nomen regis intellectualiter hoc retinet, ut subiectis omnibus officium rectoris procuret'; see Ps. Cyprian, *De XII abusivis saec.*, cit. c. 7.

[4] In this context cf. also *Cap.* 293, cc. 7, 9, 82, p. 420.

[5] See above 24 ff.

weight' (*maius pondus*) with the functions of the Old Testament priests when they anointed kings, and concluded that the ecclesiastics therefore imparted to the king the knowledge of how he should govern himself and his subjects and of how he should pay proper public tribute to the bishops. In other words, the king received his instructions relative to public government from those who conferred divine grace on him.[1] And within the precincts of public government there was no issue of more crucial concern than the idea and practical implementation of justice: there was unanimous agreement that the law must embody the abstract idea in concrete terms.

This is nothing but the enunciation of the thesis that the laws mirror the articulate and inarticulate assumptions upon which society is based; the law reflects the idea of justice which is, necessarily, a relative concept, for in a communist society the idea of justice will differ from that upheld in a capitalist society as it will differ from that upheld in a Buddhist society and in a Christian society. Here the synodists, led by Hincmar, express precisely this same principle when they declare that the laws in a Christian society must be consonant with the idea of justice and the basic tenets of Christianity of which the ecclesiastics had special knowledge.[2] Relying as he did on Old Testament models, Hincmar saw in the bishop nothing less than a *speculator*, that is, an over-seer whose main task was to inform the people in his care how to conduct their lives.[3] What the fundamental principles of justice were, was to be pronounced by the bishops, and their pronouncements were to be moulded into the language of the law by the king who, in his turn, and for the reasons stated, was bound to enforce it. The ecclesiastical verdict of what was just and unjust, was final – no better proof of a stunted sovereignty on the part of the king could be adduced. Hence in accepting the spurious submission of Constantine to episcopal judgment, Hincmar proceeds to the general thesis that secular men

---

[1] See *PL* 125. 1071, and the virtually identical passage in *De ord. pal.*, c. 5, p. 519. For this council see also Ch. de Clercq, 'La législation . . .' in *Rev. de droit can.*, 7 (1957), 255 ff., at 280–2. For some rectifications (of no direct bearing in this context) see C. Brühl, 'Hincmariana' in *DA*. 20 (1964), at 49–54. As far as I can see, the figure of King Ozias reappears here and in *PL* 125. 1058 (for the benefit of Charles the Bald) (II Paral. 26. 19 ff.), after it had been gently hinted at by Smaragdus in his *Via regia*, pref., *PL* 102. 934 C, and will not disappear again from the literature of the M.A. It achieved notoriety in the twelfth century, cf., e.g., Gratian, II. 7 d.a.c. 42; Thomas Becket in *Ep.* 153 in R.S., *Materials . . . Becket*, V. 273; Peter of Blois, *PL* 207. 30 (A).

[2] *PL.* 125. 1009; 1010 C; 1011 B–1012 C; also *De raptu viduarum*, c. 12, in *PL* 125. 1026 B.

[3] *De ord. pal.*, c. 5, pp. 519–20; cf. Ezech. 33. 7.

were dependent on ecclesiastical judgment, but, once more, there was to be no reciprocity: secular people may not impose their will upon ecclesiastics nor should the latter's decisions be open to discussion.[1] Lastly, the thesis that the king must submit to the higher law,[2] must accept the interpretation of the divine law by its qualified exponents, created the virtually monopolistic role of the higher ecclesiastics in society.

In justifying the role of the *speculatores*, Hincmar skilfully makes use of his historical as well as his juristic equipment. Once more Gregory the Great had to be harnessed: according to him, in the Scriptures ecclesiastics were sometimes called 'gods' and sometimes 'angels', and Hincmar fully utilized these Gregorian passages in his own correspondence.[3] It was also Gregory I who prompted Hincmar to repeat another spurious address of Constantine to the assembled bishops at Nicaea – an address which was invented by Rufinus of Aquileja – in which he declared: 'You are gods established by the true God'.[4] Once this path was trodden, there was nothing to arrest the direct application of certain biblical statements to the ecclesiastics, such as 'He who touches you, touches the apple of my eye'[5] or 'He who hears me and despises you, despises me'[6] or the view that the people reflect the esteem in which the clerics are held,[7] and so on. In short, the ecclesiastics claimed not merely superior charismatic qualifications, but a veritable monopoly of the interpretative fixation of the divine law as the supreme norm embodying justice.

Whether the Ruler *qua* Ruler was subjected to ecclesiastical jurisdiction was naturally a question that engaged a man of Hincmar's calibre. For all the just mentioned claims about the fundamental role of the ecclesiastical body would rightly be classed as unreal, if not irrelevant, were it not possible to exercise jurisdiction over the king. Yet, there was in the ninth century – as throughout the subsequent centuries – a widespread opinion that the Ruler *qua* Ruler was to be judged by God

---

[1] See Hincmar, *Ep.* 33, c. 4, in *PL* 126. 248 B. For a cautious assessment of Hincmar as a jurist see C. Brühl, *DA* cit. 77 n. 88; see also J. Devisse, *Hincmar et la loi* (Dakar, 1963); and M. Wallace-Hadrill in *Trends*, cit. 35 f. (A).

[2] See below 133.

[3] Gregory I: *Reg.* IV. 31 and V. 36 (*MGH. Epp.* i. 318 ff.); Hincmar in his *Ep.* 32, in *PL* 126. 232 D. The contemporary papacy adopted the same point of view, see Nicholas I in his *Ep.* 88, in *MGH. Epp.* vi. 455 f.

[4] Hincmar, loc. cit. col. 233 (A).

[5] Zach. 2. 8.

[6] Luke, 10. 16.

[7] Isai. 24. 2.

alone.[1] Hincmar was of course familiar with this point of view,[2] but stigmatized it as blasphemous, inspired by Satan: it was not 'the expression of a catholic Christian'.[3] He rejected this standpoint by adducing an abundance of Old Testament examples and also historical instances to show that Rulers had in fact been judged by clerics; for the thesis he advocated he also invoked the support of St Paul according to whom 'kings should obey those who are set over them by the Lord'.[4] Amongst the historical precedents Hincmar instanced the steps taken by St Ambrose against Theodosius I which in his opinion were clearly judicial in nature, and the more recent case of Louis I, whilst Gelasius' view was also adduced in further support of his theme.[5] In only one case would he subscribe to the thesis of the king's immunity from ecclesiastical judgment and his direct subjection to God, that is, as long as the Ruler acted as a king, that is, fulfilled the will of God, he was not to be subjected to ecclesiastical jurisdiction, a contingency which hardly constituted a problem.[6] But otherwise the general principle prevailed that the king was justiciable, since he could be compelled 'ad iustitiae observationem'[7] and since he was for his failings as a king subjected to ecclesiastical tribunals.[8] The doctrinal justification he found in Gelasius according to whom the Ruler had to follow the rulings given by the ecclesiastics and to accept their decrees in humility.[9] It would be wholly erroneous to think that these were the personal opinions of Hincmar: one of the reasons which the synod of Savonières in 859 had advanced for preserving episcopal unity was that thereby the bishops constituted a common front and were therefore in a position to rule the kings, princes and the people com-

[1] Cf. already Isidore of Seville, *Sententiae*, III. 51 no. 6; or later King Henry IV of Germany. We should take note that Ps. Isidore had also made this a general point. Cf., e.g., Ps. Alexander I in *Ep.* 1, c. 7, p. 98: 'Novit enim Deus qui sunt eius. Non potest autem humano condemnari examine, quem Deus suo reservavit iudicio.' He continued: 'Si omnia namque in hoc saeculo vindicata essent, locum divina non haberent iudicia' – which seems an unanswerable logic.

[2] See his *De divortio Lotharii*, qu. VI. in *PL* 125. 756.

[3] 'Vox non est catholici christiani,' ibid.

[4] Ibid., col. 757 A, which is a rather liberal interpretation of Heb. 13. 17.

[5] *Ep.* 12, c. 2; Hincmar, loc. cit. cols. 756–7.

[6] Ibid. col. 757 B–C. Here also (col. 758) the five ways by which Hincmar in 860 illustrated with the help of the OT how a king could be created: (a) direct nomination by God; (b) by God through the instrumentality of man; (c) by man at the bidding (*nutu*) of God; (d) hereditary succession; (e) tyrannical usurpation. He did not, however, link these various ways up with the problem of jurisdiction.

[7] *De regis persona*, c. 17 in *PL* 125. 844, very much relying on St Augustine.

[8] *PL* 125. 759 D.

[9] *Ep.* 30, c. 34 in *PL* 126. 209.

mitted to them.[1] However strange these views may appear to modern readers, only a brief reflexion suffices to demonstrate that once the Carolingian idea of a regenerated or renewed or reborn society was put into practice, the basically controlling function of the higher ecclesiastics was an ideological consequence – and this led to the stunting of the king's sovereignty.

One of the ways in which sovereignty manifests itself in a practical manner is the exercise of jurisdiction by the Ruler over his subjects: indeed, this seems to be the very hallmark of any correctly understood idea of sovereignty. In the second half of the ninth century the ecclesiastics put forward the view that a clear distinction should be made between those over whom the king legitimately exercised jurisdiction and those over whom he was unable to do so. Thrown against the ideological background I have just tried to sketch, the postulate of ecclesiastical exemption from royal jurisdiction should no longer be difficult to understand. Although this claim to the so-called *privilegium fori* had a rather long history,[2] it was not until the second half of the ninth century that the postulate could be considered a matter of practical governmental concern. That the influence of Gregory the Great could once more be detected[3] is noteworthy; it is also interesting that less genuine sources, such as the decretals in Pseudo-Isidore, greatly strengthened the case for ecclesiastical exemption from royal jurisdiction. And nothing illustrates the theme of the king's stunted sovereignty better than the operation of the *privilegium fori*, because clearly enough the ecclesiastics were thereby not considered subjects of the king. Parts, and vital parts, of the kingdom the ecclesiastics were and claimed to be, but they were not subjects, or perhaps more correctly they claimed not to be subjects of the king. This contention was the basic feature of the overwhelming number of quarrels between king and episcopacy throughout the subsequent medieval period. Because jurisdiction was an issue of sovereignty, it did not extend to those who were not subjects, the ecclesiastics.[4] Differently expressed: those who effected the king's rebirth could not – so their argument ran – also be his subjects. For an inferior, and the subject was indubitably an inferior, could not sit in judgment over a superior, who here was

---

[1] *Cap.* 299, c. 2, p. 447.

[2] A number of ancient councils had postulated it; also late Roman-imperial legislation and in Frankish times especially the Council of Paris in 614, in *MGH. Conc.* i. 187, c. 6.

[3] Cf. Hincmar in *PL* 125. 1068 C and also cols. 1044–5.

[4] For details and the historical development see the work (which is still basic) of A. Nissl, *Der Gerichtsstand des Clerus im fränk. Reich* (Innsbruck, 1886), 125 ff., 227 ff.

the king: this precisely was one of the messages which Pseudo-Isidore tried to drive home.[1] Moreover, neither could the disciple judge the master nor, particularly relevant here, the son the father – in this context the filial relationship established by unction deployed its practical effects.[2] The Ruler's rebirth thus marked the birth of the free ecclesiastic, free from royal control, free from juristic subjection to royal power. This development was perhaps not so much a revolution as a rather remarkable evolution.

You may recall that I earlier mentioned the concept of the *Munt* as a structural element of Rulership. Now in the ninth century the king's *Munt* came to be replaced by his function as a tutor or was joined with the king's *tutela*. The process began visibly under Louis I who very early in his reign recalled all charters of his predecessors in order to confirm them. As they consisted mainly of privileges of immunities, it is now especially interesting to see that Louis stipulated in addition to the immunity of churches from royal control that they were to receive royal protection: thereby charters of protection replaced charters of immunity, a step of considerable constitutional and ideological significance. It was one of the first measures by which the role of the monarchic king was almost imperceptibly changed into that of the king as a tutor or protector of the kingdom.[3] The synodists assembled at the Council of Paris (829) drawing heavily on Pseudo-Cyprian, issued a declaration which ideologically strengthened the theme of royal tutorship considerably, so, for instance, when they said that the king's prime duty was the *tutamentum patriae* as well as the *munimentum gentis*, that is, the protection of the fatherland and the military defence of the people, because his task was to provide the *pax populorum*.[4] It was not many years afterwards that Lothar I in a charter entitled himself 'Lhudarius *Galliarum gentium tutor* et rector'.[5]

---

[1] Cf. on this my *Individual & Society*, 15 f.   [2] See above 72 f.

[3] For the elucidation of this point see J. Semmler, 'Reichsidee und kirchl. Gesetzgebung' in *ZKG* 71 (1960), 37 ff., at 41–2, where the relevant literature (Sickel, Ganshof, etc.) will be found (notes 28 ff.); see especially also E. Lesne, *Hist de la propriété ecclés. en France*, ii (1926): *Les droits régaliens*, 30–62, with numerous examples of *tuitio* and tutorship exercised by the king.

[4] See Ps. Cyprian, *De XII abus. saec.*, cit. c. 9, p. 51 f.; *MGH. Conc.* ii. 650, lines 36 f.; Jonas of Orléans, *De instit. regia*, cit. c. 3, pp. 140–1. *Munt* was often joined with *tutela* or *tuitio* in the DD. of the ninth century. A particularly good example is that of Charles III in *MGH. Die Urkunden d. deutschen Karolinger: Karl III.*, ed. P. Kehr (1937), no. 21, p. 35. For Charles the Bald see especially the observations by G. Tessier in *Recueil des actes de Charles II le Chauve*, iii (Paris, 1955), at 227 f.

[5] See *MGH. Die Urkunden d. Karolinger*, ed. Th. Schieffer, iii (1966), no. 110, p. 258 (anno 850).

Now you may perhaps also recall that the king in the coronation orders was conceived in the military image of an athlete in the service of Christ, whilst the bishop was credited with the cure of souls. The significance is clear: the function of the bishop relating to the internal part of man, was to be complemented by the external power which the king wielded in his governing capacity; the sword was to support the word. This was little more than the ancient Pauline and Isidorian doctrines clothed in the symbolic language of the coronation rites. But it was left to Hincmar to express this same point of view in concrete terms which showed how stunted the king's sovereignty was. Hincmar's statement, though relating to the principle of division of labour, directly touches upon the king's sovereignty. Let us quote the view of Hincmar which, probably because of its terse and laconic character, has not attracted the attention which is its due:

> Just as the things and the estates of the church are committed to the bishop for the sake of good management and disposition, in the same way they are committed to the king for the sake of defence and protection.[1]

The distinction is crucial concerning as it does regal and episcopal functions. But what matters from the point of view of sovereignty is that the control, disposition and management of ecclesiastical goods and estates was an episcopal function, whereas the king's function consisted in effectively supporting the episcopal arrangement by his physical defence with the sword, that is, by exercising his function as a tutor, the very function which Hincmar avowed was conferred on the king by a divine decision.[2] The teleological conception of kingship seems to have prompted the transformation of the *Munt* into *tuitio* and to have facilitated the emergence of the view that the king was the *tutor regni*; and the *regnum* was nothing less than the articulate, corporate and organized Christian body. This view was adopted both by the papacy and the important council held at Tribur in 895. Pope John VIII in crowning Charles the Bald as emperor of the Romans (875) declared that he (the pope) had 'elected this king as the defender and tutor of the Church'[3] whilst the Council of Tribur designated the king as 'the always ready and ever active tutor of the kingdom'.[4]

[1] Hincmar, *Pro eccl. libert. defensione*, in *PL* 125. 1051 A ('. . . commissae sunt ad defendendum et tuendum'); further col. 1044 B.   [2] *De ord. pal.*, c. 9, p. 520.

[3] *Cap.* 279, c. 1, p. 351. Cf. also John VIII's speech at Ravenna in 877, now newly edited by W. A. Eckhardt in *DA* 23 (1967), 295 ff., at 304 ff.

[4] *Cap.* 252, p. 212, lines 30 f.

The evolution of the tutorial conception of Rulership in the ninth century marked a further ideological breach in the fortifications of the king's sovereignty. We shall see how as a result of Roman law studies this tutorial conception was to colour the whole complexion of Rulership from the late eleventh century onwards.

II

I have so far concentrated on the development in the West-Frankish realms, because intellectual leadership indubitably belonged to the West-Frankish ecclesiastics. We may, however, recall that in the first half of the ninth century the East-Frankish regions had also made considerable intellectual advances. Nevertheless, there was a gradual erosion of public authority with a consequential lowering of public security, as well as the virtual cessation of scholarly pursuits. This was due to several factors: apart from frequent famines and a sequence of bad harvests, there were numerous internal insurrections, the resumption of Norman invasions and the military aggressions by Danes and Hungarians, whilst on other borders the Slavs demanded increasing military attention. In these circumstances the internal conditions in East-Francia were not conducive to the pursuit of intellectual efforts. Devastation of churches and plunderings of monasteries, robberies, murder and manslaughter, became common experiences.[1]

In view of this state of affairs due emphasis must be placed upon Arnulf's initiative in summoning a council of all three German archdioceses (Cologne, Mainz and Trier) in June 888 less than half a year after becoming king.[2] It was a council which symbolized the beginning of the process that was to lead to an evolution in the East-Frankish kingdom similar to that concluded in the West-Frankish kingdom. Three points deserve special mentioning. Although convoked by the king, the council in its first two lengthy chapters dilated upon the nature, functions and duties of kingship: and these two chapters containing as they did a miniature *speculum regis*, were addressed to Arnulf himself: according to the synodists only in co-operation with the ecclesiastics could the king hope to establish public order and security and create conditions favourable to internal and external peace. Secondly, the same decrees were almost wholly a literal copy, including

---

[1] For details see A. Hauck, *Kirchengeschichte*, cit. ii. 626 ff., iii. 275 ff.

[2] 'Imperante serenissimo seniore nostro Arnulpho rege' (Mansi, 18. 61 E; for sources see BM 1790a).

biblical and literary references, of the respective decrees issued at the Paris Council (829);[1] this slavish dependence on a former council would prove how barren ecclesiastical thought had recently become in the East-Frankish kingdom – yet we recall that it was this Paris Council which signalled the beginning of the strong doctrinal and practical influence of the ecclesiastics in the West-Frankish realms. It was this intellectual dearth which brings me to the third point, that is, the readiness with which the synodists at Mainz availed themselves of Pseudo-Isidore.[2] This council marks the tangible beginning of the pseudo-isidorian ideology upon East-Frankish ecclesiastical thought; Pseudo-Isidore was one of the most potent agencies which was to accelerate the fusion of West and East Frankish ideology, and quite especially in regard to matters of public law and authority. What further deserves mention is the barely appreciated fact that a number of eminent West-Frankish ecclesiastics were present in this council: the archbishops of Rheims and Rouen as well as the bishops of Beauvais and Noyon.[3] What language, culture and political treaties had separated, was bridged again by the ecclesiastics, and the assumption is not unjustified that these highly educated and perceptive French bishops functioned here as consultants to their German colleagues.

Whereas the council of Mainz can be designated as the first phase in the process of assimilation of the two halves of the Carolingian inheritance, the Council of Tribur held seven years later in 895, may be called the second phase; it is also the phase in which Pseudo-Isidore figured even more prominently than in its predecessor at Mainz. Nevertheless what is of immediate concern to me is the coalition desired by the ecclesiastics with King Arnulf, in which, one may safely assume, they would soon become the senior partner. The epistle prefatory to the canons and addressed to Arnulf makes a number of statements relevant to our topic. In order to attain their goal the synodists employ a somewhat flamboyant language and assert that God Himself had set up Arnulf as a prince over both ecclesiastical orders and secular offices: they are insistent that it was no human power, but divinity itself which had elected him.[4] There is some piquancy in this highfalutin apostrophe: after all, Arnulf had rebelled against his uncle, the

---

[1] Mansi, 18. 63–5; *MGH. Conc.* ii. 649–52.

[2] Cf., e.g., cc. 11, 12, which are based on Ps. Urban I, c. 5, p. 145, and the spurious *Const. Silv.*, ibid. 449–50.

[3] See Mansi, 18. 76.

[4] *Cap.* 252, p. 210: '. . . ut totus cognoscat mundus non ab homine neque per hominem, sed per ipsum Dominum esse electum.'

Emperor Charles III, dethroned him and usurped his power, but this coup would not have been accomplished without the active assistance of the magnates who went through some form of an election at Frankfurt.[1] The aim of the Tribur synodists is clear enough: to take the place of the aristocracy as allies of the king, because they held that stability of government could be achieved only by a co-operative effort between ecclesiastics and king. To the question, in what way he envisaged the defence of the Church and an amplification of their own ecclesiastical status,[2] the king replied in an unequivocal affirmative sense by declaring that he would wage war with determination against all enemies of the Church and against all who impinged upon, or lowered, the status of the ecclesiastics.[3] Thereupon the synodists acclaimed him and intoned the *Te Deum*. What is remarkable in this Tribur Council is the rapidly growing self-awareness of the ecclesiastics and the boldness with which they pursued their aim. Not the rebellious magnates who after all had materially helped the usurper, but they, the ecclesiastics, were to be the activating and sustaining organs of public government.

The expected strengthening of royal power through the concerted efforts of king and ecclesiastical hierarchy did not come about. Four years after the Council of Tribur Arnulf was dead and his successor was the six-year old Louis IV the Child, the last of the Carolingian dynasty in the East-Frankish kingdom. Here indeed ecclesiastical influence had an opportunity of making itself felt, for Louis's guardian was the archbishop of Mainz, Hatto, and to all seeming this ecclesiastical influence asserted itself in a ritual inauguration, though there is general agreement that he was not anointed, but almost certainly crowned.[4] But the government by a minor was at all times a source of weakness for any kingdom, and in this instance the weakness amounted to another breakdown of public authority.[5] For one definite result of this minority régime was a polarization of the forces on the government side – made up of the Ruler and the ecclesiastics – and the forces represented by the particularist and ducal powers. In the late September of 911 Louis IV died, at the age of 18, unmarried and without issue.

---

[1] For sources see BM 1765a–l; for details see K. Reindel in *Entstehung*, cit. 231 f.; H. Keller, 'Zum Sturz Karls III.' in *DA* 22 (1966), at 359 ff., 374 ff.

[2] *Cap.* 252, p. 212.

[3] *Cap.* cit. p. 213, lines 14–17.

[4] Cf. W. Schlesinger, in *Entstehung*, cit. 332–3; C. Brühl, *HZ* cit. 206–9, with further literature.

[5] For details see K. Reindel in *Entstehung*, 237 ff.

The accession of Conrad I of Franconia on 10 November 911 signified that a Ruler who had only tenuous connexions with the Carolingian house[1] was chosen; his reign constituted an important period of transition in the fortunes of East-Francia from the Carolingians to the Germans. The event marked that active ecclesiastical participation which had so far not been discernible in the East-Frankish regions: it was the first occasion that the native ecclesiastics were in a position to anoint the king. Thereby they had on their own account taken the first step towards the clericalization of his office and the rebirth of the king *qua* king, precisely the features with which the West-Frankish realms had long been familiar. Here the most plausible explanation is that Conrad's lack of blood charisma had to be compensated by the charisma of grace.[2] With this unction a weighty advance was made towards the assimilation of East-Frankish and West-Frankish ideological presuppositions concerning Rulership. Mere election without the charisma of blood in the elected Ruler was obviously considered insufficient, and this all the more so as, to judge by the admittedly brittle source material, not all duchies seem to have taken part in the election of Conrad. And the more the procedure adopted at Forchheim in November 911 approached a genuine election, the more it needed a sanction other than the mere human expression of the will of the electors: it needed a sanction supplied by an organ wholly outside human intervention, and that was provided by the conferment of divine grace on Conrad in the act of unction. The polarization of the forces which I have just mentioned, had now taken concrete shape.

Altogether the ecclesiastics – with the perhaps understandable exception of Saxony under Duke Henry, the later King Henry I – stood firmly in the royal camp and made front against the lay aristocracy.[3] Hence attacks on the king's power necessarily and vitally

---

[1] For this see G. Tellenbach, *Entstehung*, 197 f. and 205 f.

[2] See the cautious formulation by H. Beumann, 'Sakrale Legitimierung' in *Sav. Z.*, *GA.* 66 (1948), at 11 ff., esp. 13–15; also W. Schlesinger in *Entstehung*, 335–6: 'die kirchliche Weihe . . . musste den Mangel des Gebluts ersetzen'. For sources see BM 2070c; and on the unction see E. Dümmler, *Gesch. d. ostfränk. Reiches*, iii. 576 n. 3; P. E. Schramm, *Kaiser*, cit. ii (1968), 301 ('Conrad bedurfte einer besonderen Sicherung' because of lacking *Blutsrecht*); C. Erdmann, 'Der ungesalbte König' in *DA* 2 (1938), 312; M. Lintzel in *Sav. Z.*, *GA* 66 (1948), at 48 f.; Kern–Buchner, 85 n. 178. The possibility that Zwentibold as sub-king of Lorraine had received unction in 895 (on the model of Charles the Bald in 869) cannot be excluded, though the source is by no means unambiguous; on this see Schramm, op. cit. ii. 297–9.

[3] Cf. also W. Schlesinger, loc. cit. 335, who speaks of an increase in ecclesiastical influence during Conrad's reign.

affected the ecclesiastical body; in addition there were some events which directly concerned the ecclesiastics. There was the murder of the bishop of Strasbourg (Otbert) in 913; the physical violence directed against the bishop of Speyer and his subsequent exoculation by a number of counts in 914; the imprisonment of Bishop Salomon III of Constance by Count Erchanger and others – all these attacks were not so much aimed against the victims because they were ecclesiastics, but because they were supporters of the king. The aim of Erchanger, for instance, was the erection of a Swabian duchy. This threat to royal power necessarily involved the ecclesiastics themselves; and royal power was at the same time also threatened from without by the incessant Magyar incursions into Bavaria and Thuringia.[1] In these conditions the 'coalition' of king and the higher echelons of the ecclesiastics suggested itself, for they constituted precisely that stabilizing element of which, internally, the king was obviously in need. Both parts had therefore a keen desire for active co-operation, and the link between them had been firmly established by the episcopally conferred unction. The tenor of some of Conrad's charters makes it abundantly clear how anxious he was to tie the ecclesiastics closely to him,[2] and thereby to strengthen his own position.

It has been advisable to go into some of these factual details because they furnish the background to the synod of Hohenaltheim in 916 which marks the fusion of German and French thought, that is, a unification of intellectual and ideological elements where diversity of linguistic, political, cultural elements had separated the two halves of the Carolingian inheritance. In this synod one may well find the lengthy West-Frankish development telescoped into some three dozen canons. On the one hand there is the very strong all-out support for the king: he was to be protected by the same measures which the French ecclesiastics had devised and which unquestionably served as models. On the other hand, there are the same immunities, the same exemptions of the ecclesiastics from royal control and jurisdiction which contributed in so large a part to the stunting of the king's sovereignty. Here indeed Pseudo-Isidore rendered powerful assistance.

The synod of Hohenaltheim was a large gathering: virtually all the

---

[1] For all details see E. Dümmler, op. cit. iii. 591 n. 1.

[2] Cf., e.g., DK. I. 20, 21, 29; further nos. 4, p. 5, lines 28 ff.; 18, p. 17, lines 39 ff.; etc. Cf. also Schramm, op. cit., ii. 301: because of his conflicts with the princes Conrad had to rely more and more on the ecclesiastics – an inevitable consequence of his having been anointed by them on his accession.

bishops of Conrad's kingdom, except those of Saxony, attended.[1] But what gave this synod an additional significance was that it marked the resumption, if not in fact the beginning, of a close relationship between the papacy and the East-Frankish hierarchy. It was for the first time that the pope – John X – took part in German synodal proceedings through his own legate,[2] and this not on his own initiative, but because he was requested to do so. It was, as if 753–4 had been put into reverse, and as if 961–2 were to be prepared. In the opening address – in substance a papal letter, here called a *carta* – the legate made the cause of the German ecclesiastics his own: he defined as the purpose of the synod the establishment of public order and authority which was the same as saying that royal power was to be strengthened. The coalition of king and ecclesiastics had now been broadened by the inclusion of the papacy: it was the first occasion that the papacy had been brought into play, and this in a German-domestic issue.

There should be no doubt about the sense of public responsibility which animated the synodists. The decline of standards in public matters peremptorily demanded their active assistance in supporting the king. But the greater this support was, the more his sovereignty came to be clipped by the same ecclesiastics. The claim to control and supervision of public matters by the ecclesiastics themselves emerges here, if possible, with still greater clarity and emphasis than in the West-Frankish kingdom. Leaving aside the decrees enacting juris-dictional exemption from royal control,[3] the decrees dealing with royal power itself can be dealt with under three different aspects.

In these canons[4] the synodists attempted to buttress the foundations of Conrad's kingship by giving him the maximum protection possible at the time: two of the decrees were actually entitled 'On the strength of the king' – *De robore regis*. They declared that nobody should under pain of excommunication and eternal damnation compass the king's death or in any way lay violent hands on or endanger the life of the king or try to deprive him of Rulership and usurp his throne in a nefarious manner or enter upon any conspiracy against the king.[5] This enactment was supplemented by stern sanctions threatened in the case of perjury or incitement to commit perjury; laymen who in violation of their oath – which was held to be a sacrament – took part in actions

---

[1] For the fundamental importance of this synod see especially M. Hellmann in *Entsteh-ung*, 289 ff., who was the first to have assessed its wider historical perspectives.

[2] See *MGH. Const.*, i. 433, p. 620.

[3] Cf., cc. 12, 13, 26, 32, 38.   [4] cc. 19, 20, 22, 23.   [5] c. 20, p. 623 (A).

against the kingdom or the person of the king, had committed sacrilege against the Lord's anointed and were visited by dire penalties, whilst bishops, priests and deacons guilty of these offences were to be degraded.[1] Now the essential point here is that these canons which protected the king so powerfully, were either straight copies of the Visigothic councils or adaptations of them. And the source which familiarized the synodists with these Visigothic councils was Pseudo-Isidore.[2] For once perfectly genuine texts were transmitted by Pseudo-Isidore: the collection served as an instrument with which the foundations of German Rulership were to be supported and to be equipped in the fight against particularist ducal and aristocratic forces. The synodists drew the legislative if not also the constitutional conclusions from the royal unction whereby the king's office had been clericalized and he himself *qua* king reborn and set above ordinary mankind. Hence any attack on him was to be visited with penalties commensurate to the unique standing of the king. The concrete measures were taken in the first council in embryonic Germany to protect the core and essence of kingship, the king's *maiestas* and to fix the *crimen laesae maiestatis*.

The second point that deserves some remark is this. It was not by royal legislation that the most severe penalties against laymen guilty of perjury, breach of oath or treason were threatened, but by a purely ecclesiastical assembly. In other words, judicial power to be exercised by ecclesiastics was to be exercised not in their own interest but in that of the kingdom so that public order and security were to be ensured. Lay magnates were summoned to appear before the synod; specifically Erchanger and his accomplices were convicted and sentenced for having nefariously raised their hands against the Lord's anointed (Conrad), in addition to having committed sacrilege against Bishop Salomo III of Constance.[3] The important point therefore is that these crimes were ecclesiastical crimes the justiciability of which belonged, for this reason, not to the king but to the ecclesiastics:[4] both the character of Rulership

---

[1] *Const.*, i. 433, cc. 22, 23, p. 624: '. . . quia sacrilegium peragit manum suam in christum domini mittens, anathema sit . . .'

[2] Hohenaltheim, c. 19 = literal copy of Toledo IV, c. 74, in Ps. Isidore, 372 and 373 col. B at end; see also Hellmann, 310; c. 20 = Toledo VI, c. 18, in Ps. Isidore, 380; Hellmann, 310; cc. 22, 23, are paraphrastic adjustments of Toledo IV, c. 74. The paper by H. Fuhrmann, 'Die ps. isidorischen Fälschungen u. die Synode v. Hohenaltheim' in *Zeitschr. f. bayr. Landesgesch.*, 1957, was not accessible to me.

[3] Hohenaltheim, c. 21, p. 623.

[4] Cf. the remark of Hellmann, 307: 'Noch niemals aber hatte ein fränkischer König sich die Jurisdiktion über Rebellen durch die Kirche aus der Hand nehmen lassen.'

and its protection stand out clearly. Rulership was an ecclesiastical office. The contours of the lines separating the two fronts were drawn in wholly ecclesiastical terms: the camp of the Lord's anointed with the German ecclesiastics and the pope facing a rebellious lay aristocracy. This, in substance, is a replica of the situation in France and amounts, here as there, to a quite severe curtailing of the king's sovereignty: understandably enough if one bears in mind that the protective measures themselves originated wholly in the religious-ecclesiastical sphere.

The third point seems obvious and needs no lengthy comment. Although there was in essential matters an assimilation of German and French conceptions of Rulership, there was nevertheless some notable difference which concerns the role of the papacy. The French had not called upon the pope in their efforts to clericalize the kingly office: it was they themselves who had, so to speak single-handedly, harnessed the actual conditions to their own designs and had forged the tools with which the designs were to be implemented, and the most the pope could do was to appear uninvitedly on the scene and to come as a supplicant on the model of 753–4, and then confirm the already anointed and crowned king in his position.[1] The pope came as a petitioner and at the very end of the impressive French development. Here in Germany proper he came at a very early stage of its history, not on his own initiative, but because he was requested to lend weight to an assembly of German bishops who for the sake of creating conditions favourable to peace and security were about to legislate on a number of points vitally affecting German Rulership. The resultant decrees were issued in the presence of, and endorsed by, the papal legate, and thus with the active participation of the papacy. The papal intervention at the synod of Hohenaltheim in 916 was to portend the future of Germany's contact with the papacy: in the decisive decades of the French development papal participation was conspicuously absent.

In one point, however, there was no divergence whatsoever between the French and German theory and practice. On the contrary, there was unanimous agreement that the instrument which brought about the rebirth of the Ruler was not credited with what was technically called a *character indelebilis*. The sacrament of unction had no 'indelible character' either in the Old Testament or in medieval doctrine or practice. Perhaps nothing illustrates so persuasively the relationship

[1] See above 99 f.

of the reborn king to those who in actual fact had manipulated his re-birth than this real and important difference between episcopal and regal anointings: for the former had that indelible character which at this very same time was denied to the latter, by the same ecclesiastics who were responsible for the introduction of both kinds of unction. Already in the ninth century there were several Rulers who experienced this lack of an indelible character of their unction. The purpose of the consecra-tory prayer inserted by Hincmar for the coronation of Charles the Bald in 869 was precisely this – that the king's suitability as a Ruler be preserved by divinity, because his suitability was the presupposition for the conferment of unction and therefore also for the continued possession of divine grace. In sum, then, and seen from a wider historical point of view, very little was left of the king who once repre-sented a new Constantine: exactly a hundred years separated Charle-magne and Conrad I – what a change in the complexion, standing and sovereignty of the king had been worked within this astonishingly brief span by the consistent and purposeful application of ideas.

This appears to be the right moment to invite your attention to a problem that has not, as far as I can see, attracted much attention, and yet it is one which seems to me to concern a crucial question in the ninth century, in the later Middle Ages, and for that matter at the present time. I do not think one could subscribe to the view that the concept of stunted sovereignty was a mere heuristic or abstract notion, one that could have little practical relevance. Let us be clear about one thing: the Frankish king, or for that matter any other medieval king, before he as a Ruler became incorporated into the body of the Church, before, in other words, he was reborn as a Ruler, was incontrovertibly and incontestably a true sovereign: he possessed that kind of sove-reignty which could have passed the most rigorous tests of any examination. Part of the explanation is ideological: his sovereignty was based on the unproven and unprovable assertion of a *direct* confer-ment of divine grace of Rulership on him:[1] this released him from all

---

[1] A clear and convincing instance of the direct derivation of ruling powers is supplied by the acclamation dating from between 783 and 792: although Charlemagne was never crowned a king the acclamation has: 'Karolo excellentissimo et *a Deo coronato* magno et pacifico rege (sic) Francorum ... vita et victoria' (B. Opfermann, *Die liturgischen Herrscherakklamationen des M.A.* (Weimar, 1953), 101). P. Classen in *Karl d. Gr.*, cit. i. 583, shows the current use of this formula in Byzantium and therefore in Byzantine Italy which is indeed what one would expect in view of the Byzantine coronation ritual where the ecclesiastical participation had no constitutive effects at all. This direct derivation of ruling power from divinity gave the Eastern emperor the kind of sovereign resilience which Western Rulers lacked; see further text.

the fetters which had hitherto bound and hedged him in, for nobody else in this kingdom could boast of this singular distinction of divine favour.

This situation changed when royal grace came to be seen as mediated by the higher ecclesiastics, when they, so to speak, began to sandwich themselves between divinity and the king. The effect on the king's sovereignty was that he now became subjected – in the literal sense – to the laws of divinity, laws, however, which were made known to him and became articulated norms, through the self-same ecclesiastics. You need only recall some of the views and statements of, say, Hincmar[1] and the other leading churchmen in the ninth century to realize how much they were concerned with precisely this stunting of the king's sovereignty. For the king's sovereignty was now limited by what may be termed the higher law, that law which, allegedly divine, was entrusted for its exposition, interpretation and dissemination to the churchmen, to those who were called the thrones of God, the most splendidly shining luminaries of the world, or whatever flowery nomenclatures were showered on them. Seen from this angle, the king's role as mediator between clergy and layfolk assumed its practical as distinct from its theoretical significance. Above all, the king's sovereign wings were drastically clipped, and he came to be subjected to a basic law of which the ecclesiastics were the expositors: in the prevailing circumstances this basic law could be none other than the divine law. Evidently, the scope of divine law as a basic law stunting the king's sovereignty could also include the ecclesiastical law itself, as, for instance, Hincmar plainly urged.[2]

The Frankish ecclesiastics had – unbeknown to, and undreamt by, themselves – made an advance which has not lost its topical relevance to this day. Especially since the end of the Second World War we have witnessed the search for a so-called higher law to which everyone, including heads and ministers of states, as well as state organizations themselves, is to be subjected: today this 'higher law' is found in a natural law the contents of which are as unfathomable as they are

---

[1] For instance the statement above 104 n. 1. M. Wallace-Hadrill, in *Trends*, cit. rightly points out that there was no contract between the king and his consecrators; see also on this below 179 f.

[2] See *PL* 125. 1068 B, where he said that the ecclesiastical laws were based on the working of the holy ghost and made known through the clerics, continuing: 'Quas (scil. leges) qui non observat, sine dubio contra Dei voluntatem et sanctae ipsius ecclesiae *statum* et *honorem* . . . suam salutem et iustitiam . . . facit.' Cf. also Hincmar in his *Ep.* 33 in *PL* 126. 245: 'sacri canones *spiritu Dei conditi* et totius mundi reverentia consecrati . . .'

elusive.[1] The modern solution is, it would seem to me, little more than a variant of the theme which the ninth century had evolved. For there royal absolutism came to be checked, since the stunting of the king's sovereignty was a necessary consequence of the conferment of royal grace by the ecclesiastics and – this is the historically crucial point – signified the implicit recognition and tacit admission that there was a 'higher law', a law that governed the cosmos as well as society, to which the king *qua* king was consequently subjected. Here indeed is the point where the coronation promises given by the kings, receive added significance: *au fond* the concern of the 'Petitions' and the royal responses to them was precisely this subjection of the Ruler to a 'higher' law that was prior to him and wholly independent of him. Seen from yet another angle, the process of subjecting the Ruler to a 'higher law' was the ostensible beginning of the long and wearisome journey that has still not come to an end – the discovery and the fixation of the principle of the rule of law in civilized communities. It is not, I think, an exaggeration to claim that as far as the history of European civilization is concerned, it was the evolution of theocratic Rulership in the ninth century which first brought about the thesis that the Ruler was subjected to a law.

This ecclesiastical complexion of, and the infusion of ecclesiastical elements into, Rulership resulted in the stunting of the Ruler's sovereignty both *ratione personae* (the ecclesiastics having been taken out of the nexus of subjects) and *ratione materiae* (the basic law and ante-legal ideas as prerogatives of the ecclesiastics). It was this kind of Rulership which with some modifications of a tangential and peripheral character the Carolingian age bequeathed to the European Middle Ages. But it was also this ecclesiastically flavoured Rulership which affected the relations of Latin Western Europe to its Greek Eastern counterpart. This will form the subject of my next lecture.

[1] Cf., e.g., the contributions to *Naturrecht oder Rechtspositivismus*, ed. W. Maihofer (Darmstadt, 1962) (A).

The Renaissance of Europe:
East and West

I

The stress which Charlemagne laid on Europe can be fully appreciated if it is set against the background of that Roman empire which was represented by its capital Constantinople. For his Roman empire was to represent the rebirth of the ancient pagan Roman empire in the guise and shape of a new Latin-Christian one which was for all practical purposes identical with the notion of Europe. In both concepts the essential ingredients were religious in subject-matter and ecclesiastical in institutionalized form.

The designation of Charlemagne in the preface to the *Libri Carolini*[1] as the governor of the 'regnum sanctae ecclesiae' is important in this context: he was the governor 'of the kingdom of the Church' which for some considerable time had been linked with the idea of Europe.[2] There is justification for saying that Gregory the Great may once more have started a line of development: it was he who, as far as I can see, first associated the Roman Church with the concept of Europe by making the papacy the centre towards which all the torn parts of Europe gravitated.[3] It should further be noted that the concept of Europe was also used with a very similar connotation by a contemporary of Gregory, Columban of Luxueil who addresses this pope as 'the most august and excellent overseer of the whole of Europe now in the process of decay'[4] the implication clearly being that Europe on the brink of withering away was to be saved or rejuvenated by the papacy. The idea aired by Gregory the Great and his contemporary experienced its effective revival by Charlemagne. This Frankish-dominated realm stretching from

---

[1] *Libri Carolini*, ed. H. Bastgen in *MGH. Conc.* (suppl. 1924), 2–3.

[2] For earlier different meanings especially mythological and geographical, see J. Fischer, *Oriens-Occidens-Europa* (Wiesbaden, 1957), 5 ff., 19 ff. and 35 ff.; especially D. Hay, *Europa: the emergence of an idea* (Edinburgh, 1957), 16 ff., 37 ff.

[3] *Reg.* V. 37 in *MGH. Epp.* i. 321–3. Cf. also G. Ladner, in *RAC* cit. col. 964.

[4] 'Totius Europae flacentis augustissimus . . . egregius speculator' in his *Ep.* 1 (*ca.* 595–600) in *MGH. Epp.* iii. 156; cf. also his *Ep.* 5, p. 170, addressed to Boniface IV ('caput omnium *totius Europae* ecclesiarum').

the Spanish marches to the far North, from the Atlantic to far beyond the Elbe,[1] could indeed be looked upon by a contemporary of his as Europe, united under one head, one government, one effective Ruler and, above all, united by the basic ingredients of one and the same religious faith: what gave this entity its unifying and cementing bond was the religious element upon which the government of Charlemagne himself was based. And this faith was of Roman-Latin provenance. Not only was he designated the 'Governor of the Church', but he was also apostrophized as the one who was called upon by divinity to govern the *regnum Europae*; he was designated as *rex pater Europae*, the *apex Europae*,[2] the 'one rector whom the catholic Church of Europe had accepted',[3] in short during his reign Europe[4] was understood as the manifestation of a religious idea in its institutional form, the Christian Church, which itself derived its sustenance from the Roman Church.[5]

Now considered from this angle, the inhabitants of this Europe directed as it was by Charlemagne, could well be called Romans: the Latin-Roman creed turned the Franks, the Saxons, and all the other peoples governed by Charlemagne, into Romans of an ideological kind, Romans in a religious sense. Indeed, the contrast between Romans and Greeks was one with which the West had already been familiar.[6] And by the same token the geographical term Europe changed into an ideological or religious concept denoting the *Romanitas* of its inhabitants: Europe was becoming a community which had undergone a transformation, which had been through a process of Renaissance from the unregenerated, territorial notion (characterized by the physical and

---

[1] For the geographical extent of Charlemagne's realms see L. Halphen, *Charlemagne et l'empire Carolingien*, cit. map no. 1; and the general map in D. A. Bullough, *The Age of Charlemagne*, cit. p. 19.

[2] Cited *PG* 106 n. 2; see also ibid. 63 ff.

[3] *Vita Willehadi* in *MGH. SS.* II. 381, lines 39 ff.

[4] But not only in his; cf., e.g., the identification of Europe with Arnulf's kingdom: *Ann. Fuld.* 116: 'multi *reguli* in *Europa* vel regno Karoli sui patruelis excrevere'. For numerous examples from the tenth century see C. Erdmann, *Forschungen*, cit. 46 n. 2; and for a later age, see L. Boehm, 'De Karlingis . . . princeps totius Europae' in *HJb* 88 (1968), 1 ff.

[5] Genetically this process begins with the papal creation of Pippin as a 'patrician of the Romans' which was a demonstration against the East, cf., *PG* 64 ff. and 466 with additional literature. See also W. Mohr, *Studien zur Charakteristik des karol. Königtums im 8. Jahrh.* (Saarlouis, 1955), 42: the pope had thereby shown 'dass er gewissermassen alle Brücken nach Konstantinopel abbrach'.

[6] See *PG* 62 n. 2 and 466 with additional material. Cf. also Walafrid Strabo's *De exordiis . . . rerum* in *MGH. Capit.* ii. 475 ff. which is replete with comparisons between Greeks and Latins.

geographical features of its natural complexion) to the regenerated, renewed, reformed conception of a community held together by the premisses of the Roman-inspired Christian creed. Here we have a transformation of a natural concept into an ideological, spiritualized and abstract conception – a Renaissance which clearly already formed part of the prophetic vision of Gregory the Great. Hence by the time of Charlemagne the terms *Latinitas – Christianitas – Romanitas* were tautological and interchangeable: they denoted the essential and vital and sustaining ingredients of the *Regnum Europae* which reappeared in the terminology of the *imperium christianum* or *imperium Romanum*. The transformation or Renaissance to be witnessed on the continental-European scale had all the appurtenances of the renaissance which the individual underwent as a result of his having received baptism. Here as there the unregenerated entity – the individual or the geographical-physical territory – lost its naturalness and became 'a new creature' by accepting the totality of the Christian faith.

The ideological concept of Europe determined its territoral extent: Europe as conceived in the Carolingian age stopped where Roman Christianity ceased to be effective. It should be made as clear as possible that structurally and substantially the new idea of Europe was a wholly religious idea which had found its concrete manifestation in ecclesiastical institutions. Hence the development and fate of this new concept proceeded exclusively on these religious-ecclesiastical lines; and not only the future development, but also, and perhaps more so, the confrontation and accommodation with the entity which was expressly excluded from this Carolingian concept of Europe, that is the Roman empire with its capital on the Bosporus. For by virtue of its essential ingredient of *Romanitas* this concept of Europe necessarily impinged upon the very nerve-centre of the Roman empire represented by Constantinople. After all, this empire was the indisputable and incontrovertible historical continuation of the ancient Roman empire. It is clear that the idea of 'Roman' had undergone an ideological transformation. The Roman in the East designated a member of the empire which uninterruptedly continued the ancient Roman empire, and however much christianized the Eastern continuation was, it was essentially and was meant to be, a historically elongated ancient Roman empire. The Roman in the West, on the other hand, was not a Roman by virtue of a historic connexion with the ancient Roman empire, but by virtue of being a Christian whose faith was expounded, fixed and regulated for him by the Church of Rome. It was not tangible history but intangible faith that was the criterion. Once again, the idea of the Renaissance can be adduced to explain the different meanings of the notion of 'Roman'. The one – in the East – was the unregenerated Roman treading the path of the predecessor of by-gone ages; the other – in the West – was the reborn Roman, reborn through the association with the Roman Church, and therefore 'a new creature' which had shed its historic roots and its 'natural' trappings and emerged as a being that bore the same name of Roman, but with an entirely different meaning.[1]

It was in recognition of this different meaning of 'Roman' that Charlemagne in a letter to his colleague in Constantinople spoke of an *imperium orientale* and an *imperium occidentale*:[2] each was a Roman empire, but each in a different sense. The occidental empire was the christianized and Romanized Europe under the government of Charlemagne. From his point of view he could very well conceive of this Europe as a unit because it had one feature common to all its tribes, regions and peoples, provinces and lands conquered and dominated by him, and that feature was the Roman-expounded faith. It is from here that we can understand the deeper significance of the religiously orientated *imperium christianum*[3] which had its capital, not in the corporeal-historical, but in the religious sense, in Rome. One of the best sources in fact tells us exactly this: for Charlemagne Rome was the mother of the empire, Rome in the sense that it was the Roman Church, the focal point of the Christian faith and the epitome of ecclesiastical institutions.[4] But by virtue of the essential religious and ecclesiastical ingredients of the Carolingian Europe, its delimitation from the other empires, and quite especially from the Roman empire of Constantinople, was not difficult: it stopped where Roman Christianity was not accepted. Moreover, because the faith as disseminated by the Roman Church was

---

[1] In parenthesis it should be noted that the Roman in the East had remained a Roman, although by this time he knew no longer the language of the Romans; moreover, his Christianity was, so to speak, appended to his 'Romanity': it was a highly complex make-up, far more difficult to analyse than that of the simple Western Roman whose steps were directed by the authority of Rome (A).

[2] *MGH. Epp.* iv. 556, lines 4–5.

[3] Of which Alcuin had spoken.

[4] See *Chron. Moiss.* in *MGH. SS.* i. 305, based on *Ann. Laur.*, ibid., p. 38: '. . . tunc visum est ipso catholico Leoni . . . reliquo christiano populo, ut ipsum Carolum regem Franchorum imperatorem nominare debuissent, quia ipsam *Romam matrem imperii* tenebat.' The singular form of 'tenebat' can refer to Charles only, but this is often overlooked and the passage given a meaning which may be open to doubt. For a facsimile of this folio of the original *Ann. Laur.*, see P. Classen in *Karl d. Gr.*, cit. i. facing 577. Whether the further statement of the *Ann. Laur.*, that is, Rome as the place where the ancient Caesars had resided, rendered Charles's reflexion correctly, is not quite certain.

for Charlemagne as for his successors the 'true' and orthodox one, the faith of the Church of Constantinople could not aspire to this distinction, with the consequence that it was more than merely tainted with heresy. The right kind of Christianity was to be found where the Roman faith ruled and that was in Europe. Hence for the Westerner the Orient embraced more than would have been justified from the mere geographical standpoint: it reached as far as the 'Greek' faith reached which included the Balkans as well as Greece herself. The West consequently excluded those parts from the concept of Europe.[1] The idea of a Roman had been widened to denote a European. Vice versa, a European was a Roman, and a non-European was Greek.

II

The choice of a succinct formula as a motto or inscription always taxes the ingenuity and imagination of its originators. In Charlemagne's case the coinage of the inscription on his imperial seal is a most adequate reflection of his ideas about the Renaissance of the Roman empire in the European context. The inscription ran: *Renovatio Romani imperii*: it was modelled on the Old Testament idea of a *renovatio* and conveyed his basic aim to resuscitate or to regenerate or renew the ancient Roman empire in the form of the Christian empire ideologically and spiritually dependent on the Church of Rome. We should take note of the depersonalized character of the appellation, for Charlemagne was not the Ruler of the Romans, as the Byzantine emperor designated himself, but a Ruler of a territorial unit, the Roman empire, of which the vital ingredient and cementing bond was the Roman-Christian faith. This is a distinction which is as yet hardly appreciated. It would seem barely possible to improve upon the diction and precision of the formula chosen,[2] especially when one takes further into account the portrayal on the seal of a city gate overshadowed by a large cross in the background under which is written the word ROMA: the combination of these individual pieces yields one sense only: through the city gate of Rome one enters the city of God, and in parenthesis we recall how

---

[1] See on this F. Dölger, *Byzanz u. die europ. Staatenwelt* (Darmstadt, 1964), 282: by the turn of the eighth and ninth centuries Europe excluded the 'byzantinische Balkangebiet'.

[2] See *PG* 112 f. with further literature; and now especially R. Folz, *Le couronnement impérial de Charlemagne* (Paris, 1964), 182, and P. Classen, loc. cit. 595: 'Renovatio is nicht Rückgriff und Wiederherstellung des Alten und Vergangenen, sondern Neuschöpfung.' Further literature ibid., note 300a (A).

avidly he devoured St Augustine's *City of God*,[1] and this through following the Church of Rome. In other words, the city of Rome is here rendered in a wholly religious and ecclesiastical sense as the Church of Rome. Here the Roman empire was reborn (renovated) as the *imperium christianum* because the old Roman empire had already been destroyed:[2] the reborn empire was the new *regnum Europae*. It was the *Romanitas* which made possible this identification of the Roman-Christian empire with Europe. In poetic transfiguration this idea of a Renaissance or rebirth concerning *Roma*, because risen again as the mistress of the 'world', was expressed about the year 805 by one of the contemporary poets.[3]

This strong emphasis on the Roman character of the reborn Roman empire in its European form was very clearly pre-portrayed in the views of Charlemagne as they were contained in the *libri Carolini*: they are a first-class testimony about the basic ideological and spiritual ingredients permeating the structure and the life of the realms under his control. Perhaps no other document of the time reveals so unambiguously the basic concern of the king to preserve intact the Roman-Latin kind of Christianity, because – and in this the acumen and wisdom of Charlemagne as a statesman show themselves – its norms were to serve as the foundations and pillars of the reborn entity controlled by him. The emphatic orientation towards the Roman Church would seem to me the most conspicuous feature of these Books: it is no exaggeration to claim that no contemporary papal communication could have surpassed in pith and maturity the theme crucial to the Roman Church and therefore to the relations between it and Constantinople, that is, the theme of petrinity.

Here I need only give a few instances of the argument pursued in the

---

[1] For its idea of Renaissance, see G. Ladner, *RAC* vi (1966), cols. 266–9.

[2] For this see Peter of Pisa's commentary on Daniel's prophesy of the four world empires of which the Roman empire was held to be the last (Dan. 7. 7 ff.). Peter's answers were made 'by order of King Charles' (*PL* 96. 1347) and were extracts from St Jerome's commentary on Daniel (*PL* 25. 531 ff.). In his c. 45 (*PL* 96. 1354) Peter said: 'In uno Romano imperio propter antichristum blasphemantem omnia simul regna *deleta* sunt' whereas St Jerome had said: '*delenda* sunt' (*PL* 25. 557 B). For this see H. Löwe in *Geschichtsdenken*, cit. 120 n. 82, who first discovered, and commented on, the discrepancy. For Peter of Pisa see W.L. 195 n. 84; also *PG* 234 n. 8 with further literature.

[3] Modoinus Naso:
> Rursus in antiquos mutataque saecula mores,
> Aurea Roma iterum renovata renascitur orbi

ed. E. Dümmler in *NA* 11 (1886), 81 ff., at 82, verses 24 ff. See also the comments on the last verse quoted by W. v. d. Steinen in *Karl d. Gr.*, cit. ii. 24 at n. 34. He became, in 815, bishop of Autun, see Manitius, I. 449.

Libri. The background was the recently held Council of Nicaea (787) which issued a number of decrees claiming universal validity because of the alleged ecumenical character of this synod. It was the claim to ecumenicity which for Charlemagne was the real stumbling block: the synod was convoked by the imperial government[1] to deal with a number of vital questions, amongst others iconoclastic problems. Yet no invitation was sent to Charlemagne, and no representative of the Frankish Church took part in it, although the Frankish Church was by all accounts the largest single organized unit; the pope was invited and attended through his legates. This failure to consult the Franks on matters of vital religious concern to them was something which Charlemagne found difficult to accept, since his own standing as the *Rector Europae* was here gravely affected. And yet, although the synod was clearly only a torso, it had, according to Charlemagne, the temerity and arrogance to clothe its decrees with universal validity. Throughout the *Libri* there is a studied emphasis on the fundamental divergencies between Orient and Occident and therefore the constant recurrence to the Latin codices and the *Latina bibliotheca* in order to verify a point or a theme.[2] Clearly, the work was one of the earliest manifestations of the youthful, dynamic and talented virility that inspired the theologians around Charlemagne. The perusal of the Latin codices shows in fact what a remarkable amount of early Christian and patristic literature was available and with what eagerness these court theologians threw themselves into the battle with their Byzantine colleagues and the imperial government. The tone throughout was bitter, vitriolic and caustic; to the authors the emperor at Constantinople represented the fulfilment of Daniel's prophesy in as much as he was the embodiment of evil and hostility against Christianity[3] – hence the advice to the Greeks that they should heed the exhortation of St Paul that Christians should not imitate the emperors, but Christ.[4]

According to the *Libri* the Roman Church was the sheet anchor of the true and correctly expounded Christian faith: this role allocated to the Roman Church was indispensable to the programme of Charlemagne, for it was the Roman Church which supplied and was to supply

---

[1] See the preface to the decrees in *Concil. oecumen. decreta*, 2nd. ed. (Basle, 1962), 109.
[2] *Lib. Car.*, ed. cit. i. 13, p. 32, line 27; p. 33, line 13. For literature see above 18 n. 1. For a survey of the *Libri*, though in a different context, see E. Ewig in *Das Königtum*, ed. Th. Mayer (Darmstadt, 1965), 57 ff. and G. Ostrogorsky, *Gesch. d. byzant. Staates*, 3rd ed. (Munich, 1963), 154, which is an excellent and fair summary; see further W. Mohr, *Die karol. Reichsidee*, cit. 45 ff. and R. Folz, *Le couronnement*, cit. 109 ff.
[3] *Libri Carol.*, ii. 19, p. 77, lines 24 ff.; Dan. 2. 40.   [4] Ibid., iii. 15, p. 133, lines 31 ff.

in future the basic religious norms – which is the same as saying that the Roman-focused faith constituted the ideological and religious essence, substance and inner core, the foundations in short, of the realms governed by him. It was to him that the Church was committed[1] and although Adrian I had endorsed the Nicaean decrees, it was his, the king's, duty to protect the papacy against Pope Adrian and against all those who 'arrogantly and in an unqualified manner' had addressed themselves 'to the venerable pope of the city of Rome'. To Charlemagne there could be no doubt that 'in matters of faith the Roman Church is held in the highest possible esteem amongst all other churches and must be consulted on these matters'.[2] The implication is clear enough: the Frankish Church because it accepted the primatial role of the Roman Church, formed an integral part of this Roman Church and for this reason, if for no other, should have been consulted. It was this integrative role of the occidental churches which prompted the authors to strike up all the resounding chords of the primatial function of the Roman Church as the mother-church, if only to refute the 'absurdities' which 'the orientals in their most inept synod had enacted'.[3] This Roman Church, the authors avow, was the most solid and firm rock which had always withstood atrocious heretical monstrosities, and what it teaches must be observed by all, because it is 'without spot or wrinkle'.[4] Wherever he, Charlemagne, ruled, the unadulterated Roman faith prevailed, and in the union and partnership with the Roman Church he saw the purity of the Christian faith preserved.[5] The discord within the Church was due to the nefarious intervention by the Greeks.[6] The work ends with the point of view which will be one of the main themes throughout the subsequent medieval period: 'What is ecclesiastical is catholic, and what is catholic is universal.'[7]

What the *Libri Carolini* therefore wished to emphasize was the religious and consequently ideological contrast between Orient and Occident, between Greek and Roman which was here clearly to be understood as a conflict between 'true' Christianity, because nurtured by the Roman Church and heretical excrescences fostered by the patriarch of Constantinople and the imperial government. The *Libri* were no more

---

[1] Preface, p. 2, lines 26 ff.   [2] i. 5, p. 19, lines 26 ff.

[3] i. 6, p. 20, lines 4 f.; the so-called *Decretum Gelasianum* (for this see *PG* 5, n. 3, with literature) served here as the main canonistic basis.

[4] *Libri Car.*, p. 20, line 38 to p. 21, line 16; Ephes. 5. 27.

[5] Ibid., pp. 21–2.   [6] iii. 11, p. 104 and p. 124.

[7] Ibid., iv. 28, p. 228. None of the passages here referred to is affected by the emendations of Miss Freeman, *Speculum*, cit. 287–9.

than a statement in plain and sometimes effusive terms concerning the role of the Roman Church as the organ fixing the true Christian faith. Hence Charlemagne's anxiety to protect the pope against himself and his insistence that Adrian I should withdraw his endorsement of the Nicaean decrees by sending legates to the Council of Frankfurt (794). This council presided over by the king was meant to be the Western counterpart of the Council of Nicaea presided over by the empress: the self-confident claim to equality of the West with the East is as conspicuous as the crucial insistence that the animating life-blood of the West was the Roman-directed faith. Nicaea and Frankfurt symbolized the cleavage between Orient and Occident, a cleavage comprehensible only against the background of the antecedent ecclesiastical development that began in the fifth century and turned on the question of the primatial position of the Roman Church within the Christian world. The Orient denied it; the Occident affirmed it.

But whilst the tension which the primatial denial created, had remained a purely domestic-internal matter within the Roman empire until the mid-eighth century from the time when Charlemagne himself began to act as the *Rector Europae*, this same tension transferred itself on to a far larger plane: the tension stepped, so to speak, outside the boundaries of the empire and engulfed the whole of the West (at least as far as it was ruled by Charlemagne) and of the East. It became a 'global' problem, in which the chief contestants were represented by the imperial government at Constantinople (and its patriarch) and by the imperial government of Charlemagne and the papacy. The coronation in 800 was the event which lifted this originally domestic and religious-ecclesiastical problem out of its narrow confines: it became one of 'world- politics' focalized in the emperor of the Romans residing in Constantinople and in the emperor of the Romans residing in Aachen. It was at this juncture that the idea of the Renaissance deployed all its potentialities, for in the Orient and Occident, as we have seen, 'Roman' and therefore 'Roman empire', had no more in common than their name: as regards their meaning, they differed from each other as the 'new creature' differed from the 'man of flesh'. The wider significance of all this is that the fifth-century conflict between papacy and imperial government in Constantinople came to be in the ninth century transposed on to the largest possible canvas, with the consequence of a divided Europe because of the division of Christendom: the Latin West *v.* the Greek East. It was in this context that the Frankish Rulers came to play an indispensable part in their role as emperors.

Ninth-century contemporaries considered the elevation of the 'patrician of the Romans' to the position of the 'emperor of the Romans' as a translation of the empire from the East to the West, from Constantinople to its original seat, Rome.[1] Although this translation was declared to be the work of the Romans – or as the papal book says: 'the whole Roman people'[2] – the moving spirit was clearly the pope. But whilst Charlemagne avoided any direct confrontation with the imperial government in Constantinople – the title chosen by him brought out exquisitely his idea of the religiously understood Roman empire[3] – maintaining parity with the 'Roman empire' in the East, his plan was either not appreciated or misunderstood by his successors. For by all too willingly becoming emperors the Frankish Rulers became to all outward appearances what the Byzantine emperor was: however little cause for apprehension there was that this Ruler in the West would implement the world-dominating role inherent in Roman emperorship, a threat certainly was perceived by the East: Constantinople could not conceive itself within the historical tradition of Roman emperorship as in any way limited in scope or extent.[4]

The very concrete and serious problem was: who *was* the real emperor (of the Romans), the one in the East or the one in the West? It was a question to which each side had an answer, and it was precisely this which widened the already deep rift. The gulf represented nothing else but the problem of history and religion (or faith) expressed in terms of Roman emperorship. To the Byzantines the assumption of a Roman-imperial role by Charlemagne (and his successors) was nothing less than sheer usurpation, because historically and constitutionally the Roman empire continued to exist in the East and was symbolically represented by its capital Constantinople, the New Rome;[5] to the

---

[1] See *Vita Willehadi* in *MGH. SS.* ii. 381, lines 39 ff., text cit. in *PG* 100 n. 1; see also W. Goez, *Translatio imperii* (Tübingen, 1958), 73; and now P. Classen, loc. cit. 579 at n. 202.　　　　[2] *Lib. Pont.*, ed. cit., ii. 7, and notes 32, 34.

[3] Cf. also F. L. Ganshof, *The imperial coronation of Charlemagne* (Glasgow, 1949) 14: the *populus christianus* as a community spiritually dependent on Rome; further R. Folz, op. cit. 164 f., 167.

[4] See J. B. Bury, *Hist. of the Eastern Roman Empire* (London, 1912), 319: 'There are many empires in the world today; but in those days men could only conceive of one, the Roman imperium, which was single and indivisible: two Roman empires were unimaginable.' For more recent views to the same effect, cf., e.g., F. Dölger, *Byzanz*, cit. 291 ff.; W. Ohnsorge, 'Byzanz u. das Abendland' in *Saeculum*, 5 (1954), 203: 'Byzanz kannte keinen ideellen Kompromiss im Punkte des Weltkaisertums.' Further P. Classen, loc. cit. 598: 'Das römische Reich war nicht teilbar und ein nicht-römisches Kaisertum für Byzanz nicht denkbar.' Cf. also *PG* 115 ff.

[5] This is also pointed out by F. Dvornik, *Byzance et la primauté Romaine* (Paris, 1964), 106 f.

papacy (and herewith also to the successors of Charlemagne) only he could be an emperor (of the Romans) who was a Roman in the religious-ecclesiastical sense, and consequently, the emperor in Constantinople illegitimately claimed a role which was not his. And by adopting the very apparel and other paraphernalia of the (Byzantine) emperor,[1] the Western emperor had indeed little reason to be surprised at the hostile reaction from the East, which considered this adoption (or borrowing) an arrogation or taking away of their own articles, symbols, emblems, and so forth. But what is more important, by accepting the papally conferred dignity with all possible alacrity, the Frankish kings also of necessity accepted not only the reasons which prompted the papacy to create the emperor, but also the title-deed upon which the papacy proceeded. And for the papacy – as for the imperial government in Constantinople – there could only be, correctly enough, one emperor of the Romans, and for the popes that was the one whom they had created.

The consequence of this fundamental papal point of view was that the emperor in Constantinople was thereby deprived of his inheritance and came to be demoted to a mere emperor of the Greeks or a prince of the Greeks. The larger problem in the background was understandably enough the legitimacy of a government within a Christian world: the papacy held that only he could be an emperor (of the Romans) who as a Roman accepted the primatial role of the papacy. By denying this role of the papacy the Eastern emperors had, as it were, sunk to the level of Greek princes. It is not difficult to appreciate that through this development on the imperial plane the papacy came to assume the role of a central pivot in the European West, at least as far as concerned the relations with Constantinople.[2] The further the ninth century progressed, the more conspicuous the leading role of the Church of Rome became in precisely those matters which touched the fundamentals of public and social life, and the more the West became dependent on it. By the transposition of the religious-ecclesiastical tension between Rome and Constantinople on to the 'global' scale, the whole of the literate West participated in the debate with Constantinople. Above all, the Frankish ecclesiastics considered themselves directly involved and although they did not always see eye to eye with each other, as far

---

[1] Such as the designation of the court as 'sacer', the change in chancery practices, the adoption of secular coronation; the planning of the residence at Aachen; and so on. The imitative rivalry reached perhaps its culmination in Charles the Bald when he was emperor (A).

[2] W. Ohnsorge's formulation deserves to be quoted: 'Das alte Rom vindizierte sich die Rechte des neuen' (art. cit. 203).

as the Greeks were concerned, there was strong backing for the papacy by the Frankish ecclesiastics. For a valid or plausible or adequate reply to Constantinople could only be given by making the Roman Church the operative platform of argument: without the arguments favoured or adopted by the Roman Church there would have remained very little with which the Frankish littérateurs could effectively have opposed the East.

But all this is overshadowed by the effects which the East–West conflict had on the Frankish (and later) Rulers whose rebirth as emperors of the Romans was effected by the papacy. By accepting this role from the hands of the pope, they were catapulted, so to speak, on to the global stage and were of necessity drawn into the conflict between the imperial government in Constantinople and the Roman Church. This was genetically and essentially a purely ecclesiastical conflict concerned mainly with the primatial role of the Roman Church. By crowning Charlemagne emperor of the Romans at the time of the supposed vacancy in Constantinople, the pope hoped to establish (or to re-establish) papal primacy in the East; in this context the plan of Charlemagne marrying the Empress Irene (a project that originated most likely in the pope's head), perfectly fits into the picture:[1] the design no doubt was a serious menace to the independence of the East.[2] Neither plan materialized, but as far as the successors of Charlemagne were concerned, they in their capacity as papally created emperors had first to take part in a conflict with which they as mere Frankish Rulers would have had nothing to do, and secondly to adopt a role towards Constantinople which tied them all the more strongly to the papacy. As we have said before, what was a domestic-internal controversy in the fifth century, had now by the ninth century become a conflict of 'world-wide' dimensions involving as it did the whole of Western Europe and the East. It is time we considered some details.

---

[1] For sources and literature on this point cf. *PG* 97 n. 1, to which I have added a few more in *Rev. Belge de phil. et d'hist.*, 43 (1965), at 1074; see now especially P. Classen in *Karl d. Gr.*, cit., i. 597 f. who is doubtful about the pope as originator of the idea. But 'Weltfremdheit' in papal history is not unknown and has even sometimes led to success. Despite some reservations on H. Fichtenau's evidential grounds, I very much agree with his diagnosis: 'Wenn der Herr von Rom und Jerusalem auch zum Herrn von Neu-Rom wurde, war die Christenheit tatsächlich geeint, musste Konstantinopel sich dem Nachfolger Petri unterordnen' (*Das karol. Imperium*, 85).

[2] This had already been stated by J. B. Bury, op. cit. 320.

III

Liturgy, symbolism, doctrine, organization had developed on different lines in the East and the West: by the mid-ninth century these differences became articulate and led to acrimonious exchanges between Eastern and Western protagonists and antagonists. Some of the controversial issues cannot be said to have reached a high intellectual level, whilst others were inflated beyond all reasonable measure. For instance, the question of wearing beards and long hair was turned into a dogmatic problem the severity of which could almost stand comparison with, say, the *filioque* question; or celibacy came to be treated with an earnestness and intellectual fervour which conveniently disregarded a great deal of Western reality and which prompted some Eastern protagonists to say that through the demand for clerical celibacy respectable girls were turned into wives without husbands as well as sometimes into mothers of children with unknown or unknowable fathers; whilst at the height of the Photius affair Western protagonists retorted that with only a modest regard to the appropriate decorum he had climbed straight from the matrimonial bed to the patriarchal throne. These and similar questions such as fasting on certain days, were no more than mere issues of ecclesiastical discipline and therefore of only peripheral interest in the East–West dispute. The reason why I mention these small matters is that in dealing with them and in trying to demolish the 'heretical' Greek argument, the safest bulwark was the Roman Church: its teaching was taken as the yard stick, as the norm or measure of what was, in these matters, right or wrong. By appealing to the authority of the Roman Church it was evidently thought that the validity of the Latin arguments was sufficiently proved over and against the Greek ones which were heretical precisely because they lacked that authority which the Latin West recognized. In other words, one of the immediate effects of Greek challenges was that strong ties between the West and the papacy were forged: implicitly and explicitly the leading role of the episcopacy in the matters under dispute was recognized – a remarkable change in comparison with, say, half a century earlier when Charlemagne himself pronounced on adoptionist or iconoclastic topics. The reliance of the West on authority rather than the inherent strength of an argument is quite a striking feature.

No pope realized the potentialities of a situation so favourable to the papacy better than Nicholas I, and no pope fostered in practice the already conspicuous Western self-awareness of Europe more than he did. The Photius affair gave him the handle; it was also the affair which galvanized the Frankish ecclesiastics of both the Western and Eastern halves of the Carolingian inheritance into action, with the result that the Roman Church could register the perhaps greatest ideological increase in authority and standing it had so far achieved. A short survey of this highly significant development should show how far East and West had already diverged and how far there was what can only be called a parting of the ways which had, except in name, all the appurtenances of a schism.

Let us begin with the pope himself. His epistolary output directed to the East alone in the Photius affair amounts to nearly 200 closely printed quarto pages in the modern edition.[1] The one theme running through all these official communications concerned the primatial position of the Roman Church and the corollary of the standing and legitimacy of the emperor of the Romans residing in Constantinople. To begin with, it was only in his first communication that Nicholas I addresses the emperor as 'Emperor of the Greeks'. whilst in all subsequent letters he was a mere 'Emperor', not even of the Greeks. Photius himself was given an object-lesson in the meaning and scope of Roman primatial rights when Nicholas with superb skill deployed all the traditional arguments of Roman petrinity which, for him, was the guarantee of true teaching of Christian norms: anyone deviating from its doctrine could no longer be said to have communion with 'the only catholic and apostolic church'.[2] The contempt and detestation which the pope had for Photius, was indeed quite without a parallel in any papal correspondence against an opponent before the Reformation. Photius was accused of robbery and theft. He was said to have occupied the patriarchal chair by violent means and to have behaved like a ravenous and roguish adulterer, guilty of patricide in that he killed his own father (Ignatius the preceding patriarch), to have resembled the Jews who had raised their hands against the Lord and rebelled and murdered their own king.[3] 'When we call you a viper, we don't go far wrong.' Whilst it may well be said that this was little else but a shower of vitriolic abuse and contributed singularly little to an intellectual discussion, these outpourings nevertheless bear some significance: they would seem to show that Nicholas I – perhaps the ablest pope of the pre-Hildebrandine era – held out no hope of achieving any sort of reconciliation with the East. And if reconciliation was not possible, then let them have the full measure of Roman haughtiness and superi-

---

[1] *MGH. Epp.* vi. 433–610.   [2] *Ep.* 87, p. 453, lines 3 ff.
[3] *Ep.* 92, pp. 533, 535; II Kgs. 4. 2.

ority: you employ such bitterly hostile language only when you are convinced that there is no reasonable prospect of arriving at an accommodation.

It cannot be said that Nicholas' official communications to the emperor himself adopted a more conciliatory tone or even held out much hope of bridging the gulf between the Roman Church and the imperial government in Constantinople. Nevertheless, they were more instructive than the corresponding letters to Photius, as they restated the theme of Roman primacy and the legitimacy of the emperor's function in concise, even if sometimes flamboyant terms. The main communication to the emperor took up no less than thirty-four quarto pages,[1] purporting to be a reply to an imperial letter since lost. The aim and tenor of the papal letter was to prove the universality of Roman primacy which, in concrete language, meant that the East was included in the jurisdiction of the pope and that, by refusing to acknowledge Roman rulings, the emperor at Constantinople had lost his status as a legitimate emperor of the Romans. Nicholas in fact began his reply with the blunt assertion that the imperial letter was a tissue of blasphemous and offensive statements which, the pope argued, only goes to prove that the imperial government had never understood the function of the Roman Church within the Christian world. Eastern insults on his own person, he declared, were irrelevant; what was relevant was the contempt, irreverence and blasphemy with which the imperial government conducted itself towards the papal office. For obedience was demanded from the pope as office holder, not from his person: the ancient Leonine distinction between office and person was here applied practically.

> Consider, emperor (!), when the Lord said that those are to be heard who sit on the chair of Moses, how much more reason is there to obey those who occupy the chair of St Peter.[2]

For the Roman Church had received its privileges directly from divinity: Peter and Paul 'were the two great luminaries divinely established in the Roman Church'[3] for the express purpose of illuminating the world: it must surely be one of the most dexterous ways of handling the claim to universality of papal rule when Nicholas declares that it was through these two apostles that the Occident became what it was and that it was also through their influence that 'factus est Oriens'.[4]

---

[1] *Ep.* 88, pp. 454 ff.   [2] Ibid., p. 456, lines 17 ff., harnessing Matt. 23. 3.
[3] 'Duo luminaria magna coeli in Romana ecclesia divinitus constituta.' This argument strongly resembles that employed by Pope Agatho in 680, also to the emperors, see JE 2109 (Mansi, 11. 239 E).   [4] Ibid., p. 475, lines 13 ff.

But – and this was the point he wished to drive home – in this apostolic making of the Orient Constantinople did not figure at all: what figured was Antioch and Alexandria (by now perfectly harmless assertions) but not Constantinople. And how did Constantinople come about? Nicholas knew the answer: of all the Eastern sees only Constantinople came about through spoliation of, and robbery from, other churches; it had therefore no apostolic link at all and no ecclesiastical standing. And as the church of Constantinople derived its whole existence and function solely from the city of Constantinople which was called 'New Rome', it was 'by favour of the princes' rather than from ecclesiastical reasons that that church came into being,[1] whereas St Peter himself 'lives and presides in his own see',[2] which therefore propounded the *recta fides*. It will be readily seen with what ingenuity Nicholas turned on its head the whole Byzantine argument – echoed and re-echoed since Chalcedon (chapter 28) – of the eminence of Constantinople as a patriarchal see – by using the same argument in a reverse order.

In a no longer extant letter the Emperor Michael had apparently referred to the low educational standards in the West and in this connexion had very likely made some pejorative remarks about the Latin language calling it 'barbarous'. Whatever was the view expressed by the emperor, Nicholas in his reply scathingly and scornfully deals with this point, only once more to drive home the papal standpoint concerning the legitimacy of the emperor. 'It is ridiculous that you call yourself an emperor of the Romans, when you don't even understand the Latin language and for this reason call it barbarous.'[3] How inconsistent of you to call yourself an emperor of the Romans and yet in the same breath to insult those over whom you claim to be emperor: it is obvious that Nicholas grasped even the linguistic aside to launch an attack on the (historic) Roman emperor. The emperor in Constantinople was no Roman, because a Roman was he who followed the Roman Church, and his addressee had amply proved by words and by deeds that he was utterly opposed to the Roman Church. Hence Nicholas told the emperor to stop calling himself emperor of the Romans – 'quiescite igitur vos nuncupare Romanorum imperatores' – because he lacked the essential qualification of being a Roman.

---

[1] *Ep.* 99, p. 597, lines 1–4.   [2] Ibid., p. 599, line 34.

[3] *Ep.* 88, p. 459, lines 19 ff.: '. . . ridiculum est vos appellare Romanorum imperatores et tamen linguam non nosse Romanam.' On the other hand, to be *latinofron* in Byzantium was an act of treason against the fatherland: Ch. Diehl, *Byzance: grandeur et décadence* (Paris, 1926), 248; here also 245 ff. an excellent portraiture of the East–West tension.

In the milieu in which the Donation of Constantine was operative, the words of the pope were at once comprehensible: the transfer of imperial power from Constantinople to Rome had become an operational factor in papal reasonings: after all, the Eastern emperors had, by their own conduct as emperors, demonstrated what ungrateful sons of their mother they were.[1] For an emperor of the Romans was he who (Nicholas asserted) received the sword from the pope on the occasion of his coronation, so that he might realize the Pauline word about the purpose of the prince's bearing his sword; it was only he who was anointed by the pope on this same occasion and was thus seen to have received divine grace; it was only he who served the Roman Church by his government and exalted that church and thereby brought peace to Christendom.[2] None of this applied to the emperor at Constantinople who, on the contrary, had furnished copious evidence of his hostility towards the Roman Church.[3] On the other hand, anyone who opposed the papally created emperor of the Romans – 'our son, the Augustus' – should know that he thereby offended God as well as the apostolic see.[4] The pope viewed the division between East and West primarily from what today would be called the political perspective.

Here precisely is the junction so vital and essential for the whole Roman complexion of Latin Western Europe. And it is from this platform of Frankish Rulership in its role of Roman emperorship that the East–West split should be considered. By becoming emperors of the Romans the Frankish kings were, so to speak, catapulted into the theatre of world politics. Created as emperors of the Romans, they of necessity had to assert the very position which was tenaciously held by the Eastern emperors until the very end of their existence: from their own point of view perfectly understandably they considered the Franks as usurpers and agents of the papacy. Having accepted the papally allocated role, the Frankish kings necessarily had to accept also the papal premises as well as aims. And the most potent and conspicuous result of the papal creation of a 'Roman' as an emperor was that upon him as the obedient son of the Roman Church and its defender

---

[1] See *Ep.* 90, p. 508, lines 30 ff.; *Ep.* 91, p. 530, lines 10 ff. This again seems to go back to Pope Agatho in 680 in the already mentioned letter to the imperial government: Mansi, 11. 235, 241. That the emperor was a son of the Church universal, was old Ambrosian doctrine applied by Simplicius, Felix III and Gelasius I. It is not, of course, without significance that Gregory I never addressed the emperor as his son. For Nicholas's view on the emperor as a son, see *PG* 201 n. 2.

[2] *Ep.* 34, p. 305, lines 4 ff.; also *Ep.* 123, p. 641, lines 23 ff.

[3] Cf. the initial statement in *Ep.* 88, pp. 454–6.

[4] *Ep.* 34, p. 305, lines 14 f.

devolved the papal opposition to the imperial government in Constantinople. Consequently, the Frankish Rulers were destined to become the protagonists of Latin Christian Europe against the 'heretical' Greek antagonists: this role of the Franks (and later imperial generations) can be understood only from the angle of the function which the papacy had entrusted to them. The ascendancy of the papacy in these decades of the second half of the ninth century as the ideological centre and focus of (Latin) Europe needs no further comment: the pull towards Rome and the Roman Church was to become, through the transformation of the Frankish Rulers into emperors of the Romans, one of the constant features of the subsequent centuries. Nevertheless, I would like to emphasize once more that this development had a long history: the roots of this rebirth of the Frankish kings as emperors can be traced back to the far distant past – in an abstract-ideological sense, to the fifth century when after Chalcedon the rift between Constantinople and Rome had become a historical fact; concretely and contingent on this historical fact, to the late sixth century when in extolling the qualities of the Franks Gregory the Great had written to their king, Childebert II:

> Just as royal dignity surpasses all individual men, in the same way the Frankish kingdom excels all other peoples.[1]

What had in the late sixth century begun as a policy of bi-furcation[2] on the part of the papacy, became now by the second half of the ninth century a single Latin-European policy executed by both papacy and Frankish Rulers.

IV

Nothing is more effective than concerted action. This realization coupled with the assessment of the Western state of ideological preparedness prompted Nicholas I to invite comments by Western ecclesiastics on the Eastern situation. What this invitation signified was that the pope was sure of the availability of sufficient, reliable and ancient material and support with which to parry the Greek attacks: after all, the issues raised were old themes which had now reached 'global' dimensions. He requested Hincmar and his suffragans to support the

---

[1] *Reg.* VI. 6, p. 384, September 595.
[2] On the concept of bi-furcation, cf. my *History of Political Ideas in the M.A.* (London, repr. 1968), 49 ff.

papacy against the heretical Greeks. The same kind of invitation was dispatched to the bishops of the East-Frankish kingdom.[1] In his circular, one of the last communications before he died three weeks later (3 Nov. 867), Nicholas tried to mobilize a 'world' protest: the Occident should rise in a united manner[2] against the arrogance, rage and frenzy with which the princes of the Greeks – now not even emperors any more – as well as their satellites and henchmen had attacked us, simply because we declined to accept their innovations which in any case contradicted doctrine and practice *in tota occidentali parte*.[3] The strong emphasis on the role played by the Greek 'princes' and their satellites is perhaps the most noteworthy feature of the circular. Upon what grounds, upon what title-deeds, could they attack Latin-occidental doctrine, laws and customs? It was a frontal assault which he launched in this letter; its highly suggestive character has not yet been properly appreciated.[4] For the papal standpoint was based on the thesis of a translation of the empire to the East: a thesis which could effectively be answered only by a recourse to the Donation of Constantine which, prudently enough, Nicholas himself never mentioned.

According to Nicholas the Eastern 'princes' justified their governmental-doctrinal measures by asserting that the capital of the Roman empire had been translated from Rome to Constantinople and simultaneously the primacy of the Roman Church and therefore also its privileges had 'migrated', that is, had been translated to the church of Constantinople.[5] This was strategy of the very first order: by this subtle suggestion of a simultaneous translation of capital and Roman Church to Constantinople and its church Nicholas delicately indicated the answer which had reasonable prospects of destroying this 'translation' thesis. The Byzantine thesis was almost imperceptibly and yet radically changed by this Nicholean strategy, for the main plank in the Byzantine argument had been that Constantinople's position as the capital was the cause of the pre-eminent position of the church of Constantinople.

---

[1] See JE 2880, and also below 160 f.

[2] *MGH. Epp.* vi. 100, p. 601 ff., at p. 605. See also Hincmar's letter, no. 14 in *PL* 126. 93 f., and *Ann. Bert.* 89. We should bear in mind that Nicholas's step was very likely prompted by his deposition and the anathema pronounced on him and the excommunication of all his followers decreed by the 'conciliabulum' of Constantinople in the summer of 867; see Mansi, 15. 803–4.

[3] *Ep.* cit., p. 605, lines 4 ff.   [4] Cf., e.g., W. Goez, op. cit. p. 54.

[5] *Ep.* cit. p. 605, lines 19 ff.: 'Sed quid mirum, si haec praetendunt, cum etiam glorientur atque perhibeant, quando de Romana urbe imperatores *Constantinopolim* sunt *translati* tunc *et primatum Romanae sedis* ad Constantinopolitanam ecclesiam *transmigrasse* et cum dignitatibus regiis *etiam ecclesiae Romanae privilegia translata* fuisse.'

This thesis of the capital as cause and of the position of the church of Constantinople as effect, appeared, amongst other testimonies, in the decrees of Chalcedon and was also re-enacted later.[1] But Nicholas unobtrusively fused cause and effect into one single simultaneous transfer of the imperial power from Rome to Constantinople and of the Roman Church with all its privileges to the Constantinopolitan church. Thereby the Byzantine thesis appeared in a wholly different light: as we shall presently see this Nicholean presentation of the Byzantine theme greatly facilitated the Western reply.

Of the West-Frankish reactions to Nicholas's initiative only two can here receive more than a mere mention.[2] The one is by the bishop of Paris, Aeneas, the other by Ratramnus of Corbie. What these replies again made abundantly clear was that the Greek views were held to be capable of refutation only by firmly anchoring the argument on papal themes. It was not much more than a century earlier that the Roman Church had to fight exactly the same battle against the East singlehandedly, a battle which was still a mere domestic matter within the confines of the Roman empire. Now as a result of the intervening development Western ecclesiastics emerged as equal participants in this what was considered to be the Eastern challenge to Latin Europe.

The details of the dogmatic and disciplinary points need not detain us. By making the legitimacy of the imperial government in Constantinople contingent upon the primatial authority of the Roman Church, Aeneas of Paris went straight to the heart of the matter.[3] In the execution of his plan Aeneas found very great assistance in Pseudo-Isidore: the usefulness of the fabrication seemed fully appreciated by the bishop of Paris. In order to prove – against Constantinople – the sovereignty of the Roman Church he made out that the Council of Nicaea was convoked by the pope, thus demonstrating that the first ecclesiastical council was assembled by papal order and was under papal control: or as he declared 'the pontiff of the Roman see was then held to have been the first of all others', a statement followed by the spurious preface of the Council of Nicaea culled from Pseudo-Isidore.[4] This

---

[1] Chalcedon, cc. 17, 28; repeated in the Quinisexta, c. 38 (anno 692).

[2] For other replies see Flodoard, in *MGH. SS.* xiii. 529 f.

[3] Aeneas, *Lib. adv. Graecos*, prefaced by an epistle summarizing the main points of the controversy; this epistle is in *MGH. Epp.* vi, *Epp. var.* no. 22, pp. 171–5; the *MGH.* do not contain the main work, for which see *PL* 121. 691 ff. All my references are to the *PL.*

[4] Aeneas, cap. 187, cols. 748–9; Ps. Isidore, pp. 254–5; there are some genuine parts in this preface, especially those from the *Decretum Gelasianum*, c. 3, ed. E. Dobschütz in *T.U.* (1912), at pp. 29–30; for the preface see app. III, pp. 85 ff., at 88 f.

sovereign status of the Roman Church evidenced in this early age, could further be proved, according to Aeneas, by the contemporaneous decree of the Roman synod chaired by the same Pope Silvester that 'neither emperor nor the whole clergy nor kings nor people can sit in judgment on the pope',[1] but quite on the contrary, it was the Roman Church which was entitled to judge all and everyone and from whose verdict no appeal lay to any higher court.[2] But above all else, the fact that Constantinople was the capital of the empire, the *urbs regia*, had for Aeneas absolutely no bearing upon the arrogant assumption of powers by the Greeks.[3]

This argument of the *urbs regia* was of course the sore point in most discussions between Constantinople and Rome, since the idea of New Rome had become an operational element in Byzantine ideology. And it was in connexion with the refutation of this dangerous thorn that Aeneas showed a not inconsiderable intellectual and literary dexterity. He managed to quote the full text of a perfectly genuine letter of Gregory the Great – incidentally not in Pseudo-Isidore: enough evidence of the wide dissemination of the pope's epistolary output – in which Gregory succinctly stated that 'who could doubt that whatever might be said about the church of Constantinople, it was subjected to the apostolic see', because both the most pious emperor and his brother bishop of that city had assiduously affirmed this subjection.[4] We are not here concerned with the veracity of Gregory's statement, but the alleged imperial and patriarchal affirmation was evidently held too weak a proof for Aeneas who considered that he had better evidential means at his disposal. For he appended to this letter of Gregory a quite adequate summary of the Donation of Constantine without, however, so much as mentioning that this formed no part of the Gregorian communication. The unwary reader could indeed be forgiven for thinking that the whole Aenean entry was simply a copy from Gregory's Register. In any case Gregory stressed, according to Aeneas, that the primatial position of the Roman Church could also be proved by many other authorities. This general statement is specifically supported

---

[1] Aeneas, cap. 188, col. 749; this is the spurious *Const. Silv.*, c. 20, in Mansi, 2. 623; cf. also Ps. Isidore, 449.

[2] Aeneas, c. 199, col. 753 = Ps. Isidore, 643 = Gelasius I, *Ep.* 26, c. 5, in A. Thiel, *Epistolae Romanorum pontificum genuinae* (Brunsberg, 1869), 399.

[3] Aeneas, c. 200 and c. 201, col. 754, and Gelasius I, *Ep.* cit., c. 10, in Ps. Isidore, 644.

[4] Gregory I, *Reg.* IX. 26 in *MGH. Epp.* ii. 59–60; Aeneas, c. 209, col. 757.

by the just-mentioned summary of the Donation, of which, we are told, there are many copies in the archives of the Gallic churches.[1]

The purpose of Aeneas in introducing the Donation of Constantine was two-fold. First, it showed that the pope had primacy over all churches permanently 'by royal right' – *iure regio*.[2] Secondly it proved the independence of Rome from Constantinople: Constantine realizing that it would do no good if two emperors – the one an earthly prince and the other an ecclesiastical prince[3] – were to govern a common empire from one and the same place, went to Byzantium, but on departing he subjected the Roman empire as well as a good many provinces to the apostolic see.[4] Clearly, the empire of which Constantinople was the capital, was not a Roman empire in the interpretation of Aeneas. In other words, Constantine's place in the West was taken by the Roman pontiff. This, we here read, was 'such a unique privilege and wondrous testament' that it was ordered to be made known throughout the whole world,[5] hence the many copies in Gallic churches. The significance clearly is this: in taking up the cue of Nicholas, Aeneas operated with the Donation and rendered the otherwise dangerous concept of the *urbs regia* innocuous by making Constantinople the capital of an empire – in the East – and by conferring on the pope true royal authority over the Roman empire – in the West. In brief, there were two quite distinct empires, of which one was Greek, and the other Roman. Constantinople was neither New Rome nor Second Rome nor for that matter had it any ecclesiastical standing; nor had Rome suffered any change since according to the wondrous disposition by Constantine it was and remained the capital of the Roman empire. The response of Aeneas, bishop of Paris, would not have disappointed Nicholas: legitimate Roman-imperial power was where it always had been – in the West.

Because it has not attracted the attention which is assuredly its due,

---

[1] Aeneas, c. 209, col. 758: after the summary: 'Haec et alia quamplurima, et ad computandum copiosissima, in eodem releguntur privilegio, cuius exemplaribus ecclesiarum in Gallia consistentium armaria ex integro potiuntur.' The genuine letter of Gregory I ends col. 758 A: '. . . contemnat' immediately followed by 'De privilegio principatus . . . Postquam enim Constantinus . . .'

[2] Ibid., col. 758: Constantine wished that the Roman pope should retain the apex of all primacy over all churches by royal right, and this for ever.

[3] 'Cum alter foret terrae, alter ecclesiae princeps.'

[4] Ibid.: '. . . denique *subrogata potestate* et solenniter *regia auctoritate* Romano pontifici *contradita*, loco cessit . . .'

[5] 'Itaque singulare privilegium et mirabile testamentum toto tunc orbe vulgatum apostolicae sedi conscribi iussit (i.e. Constantinus)' (col. 758 B).

the reply of Ratramnus of Corbie, written in the same year 868, warrants at least a summary treatment.[1] He is a writer of calibre who organized and marshalled his material according to a scheme and pursued a line which no doubt has a touch of originality; the tract shows a familiarity with literature and above all with sources which is quite remarkable even for mid-ninth century standards. For instance, he quotes from, and does not merely summarize, Justinian's Novels;[2] he was familiar with the Ecclesiastical History of Socrates[3] and cited from Paschasius, the early sixth-century deacon of the Roman Church.[4] He was clearly conversant with Pseudo-Isidore and relied on him for (pseudo) papal letters,[5] but he preferred to summarize the epistolary contents instead of quoting the text literally. The work sometimes showed a biting sarcasm, so, for instance, when he asks whether a shaved head or a long beard was really supposed to be a sign of earnest holiness.[6]

Ratramnus largely concentrated, not upon what Photius had said, but on the position which the imperial government of Constantinople had taken up in ecclesiastical, religious and dogmatic matters. He therefore goes, not unlike Aeneas, to the core of the East–West conflict: he realized that what mattered was the government, and not what patriarchs did or said or taught – they existed only on sufferance by the emperors. Moreover, Ratramnus sensed that the Eastern emperors had quite in consonance with the function of the ancient Roman emperors not only not abandoned their claim to be universal Rulers, but had in fact stepped up their claim by this time.[7] Hence the author's special concern with the Byzantines who claimed universality for their legislative enactments. In rejecting the legislation of the Greek emperors or Greek princes – the emperors are never called by any other name – as heretical, superstitious and irreligious, Ratramnus must needs pursue the same method to which we have drawn attention before, that is, he must have recourse to the Roman Church as the guarantor and focal point of

---

[1] For biographical details of him (and Aeneas) see Manitius, i. 412–13. Cf. also Laistner, op. cit. 292. His tract *Contra Graecorum opposita Romanam ecclesiam infamantium* in *PL* 121. 225 ff.

[2] For instance, *Nov.* 6. 1 in IV. 1, col. 334; *Nov.* 123, c. 29 in IV. 6, col. 330; etc.

[3] For instance, in IV. 2, col. 307.

[4] His work *De spiritu sancto* cited in II. 6, col. 266 f.; modern edition by M. Moricca in *Fonti per la storia d'Italia* (1924).

[5] For instance, Melchiades in IV. 3, col. 317 = Ps. Isidore, pp. 246–7.

[6] I. 2, col. 227.

[7] Cf. also A. Michel, *Die Kaisermacht in der Ostkirche* (Darmstadt, 1960) 113, 119 ff., 196 ff. Cf. further F. Dölger, *Byzanz*, cit. 335 ff.

true Christianity: for the Roman Church represents 'the whole Latin Church' and therefore inculpations against the former directly concern the latter.[1]

No validity could be attached to the imperial legislation which violated divine as well as human laws.[2] The emperors' lack of qualification in the matters on which they legislated rendered their laws null and void. They had no right or title-deed to issue laws in ecclesiastical or doctrinal questions and could do so only *tamquam sui iuris*, that is, by usurping this right. In a Christian world it was for the (Greek) princes to learn, not to teach, because they had no ecclesiastical function.[3] By not following the Roman Church they had ceased to be parts of the Church and had become heretics. The Greek princes had even gone so far as to usurp for themselves the *principatus ecclesiae*[4] and the underlying reason for this outright usurpation of rights was the claim that Constantinople had a rank superior to Rome, and the patriarch a consequential superior jurisdiction than the pope.

Herewith Ratramnus reached the heart of the matter – it was once more the argument of Constantinople as the *urbs regia*. But whilst Aeneas tried to demolish this argument by a recourse to the Donation of Constantine, Ratramnus adopted a different approach in which he called upon history as well as upon the source of the Donation, the *Legenda Silvestri*,[5] and hardly at all on the Donation itself. To him the essential point was the historic importance of the city of Rome and therefore of the Church of Rome, because this point was held by him capable of historic proof. For Christ Himself had sent both Peter and Paul to Rome, because Rome occupied the *principatus mundi* and just as the Saviour had chosen Jerusalem as the place of His life, burial and resurrection, in the same way He had selected Rome as the site for the apostles' martyrdom and burial place: as Ratramnus saw it, Christ's motivation for sending the two apostles to Rome was clearly that the centre of the Christian religion should be established where the centre of universal power was.[6] It was in support of this interpretation based on history that Ratramnus invoked the *Legenda* as additional evidence, because in it we read that Constantine had conferred on the Roman

---

[1] I. 1, col. 227 A.

[2] IV. 8, col. 334.

[3] I. 2, col. 288; IV. 6, col. 331.

[4] IV. 8, col. 335: 'Graecorum principes . . . ecclesiae principatum sibi usurpent.'

[5] For the *Legenda Silvestri*, cf. *PG* 75 ff.

[6] IV. 8, col. 335. This would seem to show some affinity with the *Constitutum Constantini*, cap. 12.

Church the privilege that it should be the head of all churches in the Christian world,[1] including Constantinople.

Apart from evidential reasons, the invocation of the *Legenda* had also an added significance, to which I would like to draw your special attention. This source in fact enabled him to present the Byzantine argument of the *urbs regia* and its prerogatives in exact reverse. Whereas Chalcedon and the Quinisexta had made the ecclesiastical status of a church dependent upon the civic status of the city – enactments which had of course specific reference to Constantinople – Ratramnus operated with the historical argument of the Roman empire and its capital, whence was derived the principal position of the Church of Rome: the city of Rome was the centre of the Roman empire, and consequently the Church of Rome was the centre of Roman, that is, correct Christian religion,[2] a point of view which shows substantial kinship with that held by Charlemagne.[3] By opposing the Roman Church the Greek princes were not only heretics, according to Ratramnus, but also ceased to be Roman princes: they were, he held, nothing more than ordinary princes wholly devoid of any legitimate claim to be Roman emperors. Ratramnus goes as far as to say that to the *city* of Rome the whole Occident was subjected as well as Africa and 'nearly the whole of the Orient, with the exception of only a few provinces in Europe and Asia and a few islands'.[4] This, indeed, was the traditional Byzantine argument turned upside down and was its exact counterpart. Consequently, neither Constantinople nor any other city in the Orient or Occident could obtain any powers unless they were conceded or confirmed by the Roman pontiffs: this, Ratramnus assured his readers, could be seen 'in many documents issued by the popes to all the churches'.[5]

In sum, then, the imperial government in Constantinople was heretical and deprived of any legitimate status within the Roman empire. Because Rome was the centre of universal dominion, she was also the centre of the true Christianity which was therefore Latin Christianity. As an entity in governmental or religious respects the Eastern Empire no longer existed in his thought-pattern: it was a province infested by heretics and usurpers; it had forfeited all claims to be taken in any sense as the continuation of the Roman empire or as part of Europe. It is not specially necessary for me to point out the

---

[1] See C. Mombritius, *Sanctuarium* (Paris, 1910), I. 508 ff., at 510, lines 19 ff.; shortened text also in C. B. Coleman, *Constantine the Great and Christianity* (New York, 1914), 224.

[2] See also IV. 8, col. 339.

[3] See above 138 ff.   [4] IV. 8, col. 344.   [5] Ibid., col. 344 C.

similarity between the Carolingian and the Byzantine points of view: the one was the very reverse of the other. What Rome was to the one, Constantinople was to the other. What is common to both standpoints is that the respective churches – the Roman and the Constantinopolitan – were distinguished and were what they were because of the special position of their cities.

To these two witnesses from the West-Frankish realms we may add a testimony from the East-Frankish kingdom. This witness was in no wise equal to the intellectual ingenuity, literary skill and equipment of the writers I have just surveyed. On the other hand, it should be borne in mind that this East-Frankish testimony was not an individual effort, but a conciliar decision. The matter treated in the circular letter of Nicholas I was apparently considered so important that a collective statement was called for. A synod was convoked to Worms for May 868 at which Louis the German also took part.[1] This synod devoted considerable attention to the matter and issued a declaration signed by all the participants, but this declaration became detached from the main body of conciliar decrees and was rediscovered at the beginning of last century in a Vienna codex.[2] Although, as I have just mentioned, this conciliar decision cannot bear comparison with the other (West-Frankish) replies, nevertheless the synodists were quite clear that what mattered was not the patriarch, but the imperial government: the patriarch was not even mentioned, but all the more 'the two emperors of the Greeks' (that is, Michael and Basil). On the whole, the declaration reads like a memorandum drawn up by a civil servant in a modern government department: lifeless, anaemic, dull, but very earnest, though there is one shaft of probably involuntary humour at the very end: dealing with the question of beards and tonsures, the synodists declared that 'if there is any holiness in a beard, then there can be nothing holier than a goat'.[3]

But in its ideological orientation this synodal declaration pursued exactly the same line which we have noted before: orthodoxy was only preserved in the Latin Occident; all doctrinal emanations coming from the Greeks were without further examination heretical. Once again,

[1] BM. 1468a, especially *Ann. Fuld.*: 'Synodus . . . habita est praesente Hludowico rege ubi episcopi . . . *Graecorum ineptiis* congrua ediderunt responsa.' For the great number of participants see A. Hauck, *Kirchengeschichte*, cit. ii. 733 n. 3.

[2] See T. Neugart, *Episcopatus Constantiensis Alemanniae* (St Blasien, 1803), 123–4; the declaration is printed in the appendix IX, 520 ff., headed: 'Responsio contra Graecorum haeresim de fide sanctae trinitatis.'

[3] Loc. cit., 535.

the Roman Church had become the sheet anchor, the central pivot of what was orthodox Christian doctrine. In substance, this declaration did not materially contribute to the debate, since the synodists disposed quite clearly of only a modicum of talent, equipment and authorities. Of the latter, it was St Augustine whom they seem to have known well enough; there were occasional references to, and quotations from, St Jerome and Gregory the Great[1] as well as Bede[2] and extracts from some papal decretals[3] and conciliar decrees.[4] What, however, is of some interest is that they too were quite conversant with Pseudo-Isidore as is evidenced from the quite adroit use they made of the work.[5] Pseudo-Isidore had clearly become known 'abroad' fairly quickly and the evidence would show that the Worms synodists held it in great esteem: it helped them to answer the heretical Greek arguments by its material of indubitably ancient standing and 'integrity'; its usefulness was enhanced by the plethora of post-apostolic Roman-papal decretal letters which spoke, as it were, the purest truth.

The speed with which the responses we have surveyed, were produced, and no less their tenor and argumentation, would seem to furnish adequate proof for the fructifying character of the social Renaissance accompanied as it was by a literary Renaissance. None of these responses could have been composed even a generation, let alone a century, earlier. This soaking of the Frankish soil with ancient Latin legal and patristic material made the Western orientation towards the Roman Church comprehensible. This process was greatly assisted by the pull which the papacy had by virtue of its dynamic policy and its imperial creations. Articulated Western Europe found in the Roman Church the norm and measure of Christianity. The idea of an ideological concept of Europe which had come into existence with only a modest amount of active participation on the part of the papacy, had by the second half of the ninth century found in it the focus of Christendom which was Latin: since the substructure of Western Europe was ecclesiastical and its ideological orientation Roman, the tension and conflict with the Greek world was comprehensible. The Occident was reborn as an ideological unit and had become aware of

---

[1] Ibid., 529.
[2] Ibid., 531.
[3] For example, Siricius' famous decretal to Spain, 533.
[4] For instance, Nicaea I, Sardica and Carthage, 534–5.
[5] They append, for example, to a genuine Augustinian piece part of a decretal of Ps. Melchiades, so that the unwary reader once more may be forgiven for thinking that this papal 'decretal' formed part of the original passage: 531, and Ps. Isidore, 109.

its own past, of its own self. The other half, the East, was seen as an unregenerated, unreformed and a mere historical remnant of antiquity.

It is time for us to address ourselves to the communication which the Emperor Louis II sent in reply to a no longer extant letter of the imperial government in Constantinople. Written less than three years after the ecclesiastical declarations which we have just surveyed, this communication deserves all the greater consideration as it comes from the quarter most immediately affected by the East–West conflict. There is perhaps no other testimony which in so persuasive a manner brought to light the historically understandable but nevertheless tragic dilemma which the Frankish acceptance of the papally allocated imperial role entailed. For it was quite obvious by now, by the early seventies of the ninth century, that the Frankish king as a Roman emperor had assumed the role of perhaps the most vital instrument in the conflict between Rome and Constantinople, since as far as he himself was concerned, the conflict referred to nothing less than the legitimacy of his office and function and standing, and this not within a Frankish, but within the 'global', that is, the European context. There would have been no grounds for friction between a 'mere' Frankish king and the emperor at Constantinople: they had nothing in common and no points of contact. What, for the Western Roman emperor, was at stake, was the legitimacy of his being an emperor of the Romans. Having accepted this position, he had to maintain and defend it, even and primarily against Constantinople. The letter wholly adopted the thoughts which only a short while before had been expressed by Nicholas I. It was a first-class documentary pronouncement concerning the role which the Frankish king reborn as emperor of the Romans had according to his own testimony. What the letter also indicated was an approach towards a fully-fledged Roman emperorship, that is, one in accordance with ancient Roman Rulership as universal lordship: this theme broke through in only one or two places, but this infusion on however a limited scale of the original meaning of an emperor of the Romans, is worth noting

Louis II's letter of 871 was, significantly enough, addressed to Basilius I, 'the emperor of New Rome' whilst Louis himself was 'Emperor of the Romans by divine grace'.[1] This address was in every respect irregular, as there never had been an emperor of New Rome,

---

[1] *MGH. Epp.* vii. 386: 'Lodoguivus divina ordinante providentia imperator augustus Romanorum . . . imperatori novae Romae.' See also F. Dölger, *Byzanz*, cit. 317 ff.

and it was clearly intended to be an insult. And in the body of the letter Louis flatly denied the Ruler in Constantinople any Roman emperorship: after all, he said, his own designation in Greek admitted as much, as he called himself *Basileus,* which was nothing but a king, and there had been many kings at different times and in different regions, and no one would attribute much distinction to this kind of Rulership. On the other hand, an emperor of the Romans was a unique office, a singular Rulership which the Eastern *Basileus* nowhere approached, for he was not anointed and consecrated nor had the pope any role in his creation. All this was one more sign that his function was not divinely approved; papal imposition of hands and papal prayers were guarantees that the Ruler was emperor of the Romans, but all this was absent in the case of the *Basileus* who on no account could consider himself to be called to the government of the Romans and of the Roman empire. It was, on the other hand, by the assent of God and the judgment of the Church and its supreme pontiff that after having been papally anointed his ancestors and he himself (Louis II) obtained Roman Rulership. Hence he says 'we are the successors of the ancient emperors'.[1]

The essence of the letter concerned itself, however, with the reborn Frankish king as emperor of the Romans. For this latter office did not indicate that its holder belonged to a particular nation or family or tribe, but rather expressed a new idea in old clothing and old nomenclature. Admittedly he, Louis II, was a Frank, but this did not preclude him from becoming an emperor of the Romans, just as at an earlier stage Spaniards had become Roman emperors. This concept of Rulership was not the expression of a biological or physiological or linguistic or historical or natural qualification, but rested on the Ruler's being a Roman in the sense of a follower, defender and protector of the Roman Church. Here the idea of Rulership resting on foundations other than those of a physical or purely human kind, reached its genetically and historically understandable apogee. Hence the emphasis of Louis II on the indispensable role of the pope in the creation of the emperor: both the unction and coronation performed by the pope were the means which brought about the Renaissance of the Frankish king as Roman emperor.[2] The emperor in Constantinople, therefore,

---

[1] Ibid., p. 388, lines 1 ff.

[2] See especially p. 389, lines 4 ff. and lines 8–9; further lines 29 f.: 'Ergo cum ita sit, cur nos satagis reprehendere, quoniam *ex Francis oriundi Romani* moderamur *habenas imperii* . . .?'

M

should no longer think it strange that the Western Rulers called themselves 'not emperors of the Franks, but emperors of the Romans'.[1] This idea of the king's rebirth as an emperor of the Romans emerges also in the same context of the letter where Louis compared the anointing by the pope with the anointing of David by Saul: for the whole substance of unction was that it effected a change in the man: 'you shall (prophesy and) be *turned into* another man'.[2] The Byzantine Rulers on the other hand who were not anointed at all, were unable even to begin to appreciate the profundity of the development in the West – that was the message which Louis II wished to convey.

According to Louis II there were also specific reasons why this development was divinely decreed to take place in the West, and not in Byzantium. Not only was the Byzantine exposition of the faith wrong and therefore heretical – *kakodosia* – and it was not to be presumed that divinity would appoint a heretic as Ruler over those who had the true faith and doctrine – *orthodosia* – but above all it was the predecessors of the present Byzantine Rulers who had literally speaking deserted the city of Rome and the see of the Roman empire, and had thereby exposed the Roman population to hazards: and by now they had even lost the language of the Roman emperors; they had departed to a new city, and joined a different nation, and thus forfeited all their Roman claims.[3] Hence, just as God could produce children from stones, in the same way could He bring forth Roman emperors from the Franks, and the divine prophecy was especially applicable to the *Basileus*: 'the kingdom of God shall be taken from you and given to the nation bringing forth the fruits thereof'.[4] The Rulers in Constantinople were Greeks.

In sum, then, Roman emperorship was an office which only a Roman in the religious and ecclesiastical sense could fill, because it was exercised in the service of the Roman Church. The concept was detached from its historic connexion and had become wholly ecclesiastical. Seen from a different angle, it was the manifestation of the idea of a Renaissance concerning the highest available Rulership.[5] A Roman

---

[1] 'Non Francorum, sed Romanorum imperatores,' ibid. p. 389, line 2.

[2] I Kgs. 10. 6; 16. 13.

[3] *Ep.* cit. p. 390, lines 4 ff.

[4] Matt. 3. 9; 21. 43.

[5] Almost the same arguments in the report by Anastasius the Librarian (who probably drafted Louis's letter) on the Council of Constantinople of 870: *MGH. Epp.* vii. 403 ff., esp. 410 ff.; a true Roman emperor could only be he who acknowledged Roman-ecclesiastical primacy, p. 412, lines 1 ff.

was a Latin Christian which was the same as saying that Latin Christianity constituted the life-blood and cementing bond of Western Europe: the East was Greek and therefore outside Europe. The reasons which made the Roman Church the nerve-centre and focal point of Western Europe in this scheme of things, should now be accessible to understanding. I cannot conclude without inviting your attention once more to the progress which an idea had made during the course of exactly a century: you recall that Charlemagne was hailed, and to all intents and purposes was, *Rector Europae*, and now in the seventies of the ninth century, the same appellation was conferred on Pope John VIII. It was this very same pope who had perfected the papal theme of Roman emperorship doctrinally and practically: it was he who on his own volition and resting entirely on papal primatial rights created the emperor of the Romans 'who was desired and postulated and elected by us, predestined and called by God for the sake of defending the Christian religion'.[1] No wonder this pope, a true emperor-maker, was called *Rector Europae*.[2]

After this rapid survey, I believe one inescapable conclusion emerges. Whatever guises, nomenclatures, rationalizations were employed, whatever religious, biblical, dogmatic or governmental grounds were advanced, Rulers (be they now kings, popes, emperors), littérateurs, thinkers, or ecclesiastics immersed in practical concerns, in brief whoever acted or expressed his thoughts in an articulate manner, amply testified to Europe's having become aware of itself as an entity with a common and readily comprehensible physiognomy. Europe did not constitute an economic unit in the shape of a common market, nor was it a pluralistic society, but an ideological, Latin-orientated community with common interests, aspirations and objects. The core of this community was identity of (not political, economic or even by now cultural, but) basic religious norms and principles. It was this sameness, albeit confined to basic matters affecting the fabric of the unit, which gave Europe its individuality. And this indeed seems to me the deeper significance of the Carolingian Renaissance that it replaced naturally and historically grown institutions by others which originated

[1] Some of these terms chosen by John VIII were Pauline; cf. Ephes. 1. 4–5 and Rom. 8. 29. The quotation is from his Ravenna speech, ed. cit. (above 123 n. 3), 307.

[2] See *Chron. Novaliciense* in *MGH. SS.* vii. 122, lines 26 f., to which J. Fischer, op. cit. 95, makes reference. For the role of John VIII as emperor-maker and the decisive contribution he made to the theme of the function of the pope as the creative organ of the emperor, see *PG* 161 ff.

wholly in the realm of ideas, in the realm of the spirit. Thereby something new had come into being, something that lived on norms and laws different from those which it replaced. And the result was a rebirth of Europe, which was no longer a purely geographical, physical term, but an ideological concept which from the ninth century onwards began to develop on its own bases and thereby its own history. It is a history which is founded in the religious-ecclesiastical thoughts and actions and institutions as they were evolved by the men of the Carolingian age whose heirs we are.

The Carolingian Bequest

In choosing the Carolingian bequest as the subject of my last lecture instead of offering a concluding summary, I am not unaware of the inevitable shortcomings which this approach to the subject involves. But I am inclined to think that it may perhaps be more useful and possibly even provoke agreement or, as the case may be, constructive disagreement, if now that we have surveyed at least some landmarks of the Carolingian landscape, we try to find out how far further historical development was influenced by the developments in the Carolingian epoch. It is indeed painfully obvious that the greater part of the tenth century witnessed not so much a decline as a virtual collapse of public order and safety in some of the regions which had once made up the East and West-Frankish realms. It would nevertheless be erroneous to hold that this collapse was general and that it also affected all branches of intellectual activities, including the science of government; and it would be grievously wrong to say that because the brisk Carolingian activity had been merely ephemeral and only effective on the surface, there had been nothing from which the immediately succeeding period could have benefited. I would think that juxtaposing the age preceding the Carolingian era and the one immediately following it, the latter still compares very favourably with the former in whatever field you care to draw comparisons. That the great intellectual advance – great in respect of quantity, quality and speed – of the Carolingian period could not very well have been sustained much longer, would seem to me easily explicable, if one gives due consideration to the common historically vouched phenomenon that after a period of concentrated and accelerated development there sets in a period which in comparative terms appears as one of stagnation or at any rate of retardation. The drive, the impetus and the vivifying stimulus appear to have spent themselves. The situation was aggravated by a number of external factors, such as the ending of the Carolingian line itself and its concomitant unsettling and disintegrating effects, the continued raids by land and by sea from the Vikings, the undeniable economic decline hastened by a series of bad harvests, and so on.

But even so, the advance continued, though on a much reduced scale: in coronation liturgy, for instance, the tenth century has bequeathed to us the permanent German orders and their offshoots: it was also in the same century that the English orders were to receive their structural fixation. In regard to public documents the *Diplomata* of the Saxon period belong to the finest diplomatic productions of the Middle Ages. It was in the otherwise much maligned tenth century that some of the most influential monastic foundations emerged – witness Cluny, Brogne, Gorze, Fruttuaria – and their impact upon society was detectable in the tenth as much as in the eleventh centuries. What is also frequently overlooked is that in the tenth century a great many and very important collections were made especially of the canon law – here I am considering only the contributions which were made North of the Alps – and it was these which to a not negligible extent transmitted the numerous synodal and canonical enactments of the Carolingian period to later ages, notably to Burchard in the early eleventh century and to the predecessors of Gratian in the latter part of the eleventh century; that Gratian himself drew heavily on the Carolingian legal material, is evident. Nor should we leave out of account the typically native artistic and cultural and literary revival upon which has been bestowed the name of the Ottonian Renaissance with its remarkable predilection for ancient Roman manifestations of the creative spirit. In this context special mention must be made of historiography which in the tenth century approaches professional standards and by far surpasses Carolingian historiography. It was also in this same tenth century that medical as well as mathematical studies made great strides; it was this same century which witnessed the foundation of the school of Chartres.

But about these influences I do not wish to speak. To catalogue the fate of the numerous individual strains of Carolingian provenance would be out of place in a concluding lecture which must adopt a broader viewpoint. What would seem to me a more profitable task would be an attempt to show in what cardinal respects the Carolingian age can be considered relevant to the historical development of the subsequent medieval period. The details will have to be worked out on another occasion, but what I am here concerned with is the question: how far did the Carolingian development furnish a demonstrable explanation for some at least of the more conspicuous historical features of medieval Europe which, in their turn, may even have contributed, albeit in an indirect way, to the making of modern Europe?

I

There is considerable justification for saying that the clericalization of public government, of public officers and services, was perhaps the most easily detectable bequest of the Carolingian era. Here only two outstanding forms of public government can be made the subject of a few remarks, the Roman-imperial idea of Rulership and, on a narrower, confined, but perhaps more important level, the idea of kingship. That as far as the West of Europe was concerned, the Roman-imperial idea of Rulership saw its initiation in the Carolingian period, is plain enough. The development thus set on foot produced repercussions and re-echoed down the Middle Ages and beyond. In order to appreciate the effect which the idea of Roman emperorship had it is worth while to emphasize again the incontrovertible fact that this Western Roman emperor constituted primarily a constructive device which the papacy employed in order to restore Rome and herewith the Roman Church to the position which it merited in an orthodox Roman-Christian world. For this position was denied to the Roman Church by the imperial government in Constantinople since it refused to acknowledge the primatial function of the papacy. According to papal reasoning, this refusal was based on false premisses and heretical views and therefore as advocates and defenders of heretical opinions these Eastern emperors could not be at the same time Roman emperors which position was understandably enough reserved for those Rulers who had proved themselves advocates and defenders of the orthodox, Roman-Christian point of view. Hence according to the papal standpoint, the empire in the East had ceased to be Roman.[1]

It was precisely the *Selbstverständnis* of the papacy as an institution of universal standing, authority and scope which explains the dynamic policy it pursued towards the East: for on its own premisses it could not acquiesce in the flat refusal of and hostile attitude of Byzantium to what it itself considered its own legitimate right divinely and uniquely conferred. Since it was a universal institution – at no time of its existence had the papacy any doubt whatsoever on this score – it had to view the Byzantine reactions to its claims as recalcitrant obstructionism, intolerable and reprehensible from the religious-ecclesiastical point of view, in short, heretical. This idea of universality entertained by the papacy, was, however, only a mirror of that kind

[1] For this see above 144 f., 148 ff.

of universality with which Christianity was at all times credited. In actual fact the theme of papal universality was indissolubly linked with the theme of universality inherent in Christianity itself. The papacy considered itself the epitome, the quintessence of all the universality embodied in the theme of Christianity.

Now the creation by the papacy of a Roman emperor in the West was, again incontestably, the result of precisely these thought-processes which I have just tried to present. The creation of the Roman emperor by the pope was the practical application of the Pauline and Isidorian points of view on a universal scale, for this emperor was brought into being by the universal institution of the papacy. Differently expressed, because created by the papacy, the Western Roman emperor was a reflexion of the universality which was epitomized in the Roman Church. Herewith, however, *Romanitas* and *Christianitas* flowed into one broad stream and became indistinguishable. It was the papally created, that is, reborn, Roman emperor who was to embody the confluence of the two streams in his own person, in his function and position, with the consequence that Constantinople was most directly affected by this claim to universality which in reality and in practice was a claim to universal jurisdiction. Pope as well as Western emperor shared the religious and ideological hostility to Constantinople. Consequently, the emperor of the Romans created by the papacy was, as I have termed it, a constructive device to restore the Roman Church to the universal standing and function which was its due in a Christian world. That it was on the basis of these considerations that at a later age the allegory of the sun (pope) and of the moon (emperor) arose, deserves only a passing remark. What deserves more attention is that through this development in the tenth century[1] and no less in the eleventh century (a development conditioned by the rapidly evolving papal-imperial theme) the way was cleared for the assumption of a fully-fledged Roman emperorship in the ancient sense by the Staufen dynasty. Then indeed ideological hostility towards Constantinople was to change into ideological aggression against New Rome: comprehensible enough, since the Byzantine claim to universal dominion – the

---

[1] The inscription on Charles the Bald's imperial seal was: *Renovatio imperii Romanorum et Francorum*, whilst Otto I on occasions styled himself 'Imperator Romanorum et Francorum', see DO. I. 318 (p. 432); 322 (p. 436); 324 (p. 439); 329 (p. 443); cf. also DO. I. 346 (p. 473): 'Romanorum imperator.' For an excellent introduction to the re-establishment of the empire in the tenth century, see R. Folz, *La naissance du saint-empire* (Paris, 1967) with translations from numerous chronicles, such as Flodoard, Widukind, Thietmar, etc.

very inheritance of ancient Rome – had never been given up, and by the Staufen policy it was actively and concretely challenged.

All this was clearly pre-portrayed by the dynamic policy of the papacy during the Carolingian epoch; all the essential ingredients were there, ideologically and symbolically – such as the conferment of the sword on the occasion of the coronation, the crowning with (Constantine's) crown, all accompanied with appropriate prayers, and so on – as well as liturgically, sacramentally and doxologically, such as the administration of the imperial unction, the sacramental conferment of grace and the employment of such characteristic prayer texts as the famous Latin Good Friday text of fifth-century origin, according to which it was the duty of the emperor to propagate the Christian faith and to subject all barbarian nations to his rule.[1] The coalescence of the universality enshrined in the (ancient) idea of Roman emperorship and of the universality enshrined in Christianity was thus powerfully prepared. It is therefore of some moment to stress that, so to speak, looking outward, both pope and Western emperor moved *pari passu* and were in complete harmony.

The missionary activity of the German Roman emperors was certainly furthered by the assumption of the universalist role which this Roman-Christian emperor represented and which in fact the just-mentioned Good Friday prayer imposed on him as a duty. Already in the ninth century it was held by no lesser authority than Agobard of Lyons that this duty devolved upon the Western emperor as 'head of the world' (*caput orbis*).[2] Hence a good deal of the so-called Eastern-European colonization by Germany or the euphemistically called Christianization of pagan territories could be undertaken under this umbrella; in particular the vast Slav districts in the North-East of Europe, constituted a constant attraction for the Roman emperors; thereby the frontiers of a purely Germanic kingdom came to be widened, for from the tenth century onwards as German kings these Roman emperors had few, if any, title-deeds to expand, just as the French or the English kings had none. But there was the claim to universality which furnished, if not a rationalization of the policy of expansion, at any rate an additional justification for these expansive missionary activities.[3]

---

[1] For the text said during coronation mass, see R. Elze (ed.), *Ordines coronationis imperialis* (Hannover, 1960), ii. 9, p. 6.

[2] Agobard of Lyons, in *MGH. SS.* xv. 275 f.

[3] For sources see W. Ullmann in *Trans. Royal Hist. Soc.*, 14 (1964), 98–100; F. Dölger, *Byzanz*, cit. 263, 340: German missionary activity not merely a cultural enterprise, but a

Let us, however, be clear about the difference in one point between this Western conception of the Roman-Christian emperor and his Eastern counterpart. At the coronation of the Eastern emperor no such prayer as the Good Friday prayer was said over him nor did he consider himself as an organ to spread Christianity by missionary enterprises: he was already the kosmokrator, the earthly representative of the heavenly pantokrator – he was already, in idea at least, a universal Ruler for whom there existed no need to prove and to assert his universality. In other words, the Roman empire over which he presided was the continuation of the ancient one and there was no suggestion that it was created for the sake of propagating the gospel.[1] For the Western emperor, however, the acceptance of the function of Roman emperor entailed serious conflict with the Eastern emperor who on his side sensed the attack on his most treasured and also most sensitive governmental function, that of his being the world's true monarch, the kosmokrator. As I have said, ideological hostility led to aggressive actions. In pursuit of his Roman-imperial policy Barbarossa was to claim that the *regnum Graeciae* – we note in parenthesis the choice of terms – was to be subjected to himself, because he alone was the *unus monarchos*, the one emperor of the Romans, as the Greek emperor was told in threatening language in 1189. Clearly enough, the Western claim to universality was on the point of being realized – and after fifteen years it was the papacy which had every reason to say that its primacy was now also fully established in the East: the church of Constantinople, Innocent III exclaimed after the fourth crusade in 1204, had now returned to her mother, the Roman Church.[2]

This 'common and harmonious interest' of pope and the Western emperor in Eastern affairs had its contrasting counterpart on the internal-domestic scene. Looking outward to Constantinople, pope and emperor were animated by identity of language, aim and aspirations, but looking inward a picture emerges which in all essentials is the very reverse, for this was dominated by what we may call thinking on different tiers or levels. The creation of the Western emperor was

pushing eastwards of ethnic boundaries; this led to Germanization of considerable regions in Eastern Europe.

[1] Cf. O. Treitinger, *Die oström. Kaiser- und Reichsidee*, 2nd ed. (Darmstadt, 1956), 9, 27 ff., 160; A. Michel, *Kaisermacht*, cit. 168 ff., also F. Dölger, op. cit. locc. citt.

[2] Innocent III in his *Reg.* VII. 203; VIII. 19, 24, 153; in *Reg.* VIII. 26 he applies the idea of rebirth to the church of Constantinople as a result of the Latin conquest ('Cum ecclesia Constantinopolitana in *novam* nunc quodammodo *infantiam renascatur* . . .'); see further his *Regestum super negotio Romani imperii*, no. 113.

the papal application of Pauline and Isidorian doctrine. In other words, he was created for specific purposes by the pope as an officer on a universal scale with the title of Emperor of the Romans. The clearest proof of his being no more than an officer lies in the absence of any enthronement: of course, an officer never sat on a throne, and the whole symbolism of a throne was quite inapplicable to the papally created emperor, who never possessed an imperial throne. It never existed, because there was no need for one. The underlying and basic presupposition was that the making of an emperor represented the exercise of the true sovereign will of the successor of St Peter, or in papal language was the deployment of the apostolic favour or apostolic grace (the *favor apostolicus* or the *gratia apostolica*) which transformed a mere king into an emperor of the Romans. There never was and there never could be an emperor without the operation of papal favour: vice versa, there was no right to emperorship, according to the papal standpoint, however much this right was asserted by unsuccessful imperial candidates. This is abundantly borne out by the structure of all imperial coronation orders and is also borne out by the supplications of all the kings desirous of being made emperors by the pope. In brief, this Western emperor of the Romans was made and was, logically enough, also on occasions unmade, by the pope.

What this papal ideology revealed was the absence of autonomy on the part of the emperor: he was crowned and called Emperor of the Romans and yet lacked the most conspicuous attribute of any Ruler – autonomy in his function as emperor. He had not even a throne on which he could sit and had to be satisfied with a mere royal throne, in no wise different from the Danish, English, French and other kings – those very kings whom the emperors or their ghost-writers condescendingly deigned to call 'kinglets' (*reguli*). Hence, as soon as the intoxicating effects of the imperial coronation and banquet had worn off, the gulf between form and substance was too conspicuous to be overlooked by the Western Roman emperor who could not even call Rome his capital and had to undertake innumerable military campaigns to assert and to reassert himself as a Ruler in at least some parts of Italy. The essence of the difference between the papal and Western imperial standpoints concerned the function, standing, authority and above all the sovereign autonomy of the emperor: was he only a Roman emperor in name or also in substance? That the situation harboured plenty of explosive ammunition is clear enough and is all too amply demonstrated by the ferocity of the quarrels between empire and papacy in the high Middle Ages. A vast amount of energy was spent on both sides which could well have been more usefully devoted to other tasks. This papal-imperial spectre, too, is part, and I am inclined to think, an essential part, of the Carolingian bequest and deserves to be seen in its historic and genetic context.

II

Turning now to the regional kingdoms we can say without fear of contradiction that the effects of the Carolingian development were felt both in a direct and indirect way. In regard to the concept of theocratic kingship itself I do not think much detailed commentary is called for: throughout medieval Europe, including the Eastern regions, once they were opened up, this concept became the norm, and it could become the norm, because the religious assumptions of society favoured its acceptance. And once the theocratic presupposition was accepted, the descending theme of government and law also became operative. Moreover, throughout the period the backbone of the royal coronation orders remained as devised by Hincmar. Evidently, it was in some respects only a skeletal backbone which left plenty of margin to the ideologically inclined liturgists of the subsequent ages to expand, to embellish and to rearrange texts and gestures and symbols. Nevertheless, these changes in most cases left the Hincmarian structure virtually untouched – and this is true in regard to the English as well as the Burgundian and the French and the German and the Spanish and the Hungarian orders.

What, however, received elaboration was the ideology that had found liturgical-symbolic reflexion in the royal orders. Above all, the idea of enthronement and the consequential occupying of a seat provided, allegorically, a vantage point from which the incumbent could, so to speak, survey the scene around him; and this symbolism greatly assisted in crystallizing the conception of the king forming an estate of his own, an estate which had nothing in common with any of the estates occupied by other mortals who, after all, were his subjects. What needs stressing is that within the ambit of kingship this concept of the king's forming an estate of his own, produced severely practical effects. No doubt, the idea was originally of great advantage to the king who, from the theocratic angle, could with every justification consider himself free from the fetters that at one time bound him to the people – the very people who were now entrusted or committed to him by divinity. It was in the Carolingian age that the ecclesiastics were instrumental in liberating the king from ties which had bound him to the people, but the advantage which the king thus reaped, could, as indeed it did, lead to severe disadvantages when those who had first liberated him from the people, came to be his opponents, if not his outright adversaries. Metaphorically, one might speak here of the ecclesiastics presenting their bill for professional services rendered. The Investiture Contest would seem to provide an excellent illustration of this development. Then, indeed, the idea of the king forming an estate of his own, had resulted in what one might well call the Ruler's isolation from the people, in whatever large or restricted sense the latter term is taken: it was as if the Ruler had to face his opponents without any protective armour, nakedly, and as a prisoner of the very men who long before had 'liberated' him, but from whose clutches he was now unable to escape. Having made their premises his own, he stood alone. The status of a *persona ecclesiastica* was to prove more a liability than an asset. Differently expressed, kingship was firmly embedded in ecclesiology: this ecclesiological theme was perhaps the most original of all Carolingian themes applied in practice. Through its operation Rulership became an ecclesiastical office and as such was subjected to ecclesiastical norms, laws and criteria. The Ruler *qua* Ruler had become incorporated in the structure of the Church.

The ecclesiological premisses of theocratic kingship permit us to realize a bequest of the Carolingian era which has hardly, if at all, been noticed. What theocratic kingship, as evolved in that period, expressed was the consideration that the Ruler's office was grounded in religion, hence the numerous religious attributes of theocratic kingship. The immediately important point is that this conception of Rulership contributed a great deal to the circumscription of regal powers, because the religious norms and laws applicable to Rulership and manipulated by the ecclesiastics, were not only prior to the making of the king, but also entirely independent of him. And since they were independent of him in his function as king, and since, moreover, these laws were basic to his function, the directly emerging result was that this theocratic king was placed under the law. This is a point to which I would like to attach considerable importance and to which I have already invited your attention in a different context.[1]

---

[1] See above 133 f. For a persuasive example of an expansion of this vital principle cf. the fundamental statement of Frederick Barbarossa (in *MGH. Const.* i. 233, no. 167, lines 28 ff.), according to which he acknowledged his subjection to the written and unwritten

Considered *per se* theocratic kingship contained all the makings of absolutism; this clearly inherent tendency of every theocratic Ruler towards absolutism received further nourishment through the application of some well-selected Roman law principles as soon as these were recognized in their governmental and ideological potency. In other words, the undeniably historic attainment of the Carolingian age lay in that the king, precisely because his powers were seen to be eventually located in divinity and expressed in Scripture, was subjected to a set of laws which were, literally speaking, fundamental to the whole framework of theocratic Rulership. It was perhaps for the first time in European history that this was achieved and – the paradox is only apparent – achieved it was through the kind of Rulership which bore in itself all the germs of absolutism. As I have elsewhere indicated, you have here without any high-falutin jurisprudential speculations the first European attempt at establishing the rule of law, in this instance arrived at through the operation and application of the Bible. That under these presuppositions the ecclesiastics and their influence reached a high-water mark, is understandable: the interpretation of the fundamental laws to which the king was subjected lay in their hands.

Whilst the importance of this bequest can hardly be exaggerated, there is one more item which though on closer inspection was clearly there, was nevertheless hidden from vision in the Carolingian period. It came to fruition much later, and powerfully and effectively contributed towards arresting any growth towards absolutist royal powers. In order to appreciate the genetic influence of the Carolingian development in this respect, it is advisable to keep in mind two points. The first is that this Carolingian and post-Carolingian kingship had few, if any, sharply defined contours: it bore the stamp of a religiously conceived Rulership of which the just-mentioned basic law was indeed an integral element, but in which constitutional and jurisdictional functions, in short government, were seen through the eyes of what nowadays may be called Christian morality.[1] This is not difficult at

---

laws, affirming that they were the foundations of his government and that he was unwilling to set these limits aside. For some details of this important pronouncement see *Sav. Z. KA* 46 (1960), 430 ff.

[1] A good example is Jonas of Orléans, *De instit. regia*, ed. cit., esp. cc. 3–6, pp. 138–54. Or cf. the *speculum regis* discovered and edited by G. Laehr in *NA* 50 (1935), cc. 21–4, pp. 124–6; similarly Hincmar's *De persona regis* in *PL* 125. 833 ff., the dependence of which on the *speculum* was clearly demonstrated by G. Laehr, 114 ff. Another contemporary example is Alfred's law book: after referring to Matt. 7. 12, the introduction (49. 6) declares that no other law is required to render justice: Liebermann, I. 45.

all to understand, since the king himself was 'a new creature', was reborn within the precincts of religious-biblical norms. Throughout the ninth century the Carolingians attempted by their own *Capitularia* and their charters to translate Christian-religious precepts, injunctions and prohibitions into enforceable laws, and to a very large extent succeeded in so doing, but there still remained the intellectually taxing task of supplying the well-marked contours which the kingship of Carolingian origin needed; part of this task consisted in the release of the king from the pressing religious appurtenances and their replacement by the juristic conceptualization of his office. This brings me to the second point, namely the assistance rendered by the confluence of the Germanic concept of the *Munt* with the Pauline conception of the king as a minister of God: this ministerial conception of kingship in conjunction with the Germanic *Munt* resulted, amongst other things, in the view – of which we have already the clearest possible proof in the ninth century – of the king as a *tutor regni*. And we shall presently see, how potent, influential and pregnant this confluence was when to it was added one more Pauline point of view: it was a most powerful combination of ideological (and juristic) forces which led to the constitutional entrenchment of the Ruler as a tutor. The charters and public documents of the Carolingian and post-Carolingian time reveal the familiarity with such concepts as *tuitio*, or *tuitio et defensio*, *tutela*, *tutamentum*, and so on – they all go to show how much the king's function was primarily conceived to be that of a protector, of a tutor.[1] This conception of the king as a *tutor regni* was one of the most significant Carolingian achievements. It is in this context of some importance to note that in the tenth century the king's tutorial function came to be anchored in the coronation service itself.[2]

No doubt, the tutorial function of the king was considered a structural element and an essential attribute of kingship. But as yet the

[1] See also above 102, 122 f. But papal chancery practice, too, had thoroughly familiarized itself with the king as a tutor or, later, even with St Peter exercising *manus et tutela* over the king. See, for instance, Alexander II to William the Conqueror, in Deusdedit, *Collectio canonum*, ed. W. v. Glanvell (Paderborn, 1905), iii. 269, p. 378: 'Novit prudentia tua Anglorum regnum . . . sub apostolorum principis manu et tutela extitisse.' Here the pope quite correctly couples the Roman *manus* (which is the same as the Germanic *Munt*) with *tutela*. On the juxtaposition of *Munt* and *manus* see especially L. Wenger in *Misc. Francesco Ehrle* (1926), at ii. 24 (A).

[2] Cf. the West-Frankish ordo (above 102 f.) and see the official German ordo, based on the early German ordo (above 108), where the coronator asks the king: 'Vis sanctis ecclesiis ecclesiarumque ministris *tutor* et *defensor* esse?' To which the king replies: 'Volo.' See *Le Pontifical Romano-Germanique du Xᵉ siecle*, ed. C. Vogel and R. Elze (in *Studi e Testi*, 226 (1963)), 249.

juristic contents of this notion of tuition or tutorship were, as far as I can see, not clearly formulated or stated. The very existence and constant application of this tutorial idea throughout the subsequent period potently fertilized the soil for the later reception of Roman law doctrines and principles, now better and better understood through the scholarly analyses of the Justinianean corpus. It was the application of Roman law principles to the function of the king as a tutor which not only gave precision to the royal office itself, but also filled it with juristic contents and drew sharp contours around the kingly functions. The bequest of the Carolingians then consisted in handing on an amalgamated concept of the king to later generations which were thus given an essential tool, one with which absolutist aspirations of Rulers were effectively kept in check. The tool handed on was ready to be sharpened by thoroughly juristic means.

In order to explain the ease with which Roman law principles were to be applied, it may perhaps be helpful if I invited you to recall the other thesis with which the Carolingians had characteristically operated, namely that the kingdom was entrusted to the king's care. Now this means in brief that the kingdom itself or rather its members were not only subjects of the king, but were also considered to be without the relevant intellectual equipment or political maturity and knowledge: that was the reason why they had to be guided by the king. In juristic language the people committed to the king lacked independence, lacked autonomy, lacked the essential presuppositions for governing. The kingdom was held to have been handed over to the king by divinity in order to be guided by him in accordance with the basic law as enunciated by the ecclesiastics. In the final resort the kingdom was divine property committed temporarily to the king, upon whose death it reverted by escheat to where it had come from.[1] It was divinity's trust in the king as a suitable Ruler which through the working of divine grace delivered the kingdom to him as a trustee. To this Carolingian conception of the king as God's trustee corresponded his function as the tutor of the people. Trusteeship and tutorship expressed exactly the same thing, only seen from different angles.

We may formulate this particular element of the Carolingian bequest thus: the emergence of the thesis that one of the king's functions was that of being a tutor of the kingdom, was a sure symptom that the kingdom itself was viewed as a legal entity or as a legal person-

---

[1] For some of the points here touched upon cf. my remarks in *Individual & Society*, cit. 22 f. and in *PGP* 133, 309.

ality, aside and apart from the king himself. Because eventually laid up in heaven, the kingdom was endowed with all the characteristics of sempiternity or immortality. It was the growing awareness in the Carolingian age that what constituted the material ingredients of the kingdom were the specific rights attached to it, and these specific rights were called, in the ninth century, regalian rights, originating in divinity which had conferred them on the king. Their protection was a vital element of king*ship* which was notionally set apart from the king*dom* as an entity or a body on its own.[1] It need hardly be stressed before this forum how fruitful and stimulating this particular feature of the Carolingian bequest was bound to prove itself.

The Romanist civilians in the high Middle Ages provided the legal clothing for a Rulership as yet largely without sharp juristic contours. A jurisprudential analysis shows that in Roman law the members of a corporative body, such as a municipality, were incapable of giving valid consent. And because they were incapable of expressing a legally valid and relevant will, they were put on the same level as a minor under age or an insane person or an orphan. This principle was considerably extended by imperial rescripts, and applied to the *res publica* itself which was thus put juristically on the same level as a minor under age.[2] Neither the minor nor the *res publica* was capable of expressing a legally valid will. Hence emerged the easily understandable correlate: they needed in law someone who functioned on their behalf and acted for them: they needed a tutor. It was he who transacted legally relevant business on behalf of the personal minor no less than of the *res publica*. All this, you will readily perceive, fitted perfectly into the Carolingian scheme of the king as a *tutor regni*. Moreover, because those whose affairs were in the hands of a tutor were said to be 'in aliena potestate',[3] the tutor exercised 'vis ac potestas' over his charge, with the further consequence that no contract between tutor and the minor could be established.[4] Here we have in fact a most important juristic reason why the king in his function as *tutor regni* could not enter into any contractual relations with the kingdom: no contract was ever established

---

[1] See Smaragdus, *Via regia*, in *PL* 102. 933 C, addressing King Pippin of Aquitaine: 'Superest ut haec *ipsa regalia*, quae percepisti a Domino *munera*, salva *custodias* et operibus pariter moribusque *defendas*.' For Smaragdus see above 50 n. 5. For the sempiternity of public bodies, especially in connexion with the idea of law as their 'soul' (*anima*), cf. *Individual & Society*, 46 ff., at 49 f.

[2] For details cf. my contribution to the forthcoming Memorial Volume for Francesco Calasso.

[3] Ulpian, Dig. 39. 3. 17 pr. with §2.

[4] Gaius, Dig. 44. 7. 5 (1): 'Nullum negotium inter tutorem et pupillum contrahitur.'

between king and people nor did the coronation promises create or were they intended to create a contractual relation.[1] It is as well to draw specific attention to this vital point which in a somewhat amorphous way begins to enter the historic–ideological horizon during the formative Carolingian period and comes to full juristic fruition from the twelfth century onwards.

There was, however, an additional and specific reason why the Roman law doctrine and its medieval juristic exposition met with so ready a response. However strange it may seem and however much the point has hitherto been overlooked, Pauline doctrine powerfully prepared the way for the infusion of Roman law ideas into the kingship transmitted by the Carolingians. That the Carolingian advisers and writers were as familiar with the Pauline corpus of knowledge as modern people are unfamiliar with it, is an incontestable fact. Thus, in his letter to the Galatians St Paul said that the heir, if a child, that is, a minor, must be under a tutor or a governor until he comes of age.[2] The reason was clearly that the minor lacked the legal ability to order and manage his own affairs,[3] just as the slave in the same context was pronounced incapable of entering into legal transactions. Hence the need for a tutor or governor who acted on behalf of the minor as his administrator whose supreme task was the preservation and, if possible, augmentation of the minor's goods; therefrom also – I draw attention to it now – arose the prohibition against alienating his goods: all this was old Jewish doctrine and practice,[4] which St Paul distilled into a short, but highly pregnant passage. We should also bear in mind that already patristic literature interpreted the Pauline term 'child' (*parvulus*) in the sense of 'the people' and conceived the tutors to be princes and priests.[5] Nor, and this is a most interesting point, should we omit

---

[1] I have made this point already in *PGP* 144 f. without clearly realizing the Roman law background. See further my *Papst und König* (in *Dike: Schriften zu Recht und Politik*, 3 (1966)), 52 ff. This does not, of course, affect the function of the king as feudal lord: here indeed entirely different principles prevail.   [2] Gal. 4. 1–2.

[3] See Strack–Billerbeck, *Kommentar zum Neuen Testament* (Munich, 1932), iii. 564–6. The statement in the text is derived from the fourth-century author, Marius Victorinus, who in his *In Ep. ad Gal.* (in *PL*. 8. 1174) said that the sense of the Pauline passage was to protect future heirs 'quoniam ipsi (i.e. the minors) per se agere non possunt nec capere effectum . . . sic enim actor vel curator vel tutor . . .'

[4] For the evidence see Strack–Billerbeck, iii. 565, 566–9.

[5] For the former see St Augustine, *Expos. ad Gal.*, c. 29 in *PL* 35. 2126: 'parvulus, id est, populus' and for the latter see St Jerome *In Gal.*, ad loc. in *PL* 26. 396 C: 'possunt (tutores) intelligi et sacerdotes et principes, qui tunc populo dominati, nunc formam praebere censentur'. Similarly in the ninth century Smaragdus in his *Collectiones in Epistolas* in *PL* 102. 63 A.

to refer to Justinian himself who juristically bracketed the *populus* with slaves and minors under age.[1]

It is therefore of special moment to emphasize that both Roman law and, independently of it, Pauline doctrine contained a completely identical point of view relative to the function of a tutor which, when transposed on to public government, yielded the perfect complement to the transmitted Carolingian kingship. Turning to the medieval jurists we shall find the doctrine advanced that a body public such as the *res publica* 'always is a minor and is understood in law as such'.[2] In fact, there is no jurist who had stated any other opinion than that the *res publica* was to be equated to a minor.[3] And because it was a minor, it needed someone to act as a tutor – there was however no need to create him, for he was already there in his full regalia: the king. This is how the king was designated in the Carolingian era and this is how he was to be called half a millennium later: at the very end of the fourteenth century Baldus de Ubaldis stated that 'Rex debet esse tutor regni';[4] Baldus thus moved, unbeknown to himself, entirely within the ideological framework provided by the Carolingians. Identity of premisses and principles leads to identity of language. Or as another great jurist said, the king was a warden or guardian and administrator.[5]

The operation with this Roman law principle of the *res republica* as a minor under age and the need for a tutor had, understandably enough, far-reaching consequences for the functions of the theocratic king and in a wider sense for the constitutional developments. Indeed, the full application of this principle had, in the main, three effects. The function and duty of the king as a tutor was first and last the preservation of the rights acquired by the kingdom, its possessions and assets, in short,

---

[1] Justinian in his *Institutes*, 4. 10 pr. Cf. about this also P. Cosentino, 'Sul "pro tutela agere" ' in *Studia et Documenta Historiae et Iuris*, 30 (1964), 263 ff., esp. 273 ff.

[2] Cf., for instance, Hugolinus in G. Haenel, *Dissensiones Dominorum* (Leipzig, 1834), §59, p. 299; also the anonymous author in *Cod. Chis.* ibid. p. 169.

[3] In parenthesis I should add that the church too was considered a minor and the bishop a tutor. Cf., for instance, the twelfth-century *Quaestiones Stuttgardienses*, ed. F. Thaner, *Summa Magistri Rolandi* (Innsbruck, 1874), qu. XXX, p. 284: 'Episcopus gerit personam tutoris, ecclesia vero gerit personam pupilli.' In the late thirteenth century cf. Jacobus de Ravanis, *Super Codice* (ed. Paris, 1519), ii. 54. 4, fol. 115: 'Minor et res publica pari passu ambulant . . . idem dico de ecclesia, nam ius divinum et publicum ambulant pari passu.'

[4] See Baldus, *Lectura in tres priores libros decretalium* (ed. Lyons, 1585), ii. 24. 33, fol. 234.

[5] Panormitanus, *Super decretales* (ed. Lyons, 1512), ii. 24. 33, fol. 128 vb: 'Rex est praepositus et administrator.' For an eleventh-century explanation of 'augustus' see H. Hoffmann, art. cit. (below 183 n. 1), 407 at n. 58.

the preservation of its interests was to be the sole motivating force of the king's governmental actions. The king should not only preserve – *conservare* was the term used – but also if possible enlarge the rights of the kingdom (hence his designation as *augustus*); on no account was he allowed to diminish – *minuere* or *alienare* – them. Thereby a neat distinction between the king's rights and the rights of the kingdom was achieved.[1] As can readily be understood, the full operation of this tutorial principle curtailed the king's monarchic functions and confined them to the exercise of his royal powers *qua* Ruler exclusively in the interests of his kingdom; this is the same as saying that the tutorial principle operative in kingship was a highly effective bar to the display or development of any absolutist kind of Rulership. This principle also provided a secure base for declaring a Ruler a tyrant: if he disregarded the tutorial functions inherent in his kingship, there was a perfectly valid juristic reason and justification for declaring his government a tyranny. This explanation, however strange it may seem to modern historians of the Middle Ages, would appear to have at least the merit of being in tune with those medieval conceptions with which contemporaries themselves were perfectly familiar. Not the least result of the operation of the tutorial principle was that the right of resistance could enter by the back door, so to speak: it was a right no longer as amorphous as it was in the pre-Carolingian period, but rather well defined in a juristic sense and on juristic foundations.

This brings me to the second effect. That is to say, this tutorial principle correctly understood and applied was also an important shield for the king himself against what may have been held encroachments on the part of the ecclesiastics. For their demands could perfectly lawfully be resisted by the king's referring to his function as a tutor, in other words, the condition of fulfilling the demands of the ecclesiastics was whether or not they could be squared with the tutorial duty of the king towards the kingdom.[2] That the handling of this principle

---

[1] Cf., e.g., Baldus, loc. cit.; Panormitanus, loc. cit.: 'Bona sunt dignitatis, et non propria ipsius regis . . . hinc est, quod regnum vel comitatus vel alia dignitas non dividitur post mortem regis inter filios defuncti.' Cf. further Johannes ab Imola, *In Decretales Commentaria* (ed. Venice, 1575), ii. 24. 33, fol. 211 (duty of preservation, even if no oath to that effect had been taken); Guido Papa, *Super Decretales* (ed. Lyons, 1508), ii. 24. 33, fol. 108. Hence also the slowly emerging thesis that the Donation of Constantine was invalid because Constantine had acted not as a conservator and therefore not in the interests of imperial rights; see the jurists cited, locc. citt. Despite some recent work on the juristic treatment of the Donation, this whole cluster of question relating to it needs to be re-examined afresh in the light of the tutorial function of the Ruler.

[2] This was often enough applied in the course of English constitutional history when

led to a considerable loosening of the ties between the king and the ecclesiastics, is in no need of special comment. Nothing changed, however, in his status as the personal sovereign and nothing changed in his function as a law-giver – what did change was the scope of his personal sovereignty and the extent of his law-creative powers, for each of these royal attributes was directed by the interests of the kingdom entrusted to him: each of these attributes was considered from the teleological point of view – in a word, royal functions were relative, relative to the well-being of the kingdom and the preservation of its interests.

The third effect is so intimately linked with the second that it might well be considered its appendix. During the last thirty years great advances have been made in the understanding of what is somewhat inelegantly called the principle of inalienability. Now whilst I would like to put on record how greatly indebted all researchers are for the insights so far offered, I nevertheless feel strongly that the principle of inalienability was not one which, as the common opinion seems to hold,[1] was born in the thirteenth century in the decretal of Pope Honorius III (*Intellecto* (1220)) or had developed out of the episcopal oath. What I would maintain is that the principle of inalienability received its juristic delineation, its juristic physiognomy, its juristic outfit and polish as a result of the penetration into the texture of Roman law, but in substance the principle had been there from the moment the king was considered a *tutor regni*. By failing to realize the nature of the concept or its practical impact upon the working of royal governments, current opinion has failed to grasp the intrinsic reasons for the prohibition to alienate. In fact one can go further and say that as far as the existence of the concept of inalienability comes into question, Roman law was not necessary at all. After all, it stands to reason that a tutor's primary duty is to act in the interests of his ward:[2] to give away rights or property of his charge, to alienate or dispose of these to the detriment of his charge would assuredly have seemed a travesty of the tutor's functions and duties. Upon this principle were

---

kings had to refuse ecclesiastical and especially papal demands, by referring to the *exhaeredatio coronae*; for examples cf. *PGP* 180, 311. In France, Philip IV also made great use of this principle.

[1] Cf., e.g., E. H. Kantorowicz, 'Inalienability' in *Speculum* 29 (1954), 491 ff.; id., *The king's two bodies* (Princeton, 1957), 347–55. A great step forward was taken in the excellent study by H. Hoffmann, 'Die Unveräusserlichkeit der Kronrechte im M.A.' in *DA* 20 (1964), 389 ff., especially in regard to the empire (397 ff.) and England (420 ff.). About the inadequate attempts by G. Post to clarify the problem, cf. H. Hoffmann, art. cit. 474; cf. also my criticisms concerning his insufficient equipment in *HZ* 202 (1966), 104 ff. [2] See above for the king as guardian 179 ff.

based[1] the ecclesiastically inspired Carolingian doctrine and legislation as well as the post-Carolingian practice, and the principle itself was – I must repeat this – stated in St Paul as conspicuously as one could wish.[2] The profound impact of Pauline doctrine facilitated the absorption of the Roman law principle of inalienability[3] and its incorporation into the public sector of the law.

It is not therefore surprising – although it has hitherto as so much else gone unnoticed – that Gregory VII operated with this principle of alienability, as if it had been one of immemorial standing.[4] That this showed Roman law influence would seem an assertion that is incapable of proof. His contemporary Cardinal Deusdedit incorporated relevant Roman law passages in a number of places. It is easily understandable why inalienability makes its appearance in the *Liber Censuum*, because the operation of the principle was, for obvious reasons, a matter of grave concern to the papacy, since the census was dependent on the property held by the individual churches and vassals.[5] When Honorious III therefore issued his decretal *Intellecto* which, like Gregory VII's original decree, also went to the Hungarian king, he employed the same relevant terminology – the violation of the *ius* and *honor* by the king – as his predecessor nearly 150 years earlier had done. Here, too, the juristically relevant background was furnished by the conception of the king (or for that matter the bishop) as the tutor of the kingdom entrusted to him. Inalienability, as we have seen, was consequently as much an attribute of the Jewish tutor as it was of the Roman tutor as it was of the medieval king (or bishop) in his function as a tutor. The base upon which this principle of inalienability rested, was a very strong one, but it was the Carolingian definition and articulation of the king as a *tutor regni* which set in motion the subsequent juristic clarification.

[1] See above 109 f., 174 f., and, furthermore, J. Semmler, 'Traditio und Königsschutz' in *Sav. Z.*, KA 67 (1959), 1 ff., at 27 f.

[2] See Strack–Billerbeck, iii. 565, commenting on the Pauline tutor in Gal. 4. 1–2 and the Jewish background: 'Die oberste Richtschnur für die Verwaltung der Mündelgüter war deren *Erhaltung* und, soweit es anging, deren *Mehrung*. Verkäufe, die den Wert der Güter mindern konnten, waren deshalb verboten. So durften keine Immobilien veräussert werden ... auch alle zweifelhaften Vermögenstransaktionen hatten zu unterbleiben' (italics mine). For the Jewish sources, ibid. 568–9.

[3] Cf., e.g., Cod. I. 2. 14 pr; *Nov.* 7, cc. 1, 10–12; *Nov.* 120 p.t., all incorporated in Cod. cit., post legem 14.

[4] Cf., e.g., *Reg.* II. 13, p. 145; also *Reg.* I. 18a, p. 30; further *Reg.* V. 17, p. 379 (page references to E. Caspar's edition); for the latter passage see Hoffmann, art. cit. 392 n. 11.

[5] I have dealt with some of these points more fully in my contribution to the forthcoming Memorial Volume for G. B. Borino (= *Studi Gregoriani*, ix).

I have given some prominence to this tutorial complexion of the medieval king, partly because it is a topic which has not received much, if any, attention, and yet seems to me one which holds the key to a better understanding of medieval theocratic Rulership; and partly because the juristic elaboration of the king's tutorial function signifies also the clearly discernible process of the secularization of the kingly office itself. Let us be clear that the full impact of this juristic development did not come to be felt until the twelfth century, that is, after the shattering blows which theocratic Rulership had received as a result of the Investiture Contest. And this conflict reached the dimensions which it did, precisely because of the theocratic character of Rulership; or differently expressed, it was because the king was heavily overburdened, if not virtually suffocated, by the religious-sacral appurtenances of his Rulership that he was fully and unprotectedly exposed to the ferocious ecclesiastical onslaughts. But – and this is the point I wish to make – through the juristic conceptualization of the kingly office the king gained some release from the heavy religious encumbrances: the regal office itself was to become secularized, so much so that a repetition of the conflict of the late eleventh century was ideologically and historically no longer possible.[1] This process of secularization of kingship seems to me one of the most noteworthy indirect effects of the Carolingian bequest.

At least one more consequence of this juristic development should be mentioned. For a number of reasons I was unable to deal with the contribution which the Carolingian ecclesiastics made towards the conception of crime as a public offence and its prosecution by public authority. These ecclesiastical efforts had on the whole little practical effect: the ancient Germanic and quite primitive tradition that crime was an offence, the prosecution of which did not concern public government, was apparently far too strongly entrenched to be shaken. Unless I am badly mistaken, I think that in this context too the jurisprudential development relative to kingship contributed materially to the strengthening of the conception that crime was a matter of public concern: once the tutorial function was juristically adequately appreciated, it became easier to introduce the methods of criminal prosecution which were alien to the traditional and primitive Germanic views. Was it not precisely for the very purpose of guarding the life, limb,

---

[1] The Investiture Contest was a conflict between the papacy and the king (Henry IV) and must be clearly distinguished from later conflicts between popes and emperors, where entirely different premisses prevailed.

lands and property of his subjects that the king was set up? As far as the subjects were concerned, it was in just this latter respect that they looked upon the king as their protector, as their tutor. Hence, the readiness on the part of most continental kings to adopt the Romano-canonical inquisitorial procedure for the purpose of prosecuting crime, can be easily understood. The conception of the king as the tutor of the kingdom entrusted to him, also proved itself most fruitful in this connexion.[1] The increase in royal legislation concerning crime in the whole of Western Europe from the thirteenth century onwards is certainly a well-attested feature, whereas in England there developed the comprehensive criminal concept of the disturbance of the peace which, in itself, is quite an apt term reflecting and revealing the king's tutorial function.[2]

However much bereft the king was of the means to realize his aspirations to absolutist power,[3] there was on the other hand no attribution of governing powers to the kingdom as a corporate body. The strong and repeated emphasis on the king's function as a tutor signified also the reverse, namely that the kingdom or the people was all the more considered a minor and for this very reason was in still greater need of a tutor. The more the tutorial function of the king was underlined, the more he was deprived of the possibility of turning absolutist, but the more also was emphasized the people's minority status. The king remained, as I have said, a personal sovereign who could wield an omniscient paternalistic hand as a tutor, but there was no assignment of powers to the people, and there could not be, as long as it was legally and constitutionally a minor: it could not initiate legislation or take an active share in the law-creative process. It is precisely here we should remind ourselves, that the great and still so little recognized beneficial effects of feudal kingship lay. However much the concept of theocratic kingship was secularized, it was still genetically, and remained essentially, theocratic Rulership. The king was still the superior, and his subjects the inferiors. And precisely because this de-absolutized Rulership was juristically conceptualized,

---

[1] In France and Germany the inquisitorial procedure came to be established in the course of the thirteenth century, whilst in England there were certainly some tentative beginnings in the reign of Henry II; it is not without interest that by 1160 there was at Canterbury a royally appointed and publicly paid hangman, see Liebermann, ii. *s.v.* Strafvollzug 5 (c).

[2] Cf. Pollock and Maitland, *Hist. of English Law*, 2nd ed. (Cambridge, 1926), ii. 464: the king's peace 'had become an all-embracing atmosphere'.

[3] Because he was subjected to a higher law, see above 133 f., 175 ff.

it led to a stagnation of constitutional developments – once again a conspicuous contrast to the scene where feudal kingship was operative.

The petrification of the relationship between the (superior) king, albeit as a tutor, and the (inferior) populus as a minor under age, led furthermore to an easily detectable estrangement of the people 'below' from the Ruler 'above': being entrusted to the Ruler, the people had not given him any powers – just as a personal minor under age never gave powers to his tutor – and therefore the people could not take them away, modify or circumscribe them. The king's power was still firmly anchored in divinity, and the core of the Carolingian bequest – theocratic Rulership – was not touched by the subsequent juristic development. That indeed seems to me one of the most potent reasons why the emancipation of the people from its stage of minority, why the release of the people from tutelage in the literal meaning of the term, was bound to take so long a time. Emancipation and release presupposed sovereignty on the part of the people, the very attribute which the alliance of 'Throne and altar' for so long denied to the subjects, to the *Untertanen.* What is remarkable is the longevity of this conception of Rulership – just about a millennium on the Continent. The actual open confrontation of the two opposing themes of government – of the descending-theocratic and the ascending-populist – did not take place until, historically speaking, recent times.[1]

These last reflexions prompt me to consider one more and final point which concerns the reasons for the longevity of the doctrines and governmental systems which I have had the honour of sketching for you in these lectures. There surely must be general agreement about one thing: that these governmental ideologies were kept in being long after they had ceased to present a vivifying force and long after the contingencies which had brought them into being, had ceased to exist. Assuredly, conditions in the thirteenth and fourteenth centuries had materially changed when compared with those of the Carolingian period; and this same can with confidence be said about the succeeding centuries – and yet, the basic substratum, at least as far as it relates to the doctrine of Rulership, did not undergo a corresponding change. To explain this by intellectual inertia, or by the inability to realize the need for a corresponding change, or by the incapability to devise an adequate, alternative governmental system, would seem to me wholly unacceptable solutions, because historically untrue.

---

[1] I believe it was the Prussian king Frederick William IV who said in 1848: 'Gegen Demokraten helfen nur Soldaten.'

We may hope to obtain at least part of an answer, if we proceed genetically. The originators, creators and manipulators of the kind of Rulership which we have been considering, were ecclesiastics. And we can go further and say that they had a monopoly of education, learning and scholarship, a monopoly which somehow resembles the kind of monopoly which has been characteristic of most civilized and industrially developed countries since the eighteenth century, that is, the monopoly relating to capital. This ecclesiastical monopoly was of course perfectly attuned to the intellectual and religious premises of the (Carolingian) age: it related to matters of the mind, of the spirit, in short to ideas. Indeed, this ecclesiastical monopoly was conspicuous from the ninth century down to the twelfth, and had grown on native Frankish soil. Hence not only the science of government became a department of ecclesiastical thought, but also virtually all branches of intellectual activity, yet this was basically nothing else but applied theology, and within the precincts of governmental science it specifically related to the themes of social relations and the exercise of public authority. This character of governmental science as a species of applied theology imprinted itself upon all the component parts of the science: each and every one of its particulars exhibited the incontrovertible traces of the paternal ancestry – theology. This is true in regard to sacramental theology (such as the cluster of ideas surrounding the king's divine grace) or liturgy or the thesis that all power descends from the superior to the inferior, the theme of obedience, and so on. There is no item within this ecclesiastically conceived doctrine of government which in the final resort is not traceable to a theological premiss, itself so largely derived from an interpretation and application of the Bible. The consequence of this was that *because* this governmental science was overwhelmingly applied theology, it could be safely handled only by the ecclesiastics: they laid down the norms for becoming a cleric and thus for becoming qualified to pronounce on biblical or theological questions, to pronounce in other words upon those items of Christianity which had a direct or indirect bearing on society and its government. And since Christianity seized the whole of man, the scope of this science was similarly 'totalitarian'. But it was the ecclesiastics who on the basis of their own interpretation of the Bible and of theology had determined the conditions for entry into the profession as well as for receiving the charismatic qualifications. It was a self-perpetuating process which showed all the characteristics of a monopoly and exclusiveness.

Ecclesiastical monopoly began to be broken in the course of the twelfth century when the study of Roman law not only opened up new vistas, but above all was overwhelmingly in the hands of laymen, notably at Bologna. But the effect of this inroad into the ecclesiastical monopoly should not be exaggerated. In personal respects certainly the monopoly was broken, but not in impersonal, conceptualized respects. To begin with, what became juristically conceptualized was the Carolingian-born theocratic Ruler: in other words, the subject of Rulership had not changed. And a large part of the jurisprudential armoury with which this conceptualization of the transmitted Rulership was undertaken, came in fact from Justinian's Codex, itself overwhelmingly manifesting ecclesiastical if not also theological presuppositions. Furthermore, even later, say in the thirteenth century, language and substance and argument concerned with Rulership, were still all those of the parental governmental science, which was applied theology. All this cannot surprise because of the impregnation with biblical, theological and sacramental ingredients which had made the original governmental science at once an ecclesiastical prerogative and enclave. And even when by the turn of the thirteenth and fourteenth centuries a political science in the proper sense emerged, it still exhibited a great many of the ecclesiastical trappings which had enveloped the science of government for the past five centuries: the basic vocabulary and the basic concepts had not changed, however much their contents might have been in the process of undergoing more or less drastic modification. It was this traditionalism which was the result of the ecclesiastical monopoly in all matters concerning the manipulations of ideas and which also entailed a longevity of the traditional governmental theme of the 'king by the grace of God' and all this Carolingian concept implied.

In concentrating upon the theme of Rulership and its Carolingian ancestry I have tried in these lectures to select one particular topic which has always been of crucial interest to society and its individual members. Many other topics either directly connected with this central topic or only indirectly linked with it, have had ruthlessly to be neglected, such as, for instance, the kind of law-creative process conditioned by the Carolingian-coined Rulership; or the effects which the Carolingian ecclesiastics had, primarily in their synodal procedure, upon the development of criminology and penology, for which they had quite especial expertise in view of their own peccatorial science; or the contribution of the Carolingian ecclesiastics to the polemical publicistic literature in which they were true pioneers; and a great many other topics must wait for another occasion. Nor could I do more than merely allude to the development of the principle of public interest or well-being (the *utilitas publica*) during the Carolingian period, a principle which was arrived at, be it noted, without any help from Roman law.[1] The reason why I concentrated on the theme of Rulership was that the Carolingian period was the cradle of Europe in which, for the first time in its history, fundamental questions relative to public government were asked and at least partly answered, within the confines of contemporary conditions and assumptions. And some of these very same questions are still asked today by us, the heirs of this development that began during the remarkably lively decades of the Carolingian reigns. The assumptions, cosmology and outlook of the Carolingians may well differ from our own, but it is precisely in recognizing this difference that the historian's prime task lies – to discover what we were before we have become what we are.

---

[1] Cf. as an early example Lothar's *Cap.* 165, c. 3, p. 330 (anno 825): threat of sanctions to prevent 'ut in quocumque *publica* non minoretur *utilitas*'.

Addenda

p. 7, n. 1: See also Col. 3. 9 and Eph. 4. 23. Doctrine also spoke of the *vis regenerativa* inherent in baptism, for instance, St Ambrose, *De sacramentis*, III. 1, in *CSEL* 73. 37, lines 8 ff., where the *regeneratio* was also called a *resurrectio* (cf. also ibid. II, 6, p. 33 f.); in the same sense ibid., IX. 59, p. 115, where he paraphrased the Johannine passage just referred to: 'Adepti omnia sciamus *regeneratos nos* esse.' Baptism was considered at the same time as the *sacramentum regenerationis* by Hilarius of Poitiers, see his *Opera* IV, in *CSEL* 65. 119, line 15 and p. 201, line 15; the same in Gelasius I, *Avellana* in *CSEL* 35. 419, line 7 and p. 426, line 13; cf. also, p. 425, line 8 ('*renati fonte baptismatis*'). The Ps. Augustinian *Quaestiones vet. et novi Test.*, c. 127, *CSEL* 50. 408, lines 20 f. have: '*Renasci* enim *renovari* est et qui renovatur instauratur.' Augustine himself in his *De spir. sancto*, I. 6, *CSEL* 79, 48 has: 'Morimur, ut renascamur.' In fact, the theme of *renovatio* or *regeneratio* pervaded all baptismal doctrine; for the eighth century cf., e.g., St Boniface in his *Epp.* 73, 91, in *MGH. Epp.* III. 343, line 19, and p. 377 line 10; in the ninth century cf. Jonas of Orléans *De instit. laicali*, I. 2, *PL* 106. 126 D. This theme was even made the subject of a long exposition in a letter attributed to Ps. Melchiades, cc. 6–7, in P. Hinschius, *Decr. Ps. Isidorianiae* (repr. Aalen, 1963), 245 f. For an expression in the high M.A. cf. Guido de Orchellis, *Tract. de sacr.* (*ca.* 1220), ed. D. & O. van den Eynde (Louvain, 1953), III. 19, p. 24. The conferment of a baptismal name is of course closely linked with the idea of rebirth, cf. also below 72 at n. 8, to which might be added the late eighth-century Formulae of Sens, in *MGH. Form.*, p. 208, lines 9–10.

p. 65, n. 1: The same expression (*spiritales medici*) was used by Jonas of Orléans, *De inst. laicali*, c. 10, *PL* 106. 140.

p. 73, n. 2: The Anglo-Saxon council of 787, c. 12, allegorically called the king a *christus domini* (Mansi, 12. 943).

p. 74, n. 3: But cf. Stephen Langton: 'Quaeritur, utrum in unctione conferatur character. Magister (Peter the Chanter) dicit quod non. Non enim inungitur ad misterium ecclesie, sed ut sit *subditus ecclesie*' (Quaestiones, MS 57, St John's Coll., Cambridge, fo. 38va: kind information supplied by Prof. J. W. Baldwin). On the other hand, the papacy still designated royal unction as a sacrament, cf. Alexander IV in 1257, see P. E. Schramm, 'Der König von Navarre' in *Sav. Z. GA.* 68 (1951), 110 ff., at 147.

p. 75, n. 3: Cf. also Optatus of Milève in *CSEL* 26. 60, lines 4 ff., 11 ff. For a later view cf. Guido de Orchellis, *Tractatus*, cit., IV. 51, p. 50 f.

p. 76, n. 1: See also the Frankish Council of *ca.* 819, c. 4, in *Conc.* 594: 'sacerdotes . . . sunt mediatores inter Deum et homines . . .' The designation of bishops and priests at this very time as *vicarii Christi* was to indicate that they acted vicariously as mediators of Christ, the one mediator between God and man (I Tim. 2. 5).

p. 118, n. 1: See further Agobard of Lyons, *De priv. . . . sac.*, c. 8, *PL* 104. 135–6.

p. 119, n. 1: This mode of argument was clearly preportrayed by Agobard, op. cit. c. 9, *PL* 104. 136: 'Praecipitur populo, ut eis (*scil.* sacerdotibus) *in cunctis* obediat.' In view of the Ruler's close links with the *populus* a statement such as this had a great future, esp. when *regnum* and *ecclesia*, *populus* and *christianitas* were held identical bodies, cf. *Cap.* 244, c. 6, p. 167, lines 9 f.

p. 119, n. 4: Cf. already the Council of Aachen (836), c. 45, in *Conc.* 717.

p. 129, n. 5: Cf. again the Anglo-Saxon Council of 787, c. 12 (Mansi, 12. 943).

p. 134, n. 1: Cf. now also H. Weinkauff, *Die deutsche Justiz & der Nationalsozialismus*, I (Stuttgart, 1968), advocating the natural law as the higher law comprehensible to layman and jurist alike, because it contains a basic order of 'natural' values.

p. 138, n. 1: The fundamental idea can also be expressed thus: the successorship of the Eastern emperor was based on wholly *historical* grounds; what there was of a successorship in the West was based on the *ecclesiological* grounds of Matt. 16, 18 f., and hence concerned primarily the papacy, with consequences into which there is no need to enter here.

p. 139, n. 2: See now most recently P. E. Schramm, 'Nachträge zu den Metallbullen der karol. und sächs. Kaiser' in *DA* 24 (1968), 1 ff., esp. 7 ff., with further literature, particularly Ph. Grierson's works.

p. 145, n. 1: That the designation of Charlemagne as *a Deo coronatus* was the usual Byzantine intitulation, may be seen from the oath taken by St Boniface on 30 Nov. 722; see the invocation in *MGH. Epp.* III. 265, no. 16.

p. 177, n.1: The view expressed by Maitland in Pollock & Maitland, *Hist. of Engl. Law*, 2nd ed. (Cambridge, 1926), II. 445, deserves here quotation: 'That the king is the guardian above all guardians is an idea which has become prominent in this much governed country.' A justice in the reign of Edward II declared: 'The king is no more than a mere guardian of the crown.'

Index

Aachen, council (816), 26; (817), 26n; (836), 27n, 40nn, 57n, 58n, 59n, 60n

Absolutism, royal, 109 f., 176, 178, 182, 186

Adoptionism, 79, 147

Adrian I, 11, 44n, 142, 143

Adrian II, 87n

Adventius, of Metz, 88 f., 91, 92, 93

Aeneas, of Paris, 154 ff., 158

Agatho, pope, 149n, 151n

Agobard, of Lyons, 35, 76, 171

Alcuin, 11n, 19, 25, 35, 38n, 41n, 83n, 138n

Alexander II, 177n

Alexandria, 150

Alfred, king, 176n

Alienation, prohibition of, 180, 182, 183 f.

Allegory, in documents, 49, 73n, 94; in sermons, 38; of sun and moon, 170

Amalarius, of Metz, 73n, 75n

Ambrose, St, 27, 38, 75, 120, 151n

Ambrosiaster, 107n

Anastasius II, pope, 60n

Angilramn, bishop, 28

Anglo-Saxons, 2, 3, 176n; councils, 23, 24

Anointing, *see* Unction

Ansegisus, of St Wandrille, 21n, 32nn

Antioch, 150

Aristocracy, 88, 111 ff., 114 f., 117, 126, 130, 131

Arno, of Salzburg, 39n

Arnulf, king & emperor, 33, 124 ff., 136n

Ascending theme of government, 9n, 109, 187

Augustine, St, 3, 15, 27, 38, 57, 72n, 120n, 140, 161, 180n; *see* also Pseudo-Augustine

Augustus, 181, 182

Autonomy of Ruler, 63, 173; *see* Emperor; Monarchic Rulership; of people, 178

Baldus de Ubaldis, 181, 182n

Bannus regius, 34

Baptism, individual, 6, 9, 92, 137; collective, 8, 9, 137

Baptismal fonts, 30; anointing, 75 f., 114n

Basic law, *see* Law, higher

Basilius I, 160, 162

Beards, wearing of, 147, 157, 160

Becket, St Thomas, 68, 118n

Bede, 161

Benedict, St, 12; of Aniane, 12

Benedictus Levita, 28

Bible, cited, 6nn, 7n, 8, 37n, 38n, 50n, 51, 52n, 53, 55, 63n, 71n, 72nn, 116n, 120, 123, 140n, 148n, 149n, 170, 173, 188; role in Renaissance of society, 18 ff., 37, 44, 50, 57, 139; role in rebirth of Ruler, 71 ff., 75 f., 77n, 84, 85, 89, 91, 95n, 98, 102, 108, 110n, 118, 176, 177; role in protecting reborn king, 113 ff.; role in protecting bishops, 119; Bible and tutorial function of king, 180 ff., 184

Bishops, functions, 123 f.; judicial capacity, 32, 112, 118 ff., 135; king-makers and royal collaborators, 71 ff., 111, 112 f.; obedience to, 118; people committed to, 86; as tutors, 181n, 184; unction of, 131 f.; vicars of Christ, 58, 84; *see* also Ecclesiastics; Mediatory role

Blood charisma, 54, 55n, 77, 111, 127; *see Geblütsrecht*

Boethius, 15

Boniface IV, pope, 135n

Boniface, St, 2, 20, 43, 78

Boso, 79n

Brogne, 168

Burchard, of Worms, 168

Burgundy, 101, 104n

Byzantium, as capital, 153 f. (*see* also Chalcedon); as *urbs regia*, 155, 156, 158 f.; church of, reborn, 172